D0221526

3 0700 10857 1141

Growing
Your Business
in Emerging Markets

Growing
Your Business
in Emerging Markets

Promise and Perils

John A. Caslione
and Andrew R. Thomas

Foreword by Joseph Tan

QUORUM BOOKS
Westport, Connecticut • London

Library of Congress Cataloging-in-Publication Data

Caslione, John A.
   Growing your business in emerging markets : promise and perils / John A. Caslione and Andrew R. Thomas ; foreword by Joseph Tan.
       p.   cm.
   Includes bibliographical references and index.
   ISBN 1–56720–339–6 (alk. paper)
       1. Export marketing.   2. Marketing—Developing countries.   I. Thomas, Andrew R.   II. Title.
   HF1416.C367   2000
   658.8'48—dc21   99–056359

British Library Cataloguing in Publication Data is available.

Library of Congress Catalog Card Number: 99–056359
ISBN: 1–56720–339–6

First published in 2000

Quorum Books, 88 Post Road West, Westport, CT 06881
An imprint of Greenwood Publishing Group, Inc.
www.quorumbooks.com

Printed in the United States of America

The paper used in this book complies with the Permanent Paper Standard issued by the National Information Standards Organization (Z39.48–1984).

10 9 8 7 6 5 4 3 2 1

JAC

To Andrea, who has enabled me to pursue a life of exploration.
And to Allison and Christopher, who help me maintain perspective in
all that I pursue.

ART

Para Jacqueline. Hoy dia y para siempre.

Contents

Illustrations   ix

Foreword *by Joseph Tan*   xi

Preface   xiii

Acknowledgments   xv

1   Global Manifest Destiny   1

2   The Promise of Emerging Markets   15

3   Perils: The Inherent Realities of Emerging Markets   37

4   Seizing the Advantage: Defining Your Company's Role in
    Emerging Markets   59

5   The Local Presence: Selecting and Recruiting Emerging Market
    Distributors   91

6   Maximizing Your Assets, Minimizing Your Risk: Training,
    Communicating with, and Controlling Your Emerging Market
    Distributors   117

7 Bound Relationships: The Distributor Agreement   145

8 The Final Imperative: Forging Global Manifest Destiny   181

Appendix: Emerging Market Local Information Sources   191

Selected Bibliography   249

Index   251

Illustrations

TABLES

1.1	Investment in Russia, Decelerated Pro-Activity Phase	13
2.1	Emerging Markets: Rates of Growth of GDP, 1981–1999	16
2.2	Rates of GDP Growth, Selected Countries, 1999	17
2.3	Rates of GDP Growth, Selected Countries, 1981–1999	18
2.4	World Population, 2000, 2025, 2050	19
2.5	Projected Population Growth, Selected Countries, 1998–2050	20
2.6	Migration to Developed Countries, 1975–1998	21
2.7	World Population, Aged 60 or Older, 2000–2050	22
2.8	World Population, Percentages of Youth and Elderly, 2000–2025	23
2.9	World's Leading Importers, 1998	24
2.10	Communications Access, Selected Countries, 1998	25
2.11	Rates of GDP Growth, Countries in Transition, 1989–1999	26
2.12	Changes in Human Settlements, Urban and Rural, Selected Countries, 1995–2000	28

2.13	Direct Foreign Investment in India, 1993–1998	30
2.14	Direct Foreign Investment in China, 1996–1999	31
3.1	Currency Fluctuations, Selected Countries, 1999	41
3.2	Inflation Rates, Selected Countries, 1999	42
3.3	Emerging Markets: Consumer Price Inflation, 1989–1999	43
3.4	Telephone Lines per 100 Persons, Selected Countries, 1998	46
3.5	Water Supply and Sanitation, Selected Countries, 1998	47
4.1	Channel Analysis (Economic Analysis)	87
4.2	Distribution Channel Analysis (Cost Analysis)	88
4.3	Distribution Channel Analysis (ROI Analysis)	89
5.1	Distribution Profile Evaluation Worksheet	101
5.2	Initial Investment in Inventory Worksheet—Method 1	111
5.3	Initial Investment in Inventory Worksheet—Method 2	113
6.1	Content Areas for Distributor Training Programs	133
6.2	Typical Communication Problems Between Manufacturer and Distributor	134
6.3	Confidential and Protected Communications	136
7.1	Key Provisions in the Distributor Agreement	150
7.2	Sample Distribution Agreement	156

FIGURES

4.1	Factors to Consider in Setting Realistic Objectives	63
4.2	Emerging Markets Tolerances and Expectations Map	72
4.3	Degree of Control Varies	73
4.4a	Sales and Distribution Strategy Development Flowchart (1)	82
4.4b	Sales and Distribution Strategy Development Flowchart (2)	83
4.4c	Sales and Distribution Strategy Development Flowchart (3)	84
4.5	Determining the Intensity of Distribution	85

Foreword

As the authors creatively and accurately state in this book, "Global Manifest Destiny is the inevitable march towards the economic integration of all of the world's people." From where I sit today, they are the first ones to have truly captured the essence of globalization and how it impacts business today.

For companies like ours, this movement in the direction of a truly global economy is providing some of the greatest opportunities anyone in our organization can remember. Within our industry as well as countless others, the rising tide of economic integration is compelling leaders to rethink their global corporate strategies.

Along with the tremendous opportunities in high technology and e-commerce throughout both industrialized and emerging markets, emerging markets themselves undoubtedly represent the best growth potential for those companies in all industries seeking to secure long-term profits and market share far into the foreseeable future. In addition, emerging markets provide companies with the opportunity to further influence the evolution of their businesses and the sales and distribution structures within them. Unlike the rigid systems that exist in the industrialized world, emerging markets are by nature more malleable.

Nevertheless, doing business in emerging markets is not easy. Indeed, emerging markets are often laden with high risk, complicated by unforeseen reversals, and sometimes even fraught with danger. Without recognizing the realities inherent to emerging markets and implementing strategies sufficiently durable and flexible to withstand them, businesses are doomed to fail.

In our most successful international ventures, including our biggest and most difficult market, Russia, the sales and distribution strategies we have employed are grounded in the teachings of this most valuable book.

Joseph Tan
Vice President and General Manager—Russia and Baltics
R.J. Reynolds International

Preface

Global Manifest Destiny is the inevitable economic integration of all humankind. "Globalization," however, is not merely the "Americanization" of the world economy but something deeper and much more profound. In fact, "globalization" is merely the contemporary label for Global Manifest Destiny. The economic integration of all humankind is inevitable. It is undeniable. It has been with us from the origins of human civilization, and it has always been our destiny.

Nowhere is Global Manifest Destiny—today's "globalization"—more evident than in emerging markets. The logarithmic rise of populations, per capita income, infrastructure demands, and consumer spending in emerging markets are providing some of the greatest opportunities for business since the dawn of the Industrial Age.

Nevertheless, the tremendous promise that emerging markets hold is fraught with danger and often unseen perils. Far too many companies fail to distinguish between merely doing business internationally and doing business in emerging markets. Emerging markets are fundamentally different. Regrettably, companies across the United States, Canada, and Europe have neglected to recognize these underlying, vital differences and have fallen short in actualizing their full growth potential in these markets.

This book will provide readers with the knowledge, the hands-on experience and skills, and the critical tools necessary to successfully and effectively develop their companies' business in emerging markets. The proven, powerful processes put forward here will provide the reader an insider's view of emerging markets (through a discussion of the "Promise" and the "Perils"), how to develop new market entry strategies (Tolerances and Expectations Map), the methods for securing the proper distribution channels (Sales and Distribution Strategy Development Flowchart), and how to best monitor and control those channels from the inception of the relationship through the execution of the distributor agreement (Model Distributor Agreement). No book we know of has ever provided *the* complete guide to doing business in emerging markets. It is our sincere wish to deliver just that.

Acknowledgments

As I reflect upon my countless journeys to emerging markets around the world, I cannot help but be reminded of the people who have contributed to my many wondrous experiences in these markets and ultimately, to the writing of this book. In completing this, my most current journey, I am most gratified to finally be able to acknowledge those special people who have all shared a part of themselves in the writing of my first book.

First, I would like to thank my clients and all of their devoted people, many of whom have become lifelong friends. Without their confidence and trust, this book could not have been written.

Second, I want to extend a very special thanks to my one and only true mentor in business, Michael Hunter. Mike's unconditional and unwavering support provided the platform on which to build a lifetime of knowledge and experience that I never dreamed possible.

Finally, all that I have accomplished in my life including the writing of this book, I owe in great part to Andrea, my beloved wife, and to Allison and Christopher, our precious children. I can never forget the personal sacrifices they have endured through the many years of my seemingly endless travels. Through it all and despite the great distances, they always made me believe I was never too far from home.

John A. Caslione

I have been truly blessed to have seen so much of the world at an early time in my life. The doors of new cultures, places, and ideas were opened to me by countless individuals across the planet from the End of the World to Timbuktu. Thank you for welcoming me.

Warmest gratitude is for my parents. My mom showed me the true meaning of character and always let me know where home was. My dad, my champion, has listened all the way through, from the innumerable afternoon chats on the porch to the back-nine at Brandywine. The faithful support and love from both of them continue to carry me through.

To my sisters, Emily and Ann Marie, I will always be thankful for the love we share together.

Both of my grandmothers have served as inspirations for what life can be if lived to its fullest. Grandma Thomas, your laughter is one of the greatest sounds I will ever know. Nana Grey, your steadfastness in always reminding me what is most important will never be forgotten.

To Chino, the most interesting person I know, I cannot imagine my life without you in it. I trust one day the stories told here will inspire you to dream about far away places and discover the beauty found in always learning new things.

And to Jacqueline, whose beauty, grace, and patience never cease to amaze me. You are my true love and my best friend.

Andrew R. Thomas

1

Global Manifest Destiny

> Because of the transistor radio, we live in an era when, for the first time in
> recorded history, the poor people of the world know they are poor.
> Mohandas K. Gandhi, 1941

Every July, the southeastern United States makes its annual preparations for the coming hurricane season. Homeowners brush away the cobwebs to make sure their plywood supply is in order. Local governments run over again and again the contingencies for their emergency response programs. American Red Cross offices stage mock drills testing the effectiveness of their relief plans. Insurance companies send additional agents to their Atlanta and Charlotte offices to be ready for the mountain of claims sure to follow. Meteorologists, aided by new developments in satellite technology, stand at the ready to predict where and when the hurricanes are likely to hit. Yet, with all of this preparation, high technology, and valuable information, hurricanes devastate thousands of lives each year.

Like the annual hurricane season, the same can be said of the economic integration of humankind. To prepare themselves for the coming storm of "globalization," workers learn new skills that they believe will make them more employable. Governments make public policy that they hope will prepare their nations for the next turndown in GDP. Non-governmental organizations like the United Nations try to anticipate which flash point will next require their assistance. Corporate leaders endeavor to predict which country or region will bring the highest profits. Economists, armed with more and more "real time" data, attempt to forecast which economy will be most affected by events in another part of the world.

However, when the next storm arises, tragedy inevitably strikes. Workers never seem to have the right skills. Governments appear to flounder. Non-governmental organizations look overwhelmed. Corporations incredulously complain that local issues are preventing them from making a profit. Predictably, economists scream for more data. And, all the while, the financial markets continue their slash and burn tactics in order to satisfy their insatiable appetite for easy and fast money.

Blatantly put, hardly anyone really knows what is going on. Nevertheless, the storm over the world's population continues to churn. Southeast Asia melts down, seemingly overnight. Confidence is lost and currencies plummet. Investors pull their money out of Russia and Argentina. Billions of people lose their life savings. Governments collapse. Multinationals that days before were liquid are nearly bankrupted.

We look for answers but find none. The old explanations fail to tell us what is happening. Yet, we know there is something more out there, something greater than anything we have previously observed. What is it? How can we be ready for it?

Standing at the gate of the Third Millennium, we see on the horizon Global Manifest Destiny—the complete economic integration of all of humankind. Global Manifest Destiny has been around since human beings first lived together in organized societies. Today's events can only be explained in light of this march, which we as a species embarked upon thousands of years ago.

Global Manifest Destiny is compelling organizations to look at themselves in completely new and revolutionary ways. For businesses, the markets for goods, services, finance, and information have become rapidly and tightly synthesized across borders. Barriers to the flow of trade and investment have fallen and deregulation has spread throughout the world, as ideological divisions have collapsed and the cost of communications and data transmission has plummeted. Because of Global Manifest Destiny, firms in the new millennium will have enormous opportunities not only to sell and invest in previously sheltered markets and form growing global alliances but also to leverage technological breakthroughs by selling on an expanded international scale, accessing components and technology globally, securing financing by tapping world markets, and obtaining human talent from a multitude of nations. In light of such a compelling and inevitable reality, the lack of vision on the part of the financial markets is obvious and disappointing.

The opportunities appear limitless, but they will not be achieved without insight and understanding. Only those organizations that grasp the magnitude of Global Manifest Destiny and adapt their corporate culture to it for the long term will achieve greatness.

Companies that recognize, embrace, and assimilate Global Manifest Destiny as part of the very fabric of their organizations will become the leaders in their respective industries and will be best positioned to exploit the business opportunities of the coming economic integration. Those who don't will be relegated to a status of irrelevance within the total scope of history.

On a more tangible level, Global Manifest Destiny provides business, non-governmental, and government leaders the mandate to direct their resources toward the development of operational infrastructures that have as their goal a greater connection with people worldwide. Whether it is investments in information systems or information technology that seeks to link individuals by the latest means of communication, accelerated foreign-language programs for managers and employees, or the development of cultural awareness skills, organizations must prepare their stakeholders for the economic integration of humankind.

Primary and secondary school curricula must begin to prepare children at an early age to be better able to function in the new global environment. Non-governmental organizations and governments must begin to develop similar IS/IT infrastructures as well as the same skills training as their private sector counterparts. Political leaders must actively pursue positive modifications of their trade policies—as politically charged as that might be—to best position their countries to decisively leverage the opportunities that Global Manifest Destiny affords them.

Terms like "globalization" and "the global economy" are so rampant in the current-day lexicon that they are increasingly viewed by many as trite or meaningless. They are too often used to explain, justify, permit, and endorse the actions of one group against another. Speculators tell us that because of "globalization," seemingly stable economies can be brought down to their knees almost overnight. Yet, does the use of the word "globalization" justify the actions of self-absorbed individuals and institutions as they almost instantaneously bankrupt 45 million Brazilian farmers? Shareholders and investors use the term "global economy" when they demand that companies turn immediate profits or else face retribution from the markets. Yet, does the assertion of the phrase "global economy" give traders the right to compel a company to forgo its long-term strategy in favor of constantly producing damaging short-term returns? In both cases, the answer is a resounding and unequivocal "no." Still, why is it that, at the beginning of the twenty-first century, governments and businesses across the world are being held hostage by the financial markets under the auspices of "globalization" and "the global economy"?

Nick Ringer, president of R.J. Reynolds International CIS, best articulates the near-mad preoccupation with short-term profits at the expense of long-term business development, when he says, "Investment in emerging markets must be a strategic decision for the long-term. All too often, the investment community's expectations are for quick returns rather than encouraging investors to penetrate new, high-growth markets. This is crucial not only to build long-term equity value, but to balance new, emerging market portfolios with those of developed markets. Failing to do so jeopardizes a company's long-term viability in the face of Global Manifest Destiny."

The financial markets are constantly punishing forward-thinking organizations for doing the right thing, which is to make the necessary investments in these high-growth-potential markets at the expense of maximizing short-term profits. Preoccupation with instant gratification has become a "day-trading mentality" for evaluating business performance.

Hedge funds, mutual funds, and other big financial institutions that hold global portfolio investments are happy to pour money into a country or a firm during the good times, only to take it back in a hurry if the going gets even the slightest bit tough. The financial community is acting more and more like a hard-core drug addict: gregarious and energetic at the beginning, but noticeably desperate and frantic as time wears on. The "day-trading mentality" seriously retards the ability of companies to make strategic, long-term investments to develop their businesses in light of Global Manifest Destiny. Unfulfilled short-term expectations compel financial markets to lower the ratings of these companies, which in turn raises the cost of much-needed capital for investments in their emerging markets operations.

For companies dealing in this upside-down world, Helmut Maucher, chairman of Nestle SA, may sum up the desperation of fund managers' obsession with short-term value when he says, "Because of this now fashionable short-term shareholder value thinking, companies must get out of any venture if they don't get some return within six months."[1] It is becoming clear that the financial markets are out of control and often make an enemy of any government or company who is seeking to effectively prepare for the future.

Malaysia's former prime minister Mahatthir Mohamad spoke for hundreds of world leaders when he commented about the Asian financial crisis of 1997, "Institutional speculators were not only involved in manipulating stock prices, but they also had the ability to plunder central banks' foreign exchange reserves, undermining sovereign governments and destabilizing entire national economies." He correctly added, "This deliberate devaluation of the currency of a country by currency traders and speculators purely for profit is a serious denial of the rights of independent nations."[2]

What is the future? Is it merely a vicious cycle where the strong, in this case the financial markets, will continue to dominate the weak? Or is it something different? We firmly believe the events of today are manifestations of something much greater than merely "globalization," the expansion of "the global economy," or the financial markets themselves.

Nowhere is the reality of global economic integration today more striking than in the legendary city of Timbuktu. Formerly the legendary center of the Trans-Sahara trade route in the fifteenth century, Timbuktu is once again one of the world's more important commercial destinations.

On our last journey to Timbuktu, we held a seminar at Le Centre du Culture du Tombouctou, where local businessmen from all over Mali had gathered to learn what Global Manifest Destiny means to them. They had traveled to Timbuktu from even more remote places like Gao and Mopti. The local Malian who was running the meeting stood and introduced us, two American businessmen from the Midwest. We took turns speaking in French about the fantastic changes that Global Manifest Destiny will bring to these most distant places. It was necessary to pause every few sentences as a man from the southern part of the country translated the French version into Bambara. Then, a man from the east translated the Bambara into Wolof. And finally, a man from the west translated the Wolof into Fulani.

At the end of the meeting, we were taken across the street to the camel market and shown by our friendly hosts how Global Manifest Destiny is already unmistakable in this corner of the world. We were introduced to a nomad from Sudan, who called himself Tessema. Tessema told us that, like his forefathers before him, he journeys twice a year across the Sahara Desert on his camel to Timbuktu—more than 4,000 miles each way! He showed us the new pair of Nike Air Jordans and the beautiful gold Cartier watch he had just purchased at a kiosk next to the saddle maker. He proudly announced the shoes were for himself. "They make the camel ride much more comfortable!" The watch was a birthday gift for the sixth of his eight wives. Tessema let us know he was also looking to buy a Honda generator. He noted the power source would come in handy as he crossed the desert, letting him watch NBA games on satellite television from his tent and operate a blender to make his favorite drink—margaritas.

It is the inevitable nature of Global Manifest Destiny that, like the coming of the annual hurricane season, makes it compelling to organizations and the people who lead them. Just as information technology has become a fundamental truth within the structure of any organization—private or public—so too must be the application of Global Manifest Destiny. Even the most backward-thinking organization will admit, probably grudgingly, that information technology has become an inescapable reality and one of the most important strategic assets of any organization. Many of the products we buy today didn't even exist twenty years ago, and a staggering number of the world's largest and most successful organizations were just being created. Many of the products and organizations that will best succeed in the next few decades may not exist today.

Global Manifest Destiny must be viewed in the same way. To fail to recognize and respond to the inevitable integration of humankind is to insure failure for any human enterprise. Those organizations that firmly acknowledge and successfully reply to the mandates of Global Manifest Destiny will invariably be the next leaders in their respective spheres of influence. Just as those organizations that embraced information technology have often become key players within their environments, so too will those who understand and embrace the precepts of Global Manifest Destiny.

If anything is obvious in our world today, it might be that all this "coming together" is a new and powerful force linking the world in a web of trade and investments.[3] However, from the earliest of historical writings, it is clear that human beings have always sought to be economically integrated. The "new globalism" of today is a vision as old as time, one that arguably did not begin with the European age of maritime exploration five centuries ago but was also dreamed of by the Phoenicians, Vikings, Chinese, and other great trading peoples, who also dreamed of the unification of markets and of economic space on a planetary dimension.[4] "Globalization" in its present form is merely a manifestation of the recent analysis of Global Manifest Destiny within the second half of the twentieth century. The expansion around the Nile in 3000 B.C. and the colonialism of the eighteenth and nineteenth centuries, were both resultants of Global Manifest Destiny in their eras; so too is globalization today.

From Mesopotamia, the birthplace of recorded civilization, to the later empires of Egypt, classical Greece, and Rome, we read about events shaped by individuals seeking to expand trade beyond their borders. The march of Global Manifest Destiny toward the economic integration of the then-known world's people was readily evident, at least on a regional scale, during the beginnings of civilization.

The Renaissance in Europe between 1350 and 1600 was to become an international movement, aided by the spread of movable type, invented by Gutenberg in the fifteenth century. Like the Internet today, this radical form of communication was to aid in the expansion of Global Manifest Destiny. The discoveries by Europeans of new trading routes caused a rapid European economic expansion from 1500 to 1700. Stimulated by the new trade with the East, by New World gold and silver, and by a doubling of the population, new business and financial techniques were developed and refined, such as joint stock companies, insurance, and letters of credit and exchange. The Bank of Amsterdam (1609) and the Bank of England (1694) broke the old monopoly of private banking families.[5] The rise of a business mentality was commonly typified by the spread of clock towers in the cities. By the mid-fifteenth century, portable clocks were available, and the first watch was invented in 1502.[6] This period was the beginning of the rapidly expanding economic integration that was to mark most of humankind until World War I. The "ebb and flow" nature of Global Manifest Destiny is evidenced here as the antithesis to the entrenchment and lack of integration of the earlier Dark Ages.

The eighteenth and nineteenth centuries witnessed the emergence of Europe as the world's economic superpower. The imperial conquest of Africa, Latin America, India, China, Indonesia, and the Philippines were undertaken to tap the material resources of these regions in order to resolve internal European conflicts. In its day, colonialism may have best embodied Global Manifest Destiny—as "globalization" does today. Whatever the language, however, the point remains the same: humankind will be integrated, and by economic means. Global Manifest Destiny is inevitable. Sometimes, however, it is also bloody and inhumane in its direction.

Shaped by the colonial domination of Europe as well as remarkable advances in technology, the late nineteenth century would reach a pinnacle of international trade and commerce. The railroad and the telegraph came to dominate the transportation of goods and communication. Railroads were built all over the world and connected coastal regions to the interiors of many previously remote countries. Historians agree that because of the telegraph, 90 percent of all Americans learned of Abraham Lincoln's assassination in 1865 within twelve hours after it happened. Such a quick transmission of news of a major event may have very well whetted the appetite of individuals and merchants to further the advancement of Global Manifest Destiny and the integration it naturally encourages.

The ebb and flow of Global Manifest Destiny is one of its most compelling characteristics. It has been marked by moments of fantastic expansion as well as deep retrenchment. Most of the twentieth century may best be remembered as a retreat from the economic integration of the previous era. The isolationism of World War I, the despair of the Great Depression, and the horrors of World War II temporarily pushed back the march of Global Manifest Destiny in the first half of this century. Only within the last few decades have we been able to approach the levels of commerce that existed in the 1880s and 1890s. Freer world trade led to an explosion of American exports in 1896. In that year, American exports soared to 7 percent of the Gross National Product. In 1938, the number had fallen to 4 percent. By 1998, it was 8 percent.[7]

The fervent nationalism that climaxed in World War I was building for two generations across Europe. The destruction caused by the world's first total war would provide the foundation for the next global war just twenty years later. During this time, the rapid economic integration of humankind would suffer an enormous setback.

The period of the Great Depression from the early 1930s until the arrival of World War II witnessed an astonishing implosion of global trade and economic integration. Between 1929 and 1932, the value of world trade in current U.S. dollars fell by a full 50 percent. Though deflation contributed to the collapse, even at constant prices the volume of world trade in 1932 was nearly 30 percent below its 1929 level. As late as 1938, trade volume was still barely 90 percent of that of 1929, despite the nearly complete recovery of the production of primary products and manufactured goods.[8]

Adding to this decline was a dramatic shift in the direction and pattern of economic integration. Trade and the flow of capital constricted from its multilateral constructs and was channeled into self-contained regional and colonial blocs such as the British Commonwealth, a group of European gold-standard countries centered around France, a Central European trade bloc linked to Germany, and a group of Western Hemisphere countries trading with the United States.[9]

Even beyond the cataclysm of World War I and the upheaval of the Great Depression, World War II shaped the current structure of global economic power more than any other single event. The ending of the colonial system, the worldwide presence of the Soviet Union, and the preeminence of the United States were all direct results of World War II. The shift in global hegemony away from Europe caused a retrenchment in the global economy that has still not regained the ground of the nineteenth century.

Still, today's advance towards Global Manifest Destiny may very well touch many more people than the earlier kind. Like Tessema, the nomad NBA fan, billions of human beings are facing a world they have never seen before.

THE PRESENT DAY AND GLOBAL MANIFEST DESTINY

With all due respect to the strength of the United States as the leading player on the world's economic stage today, Global Manifest Destiny is not simply the "Americanization" of the world's population. Global Manifest Destiny is much deeper and more profound than the influence of solely one nation or culture. Just as the Europeans, Chinese, Africans, Romans, Greeks, Egyptians, and Phoenicians before them, the Americans of today are merely the most visible, yet unknowing, flag bearer of Global Manifest Destiny. The Europeans and Romans, for example, probably dominated more of the world and were the unaware carriers of its flag in their day. Certainly, these cultures influenced the course of events for a much longer period of time than the United States has. When the hurricane comes, it doesn't matter if you live in multimillion-dollar mansion or a modest four-room home. Similarly, when the march of Global Manifest Destiny passes, it doesn't matter if you're in a wealthy nation or an emerging market. All of humankind is becoming economically integrated.

In fact, the best place to view the march of Global Manifest Destiny today is not in North America, Western Europe, Japan, or other industrialized nations, but in what is commonly referred to as the emerging markets of the world. The magnitude and ferocity of economic integration in places like Almaty, Mumbai, and Timbuktu is striking to even the most seasoned observer of Global Manifest Destiny. In these and countless other places like them, billions of people are becoming economically integrated with their global counterparts for the first time in an increasingly rapid fashion.

The focus of this book is to show readers how to grow their business in emerging markets and take full advantage of the extraordinary opportunities Global Manifest Destiny presents there. (For a broader discussion of Global Manifest Destiny and how leading corporations and other organizations are leveraging their knowledge and understanding of Global Manifest Destiny to propel them to dominate their present industries or in industries yet to be launched, our upcoming book entitled *Forging the Global Company* will better serve to expound upon and detail these issues.)

THE PHASES OF GLOBAL MANIFEST DESTINY AS THEY RELATE TO EMERGING MARKETS

From a business perspective, Global Manifest Destiny has traditionally revealed itself in two forms: one is a period of rapid growth, high sales, and often, but not always, high profits. During this period of rapid growth, there is clear evidence of heightened competition for limited resources and arrogance on the part of customers, suppliers, and governments; constructive partnerships among and between customers, suppliers, and governments are relatively low. During this period, a specific infrastructure and unique behavioral mode of collective thinking and action prevail. We call this the Accelerated Re-Activity phase of Global Manifest Destiny.

The contrasting period of slower economic growth is characterized by comparatively lower sales and profits; reduced competition for limited resources such as the talent pool of workers; and much easier compliance on the part of customers, suppliers, and governments, with a bias for more constructive alliancing and partnerships. During this period a very different, but equally specific, infrastructure dominates and a very different mode of behavior tends to prevail. We call this the Decelerated Pro-Activity phase of Global Manifest Destiny.

The phase of Accelerated Re-Activity is the time when companies most often build greater profits. The pace of business is usually faster and more subject to wild fluctuations in the marketplace than during the Decelerated Pro-Activity phase. The Accelerated Re-Activity phase typically reveals higher growth rates in both sales and profits than does the Decelerated Pro-Activity phase.

As the vast majority of companies during the Accelerated Re-Activity phase see their profits increase, often at astounding rates, a premium is placed upon resources that become increasingly scarce. This scarcity and higher cost of resources places an increasingly heavier burden on the existing infrastructure to create more of what is needed to sustain the Accelerated Re-Activity phase. During this time, few people seek to improve the infrastructure. The primary focus is upon generating higher and higher profits, rather than to pro-actively pay attention to what is most certain to follow: the eventual ramping down and conclusion of the Accelerated Re-Activity phase. Individuals and organizations merely "react" to what is going on around them, comfortable with the current climate and not wanting to rock the boat. The inevitable overstressing of the inadequate infrastructure in the Accelerated Re-Activity phase is typically the driving force of the transition to the Decelerated Pro-Activity phase.

Once the high profits and relatively easy money begin to evaporate, priority is placed upon fixing the infrastructure and trying to get back to the Accelerated Re-Activity phase. Enlightened organizations embrace initiatives to repair and minimize the shortcomings of the current system and build new infrastructures in a pro-active manner during these times of economic deceleration. For enlightened companies, the Decelerated Pro-Activity phase is the time to keep and build market share first. Once market share is secured, these companies then extend their focus to profits.

While many Western businesses were escaping the problems plaguing Russia in late 1998 and throughout 1999, Nestle SA was continuing to prudently invest there; those investments centered upon building better infrastructure within their business in Russia. "This was the time to get in. When everybody was scared and got out," says Helmut Maucher, chairman of Nestle. When the ruble crisis came, Nestle's rivals either cut operations or pulled out. Nestle, however, stayed put and doubled market share. Minimally, almost all consumer products competitors that remained turned abruptly away from the Russian ruble and forced their customers to trade in only U.S. dollars, the hard currency of choice. More enlightened companies such as Nestle and R.J. Reynolds International restrained themselves from such overreaction and continued to trade in Russian rubles by simply keying the Russian ruble rate to the U.S. dollar on a daily basis.

From Nestle's point of view, the Russian crisis of late 1998 didn't look so desperate. "Lots of people are saying Russian people are starving. But at the same time you have 60 to 70 million people there with incomes who can buy Nestle Products." Adds Haucher, "Russia will certainly be one of the biggest markets in the world for Nestle."

Recent events in Southeast Asia further illustrate how the phases of Global Manifest Destiny reveal themselves. From the late 1980s onward, many East Asian "tiger" economies were viewed as "can't miss" opportunities for foreign investors. International lenders bankrolled everything from empty high-rises in Bangkok to South Korean companies' speculation in Brazilian bonds. Sakura Bank Limited and Bank of Tokyo–Mitsubishi led a long line of Japanese banks that more than doubled their lending to Thailand between 1993 and 1996. Germany's Deutsch Bank made risky temporary loans across Russia and the CIS as well as Asia so that it could be first in line for corporate bond deals. "All the banks would be standing in line—J.P. Morgan, Deutsche, CitiBank, Dresdner," said Klaus Friedrich, chief economist at Germany's Dresdner Bank. "We were all queuing up trying to help those countries borrow money. We would all see each in the same places. We all knew each other."

However, beginning in early 1995, fast-track economies like Indonesia, South Korea, Thailand, and Malaysia, all characterized by loosely controlled banking systems and political corruption, began to experience a decrease in their annual growth. The slowdown in the revenue stream made it increasingly difficult for the "tigers" to pay back the Japanese banks and other international investors who had financed their fantastic growth over the previous years.

Nevertheless, governments and business leaders in these countries, as well as the foreign lenders that were providing the much-needed capital, failed to recognize the natural shift that was occurring and continued to behave as if they were still at the beginning of the Accelerated Re-Activity phase, rather than its end.

The behavior exhibited by leaders in Thailand during the early 1990s is typical of what happened in many other countries throughout Southeast Asia. The nation launched its own satellites, constructed taller and taller skyscrapers, built automobile plants faster than highways were laid, and expanded its telecommunications network at a record pace.

By the time first-time visitors arrived at their hotel from the Bangkok airport, they would all be asking the same question, "Where did all the money come from?" Most of the mega-projects were financed with so much overseas money that, during the boom times, the political and economic shortcomings within the system could be covered up. However, as the returns on these foreign investments shrank, cracks started to appear in the local economies.

The discipline which the country's political and financial leaders needed was nowhere to be found. Politicians kept on promoting the promise of Thailand and constantly sought to lure foreign firms to set up shop there, regardless of the real needs of the marketplace. In one six-month period during 1995, three new tractor factories and four new automobile plants broke ground. Nobody stopped to ask if demand existed to sustain these new facilities. Instead, the focus was on development, and development alone. Thailand's financial sector continued to lend money on the assumption that real estate values could only appreciate. Words like "depreciation" and "negative equity" were alien concepts to a generation of Thai bankers accustomed to annual growth rates of 8–10%.

As the cracks became more visible in 1996 and early 1997, rumors about a correction to the Thai economy began to spread as international investors began to call for the Thai economy to increase its productivity, lower wages, and deal with the banking sector.

When faced with these demands from their financial benefactors, Thai leaders proved impotent in addressing the concerns. On July 2, 1997, the Thai government, under tremendous pressure from international lenders, stopped using public funds to peg the bhat to the U.S. dollar. Currency speculators and investors immediately pulled their money out of Thailand and the other countries of the region.

Two months later, Thailand became the first Asian country to appeal to the International Monetary Fund for short-term loans to maintain its economy. In Japan, political leaders remained unable to reach consensus on how to revive the beleaguered banking system, while on Wall Street, fears of an Asian recession forced the Dow Jones Industrial Average to fall more than 557 points on October 27, 1997.

Soon, other nations like South Korea, Indonesia, the Philippines, and Malaysia found themselves in the same dire situation as Thailand. The failing economies created political and social unrest—particularly in Indonesia. Lenders and investors who were slow to pull out their money were harder hit, as the situation seemed to be spinning out of control.

In mid-1998, international investors began to realize the "Asian Flu" might spread to other emerging markets. In Russia, President Boris Yeltsin turned to the IMF for help. The fund loaned out billions of dollars, but it did little to help the sagging ruble. Brazil's economy imploded as the real was floated, falling more than 30% in value within a week. By the end of the year, the world seemed to awaken to the possibility of a massive economic downturn fueled by increasingly accelerated fear.

The culmination of these events was the inevitable movement into the Decelerated Pro-Activity phase, where we are today. Nevertheless, opportunities still exist. These opportunities, however, are different from the ones that existed in the preceding phase, the Accelerated Re-Activity phase. As previously discussed, market share expansion is a key component of the Decelerated Pro-Activity phase. With proper strategies, enlightened companies can increase their international presence and build the necessary infrastructure for the next inescapable round of Accelerated Re-Activity. Muthiah Alagappa, a Malaysian scholar at the East-West Center in Honolulu, may best describe the current situation when he says, "This [Asian situation] is a crisis, but also a tremendous opportunity for Western companies. The situation strengthens the position of Western companies in Asia." Jeffrey Garten, dean of the Yale School of Management, adds, "Most of these countries are going to pass through a deep and dark tunnel. But on the other end there is going to be a significantly different world, and it will be one in which Western firms have achieved much deeper penetration." Such an example distinguishes the transition between phases of Global Manifest Destiny.

Moving back and forth between the phases of Decelerated Pro-Activity and Accelerated Re-Activity is often times not a clean, uniform, and painless transformation. Some industries will change phases faster or slower than others. Certain countries will rise or fall before their neighbors do. A few companies will be able to adjust to the natural changes of Global Manifest Destiny much more smoothly than their competitors. Those companies, industries, and nations that adapt their cultures to better leverage the advantages afforded them in each of the inevitable phases and transitions of Global Manifest Destiny will undoubtedly be the leaders in their respective universes.

In the Asian markets, among the most important beneficiaries of the Decelerated Pro-Activity phase are financial service companies, especially those, like CitiBank, that have already begun to expand their presence there. Opportunities also exist for companies like General Motors or large retailers like Wal-Mart, which operates in sectors where barriers to entry were common during the Accelerated Re-Activity phase.

Leading multinationals like Nestle are convinced that Russia, economically steady or not, is simply too big to be disregarded. In the mid-1990s, companies like Caterpillar, Ford, International Paper, Lucent Technologies, Nestle, Philip Morris, and Wm. Wrigley Jr., Inc. went against the conventional wisdom and began to establish their presence in Russia. Attracted by Russia's enormous potential to consume and produce their goods, these corporations made a long-term commitment regardless of short-term conditions.

Despite the financial shock of August 1998 and Russia's entry into the Decelerated Pro-Activity phase, several leading companies have decided to take advantage of the new opportunities that have been created and continue moving ahead with their earlier planned investments, albeit presumably with a different perspective than in the earlier phase of Accelerated Re-Activity (see Table 1.1). For these companies and others, their relationships with local governments, in many cases, have dramatically improved. "Before, St. Petersburg's attitude was

Table 1.1
Investment in Russia, Decelerated Pro-Activity Phase

COMPANY	PROJECT	INVESTMENT	FINISH DATE
BMW	Auto assembly joint venture	US$27 million	1999
Caterpillar	Fabrications and equipment plant	US$50 million	End of 1999
Gillette	Razor blade manufacturing plant	US$40 million	Fall 1999
International Paper	Paper mill joint venture	US$65 million	Spring 1999
Lucent	Fiber optic joint venture	US$7 million	Spring 1999
Nestle	Investment in six existing plants	US$30 million	Spring 1999
RJ Reynolds	Tobacco manufacturing plants	US$400 million	End of 1999

Source: Russian Ministry of Foreign Trade and Economic Cooperation.

something like 'Kiss our ring and maybe we'll do a deal with you,' " said James T. Hitch, managing partner of the St. Petersburg office of Baker and McKenzie, the law firm. "Now it's like: You've decided to stay in Russia after the crisis? You're dedicated to us? Well, how can we now work together?" As in Asia, smart companies who understand the opportunities in Russia will be ready to take full advantage of the next round of Accelerated Re-Activity that is certain to come.

Savvy investors all over the world should also be increasingly paying closer attention to how a company's strategic planning manages each phase of Global Manifest Destiny within emerging markets and the transition between the two phases. Opportunities will always exist, but in different and ever-changing forms. To focus only on the short term in the face of Global Manifest Destiny should be recognized as utter folly for the smart investor.

The business leaders, organizations, and financial investors who will succeed in the new millennium are those who seize the initiatives that each phase of Global Manifest Destiny offers. More than ever, business will have the opportunity to improve virtually every aspect of human life. But the emerging, high-tech supercharged economy being shaped by Global Manifest Destiny will not be the end of human strife, economic calamity, or social upheaval. The new century opens full with promise, but whether decision makers fulfill that promise may largely turn their ability to leverage the tremendous power that can be unleashed through an intimate understanding of Global Manifest Destiny.

NOTES

1. "Nestle Chairman Sweet on Russia," *Financial Post—Canada*, November 1, 1999.

2. Statement at the Meeting of the Group of 15, as quoted in the *South China Morning Post*, November 3, 1997.

3. Nicholas D. Kristoff, "At This Rate, We'll Be Global in Another Hundred Years," *New York Times*, May 23, 1999.

4. John Dunning and Khalil Hamdani, *The New Globalism and Developing Countries* (United Nations University Press, 1997), p. 16.

5. *World Almanac Book of Facts 1999*, World Almanac Corporation.

6. Ibid.

7. Ibid.

8. Barry Eichengreen and Douglas Irwin, "Trade Blocs, Currency Blocs, and the Disintegration of World Trade in the 1930's," *National Bureau of Economic Research Working Paper Series*, No. 4445, 1993.

9. Ibid.

2

The Promise of Emerging
Markets

I'm living in a world only the wildest dreamer could have ever imagined.
(Rogelio, a Peruvian accountant who just moved with wife and six children
from a shantytown on the outskirts of Lima to the new, middle-class district of Miraflores.)

Tom was once again running a little late for work this morning. He got home
late last night because he took his family out to TGIFriday's for his daughter's
birthday and then went dancing with his wife at the new jazz club that had just
opened in town. As he gets into his Jeep Grand Cherokee and heads out onto
the freeway, he realizes he forgot to tell his wife which wine to buy at the
supermarket for tonight's dinner party. While waiting his turn at the McDonald's
drive-thru for his customary coffee and Egg McMuffin, Tom calls home on his
Nokia mobile phone and asks his wife to buy a Chilean red wine recommended
in an airline magazine he read on a recent international flight. When he arrives
at the office, he immediately goes on-line, checking his e-mail and, more important, how his stock portfolio performed overnight.

Tom's morning is not much different than that of tens of millions of Americans or Europeans. However, Tom doesn't live in New York or London. Instead, he lives in Shanghai. It is in places like Shanghai, Almaty, Timbuktu,
and thousands of lesser-known places around the world that Global Manifest
Destiny can best be observed.

From a business point of view, the engines of growth within this new global
paradigm are increasingly found in the emerging markets of the world, that is,

Table 2.1
Emerging Markets: Rates of Growth of GDP, 1981–1999 (Annual % Change)

	1981-1990	1991	1992	1993	1994	1995	1996	1997	1998	1999
All Emerging Markets	2.3	3.3	5.1	5.2	5.6	4.6	5.7	5.7	5.0	6.2
Latin America	1.2	3.6	3.3	3.6	5.5	-0.1	3.7	5.2	3.5	3.5
Africa	1.9	0.8	-0.3	-0.4	1.9	2.7	4.4	3.1	4.3	4.9
Western Asia	-2.2	-5.2	5.5	4.3	-0.9	4.1	4.8	5.9	4.6	4.9
Eastern & Southern Asia	7.2	6.9	7.8	7.9	8.6	8.2	7.4	6.5	6.3	6.9
China	9.1	9.2	14.2	13.5	12.6	10.5	9.7	9.3	10.1	7.0

Sources: UN/DSEA, based on IMF, *International Financial Statistics*, 1999.

in those countries outside of Western Europe, Canada, the United States, and Japan.

The spectacular economic growth in emerging markets is the beginning of the biggest "consumer boom" in history. More customers with more income than ever before will provide manufacturers and distributors with the greatest money-making opportunity in the Industrial Age. In short, the place to strike it rich is in the emerging markets of the world, and the time is now.

Emerging markets are seen by business leaders across the globe as the place to stake their future prosperity. General Motors, McDonald's, and the Hollywood studios have already realized this. Throughout the last decade, the greatest portion of their profits and growth have come from emerging markets. In comparison to the industrialized nations, emerging markets are growing at an increasingly faster rate (Table 2.1). For the year 1999, the Gross Domestic Product in most regions of emerging markets grew at a faster rate than that of Britain, Japan, or even the United States (Tables 2.2 and 2.3). Moreover, every Asian region within emerging markets will exceed the 1999 growth of Japan—their biggest economy. According to the World Bank, Japan's GDP will rise by 0.4% for 1999, versus 4.9% for Western Asia, 6.85% for Eastern and Southern Asia, and 7.0% for China.

Although the opportunities may seem limitless, the pitfalls are equally formidable. The following chapters of this book will show you how to successfully navigate the minefields of sales and distribution in emerging markets to reach your full business potential there.

For now, it is incumbent to explore the factors leading to the high growth of emerging markets within the pillars of Global Manifest Destiny. The most important are demographics, communication, governmental action, and urbanization. An understanding of these critical elements will illuminate the fantastic promise of emerging markets.

Table 2.2
Rates of GDP Growth, Selected Countries, 1999

COUNTRY	GDP Change
Argentina	-4.9
Brazil	-0.3
Chile	-3.6
Colombia	-7.6
Mexico	4.6
Panama	2.4
Venezuela	-9.6
China	7.1
India	5.5
Indonesia	0.5
Malaysia	4.1
Pakistan	4.7
Philippines	3.6
South Korea	9.8
Taiwan	6.5
Thailand	3.5
Egypt	6.2
Greece	3.5
Israel	0.7
Nigeria	4.8
South Africa	0.0
Turkey	-2.5
Zimbabwe	3.2
Czech Republic	0.3
Hungary	3.8
Poland	3.1
Romania	2.6
Russia	1.8
Britain	3.7
Japan	0.4
United States	4.1

Source: Department of Social and Economic Affairs, United Nations.

Table 2.3
Rates of GDP Growth, Selected Countries, 1981–1999

COUNTRY	1981-1990	1991	1992	1993	1994	1995	1996	1997	1998	1999
Argentina	-1.4	8.9	8.7	6.4	7.4	-4.6	4.4	7.8	4.5	-4.9
Brazil	1.5	0.9	-0.8	4.1	5.8	4.1	3.0	3.5	1.1	-0.3
Mexico	1.7	4.3	3.7	1.9	4.6	-6.2	4.1	6.8	5.1	4.6
China	9.1	9.2	14.2	13.5	12.6	10.5	9.7	9.3	10.1	7.1
India	5.3	2.1	4.1	3.9	5.4	6.7	6.4	5.8	6.5	5.5
Indonesia	5.5	7.1	6.5	6.5	7.5	8.1	7.8	6.1	3.5	0.5
South Korea	9.1	9.1	5.1	5.8	8.6	8.9	7.1	6.1	3.1	9.8
Taiwan	7.9	7.6	6.8	6.3	6.5	6.1	5.6	6.1	5.5	6.5
Thailand	7.8	8.5	7.8	8.3	8.7	8.6	6.4	-1.5	2.1	3.5
Israel	2.8	6.2	6.6	3.4	6.6	7.1	4.5	2.1	2.8	0.7
South Africa	1.5	-1.1	-2.2	1.3	2.7	3.4	3.1	2.1	3.3	0.0
Turkey	4.3	0.8	5.1	8.1	-6.1	8.1	7.1	6.1	5.2	-2.5
Czech Republic	N/A	N/A	N/A	0.5	2.7	4.8	4.1	1.4	3.2	0.3
Hungary	N/A	-11.7	-3.1	-0.6	2.9	1.5	1.3	3.6	3.7	3.8
Poland	N/A	4.1	-7.1	2.7	3.8	5.3	6.9	6.2	5.8	3.1
Romania	N/A	-12.9	-8.8	1.6	3.9	7.1	4.1	-2.2	7.5	2.6
Russia	N/A	N/A	14.5	-8.6	12.8	-4.1	-5.5	0.5	1.5	1.8

Source: Department of Social and Economic Affairs, United Nations.

DEMOGRAPHICS

The changing demographics of the world population are profoundly changing the impact of emerging markets in the wake of Global Manifest Destiny. The growth of populations in developing countries, the movement of populations between nations, and the aging of populations in the industrial world all play key roles in the impact demography has on the economic integration of the planet's residents.

Population Growth

World population growth is taking place almost exclusively within developing nations and emerging markets. By the year 2020, only one-fifth of humankind will live in the industrial world. Nearly all of the 3 billion increase in global population expected by 2025 will be in developing countries (Table 2.4).

In addition, a substantial portion of the world's population is today living within countries described as emerging markets. China and India together alone represent 40% of the world's total population. When combined with the formidable populations of other emerging markets like Brazil, Indonesia, Nigeria, Vietnam, Russia, and the Philippines, it becomes quite clear that the vast majority of human beings are currently living in emerging markets (see Table 2.5, first column).

As Table 2.5 demonstrates, most young people today are living outside of developed nations. Fifty-two percent of all Asians are under the age of 25 while only 35% of Americans and 28% of Germans are as young. Coca-Cola sees Indonesia—a Moslem country of 180 million people where alcohol is forbidden

Table 2.4
World Population, 2000, 2025, 2050 (in thousands)

	2000	% of Total	2025	% of Total	2050	% of Total
WORLD TOTAL	6,003,054	100.0%	7,823,703	100.0%	8,909,095	100.0%
DEVELOPED COUNTRIES	1,182,184	19.6%	1,214,890	15.5%	1,155,403	13.0%
DEVELOPING COUNTRIES	4,820,870	81.4%	6,608,813	84.5%	7,753,692	87.0%

Source: Population Division, Department of Economic and Social Affairs, United Nations Secretariat.

and the median age is only eighteen—as "heaven on earth" for its product, according to the former CEO Roberto Goizieta. In Latin America and Africa, the fertility rates among women are nearly three times higher than in Western Europe and the United States. Latin women produce on average five children in a lifetime, while African women will deliver nearly six.

Asia is currently home to almost 50% of the world's total population. At the beginning of the century, Asia will account for 3.6 billion of the world's 6.2 billion people. The World Bank has estimated China's population in 2010 will be 1.6 billion and in 2025, nearly 1.8 billion—18% of the world's total population. India's population is rapidly approaching 1 billion inhabitants and may already have exceeded that number, given the Indian government's inability to accurately count its massive population. The World Bank estimates that the number of Indians in 2025 will reach 1.4 billion. Today, Indonesia is home to more than 193 million people. By 2005, it is expected to reach 227 million.

The expanding large populations of emerging markets are being coupled with a dramatic rise in per capita income in some markets. According to the Organization for Economic Cooperation and Development (OECD), the forecast for economic growth in the developing world is projected at 5% annually over the next ten years. If China, India, and Indonesia grow by an average of 6% per year through the year 2010 (still below their projections), approximately 700 million people will live in those countries with an income equivalent to that of the average American household. This group would equal the combined populations of the United States, the European Community, and Japan.

Population Movements

Massive shifts in population are occurring as the disparity between rich and poor countries becomes more noticeable. The largest single group to enter the United States has been Hispanics. By 2025, the United States will become a nonmajority nation for the first time in its history—dramatically affecting the social, political, and economic makeup of the nation.

Table 2.5
Projected Population Growth, Selected Countries, 1998–2050 (in thousands)

COUNTRY	1998 POPULATION	COUNTRY	2050 PROJECTION
China	1,255,698	India	1,528,853
India	982,223	China	1,477,730
United States	274,028	United States	349,318
Indonesia	206,338	Pakistan	345,484
Brazil	165,851	Indonesia	311,857
Pakistan	148,166	Nigeria	244,311
Russia	147,434	Brazil	244,320
Japan	126,281	Bangladesh	212,495
Bangladesh	124,774	Ethiopia	169,446
Nigeria	106,409	Congo	160,360
Mexico	95,831	Mexico	146,645
Germany	82,133	Philippines	130,893
Vietnam	77,562	Vietnam	126,793
Philippines	72,944	Russia	121,256
Egypt	65,978	Iran	114,947
Iran	65,758	Egypt	114,844
Turkey	64,479	Japan	104,921
Thailand	60,300	Turkey	100,664
Ethiopia	59,649	Tanzania	80,584
France	58,683	Thailand	74,188
Britain	58,649	Germany	73,303
Italy	57,369	Colombia	71,550
Ukraine	50,861	Myanmar	64,890

Source: Department of Social and Economic Affairs, United Nations, *World Almanac, 1999.*

Southern Europe has seen a strong influx of immigrants from North Africa, while the more affluent parts of Asia are under pressure from their poorer neighbors. According to the population report bureau of the European Union, immigration from Northern Africa has increased annually by about 15% since 1990.

From 1975 to 1998, there has been a tremendous migration from developing to developed countries (Table 2.6). Much of that migration has taken place to Western Europe—primarily France and Germany—and to North America—primarily the United States.

The Aging of Populations

The developed nations are facing an increasingly older population as people live longer and birth rates continue to plummet. By 2050, more than 1 of every 3 people in the world will be over age 60, as compared to 1 of 5 today (Table 2.7). Adding to this will be the increasing number of persons aged 80 or older. Today, this is a substantial 16% of all residents in developed nations. By 2050, fully 27% of all persons in developed nations will have completed their eighth decade of life.

Table 2.6
Migration to Developed Countries, 1975–1998 (in thousands)

	1975-1979	1980-1984	1985-1989	1990-1994	1995-1998
TOTAL TO NORTH AMERICA	758,523	915,244	830,160	956,890	890,562
TOTAL TO OCEANIA	84,307	105,692	114,485	95,879	78,952
TOTAL TO WESTERN EUROPE	982,290	922,868	1,229,489	1,768,596	1,086,549
TOTAL TO DEVELOPED COUNTRIES	1,825,120	1,943,804	2,174,134	2,821,365	2,056,063

Source: Population Division, Department of Economic and Social Affairs, United Nations Secretariat.

For the industrial world, over the next 25 years, the number of persons of pensionable age (65 and older) will rise by 70 million, predicts the Organization for Economic Cooperation and Development (OECD, 1999 Annual Report), while the working-age population will rise by only 5 million. Japan, for example, will suffer a 25% decline over the next decade in the number of workers under 30.

Today, working taxpayers outnumber nonworking pensioners in the developed world by 3 to 1. By 2030, this ratio will fall to 1.5 to 1. In Italy and other West European nations, it will drop to 1 to 1 or lower![1] An inevitable result of the aging of the industrial population will be less growth.

It is completely the opposite in the non-industrial world. The number of young people, already much higher than in the developed world (Table 2.8), is expected to logarithmically increase over the next few years. Sub-Saharan Africa, Latin America, and South Asia are all experiencing huge rises in the numbers of women who produce more children than their mothers. Further, medical care, although still way behind its level in industrialized countries, is improving in these countries. Life expectancies are increasing as, for the first time in many places within developing countries, the average person is expected to live beyond fifty years.

The expanding, large populations of emerging markets are being coupled with a dramatic rise in per capita income in some markets. According to the Organization for Economic Cooperation and Development (OECD, Annual Report), the forecast for economic growth in the developing world is projected at 5% annually over the next 10 years. If China, India, Pakistan, Brazil, and Indonesia grow by an average of 6% per year through the year 2010 (still well-below their projections), approximately 900 million people will live in those countries with an income equivalent to that of the average American household. This group would represent the combined populations of the United States, the European Community, and Japan.

The number of emerging markets that belong to the group of the world's leading importers is quite large (Table 2.9). As the middle classes increase

Table 2.7
World Population, Aged 60 or Older, 2000–2050

	% AGED 60 OR OLDER		% AGED 80 OR OLDER	
	2000	2050	2000	2050
WORLD TOTAL	19	22	11	19
DEVELOPED COUNTRIES	19	33	16	27
DEVELOPING COUNTRIES	6	15	7	12

Source: Population Division, Department of Economic and Social Affairs, United Nations Secretariat.

in these countries, the demand for imported goods will also continue to increase.

COMMUNICATIONS

Worldwide communications networks are touching every corner of the planet. During the writing of this book, the authors communicated instantaneously from some of the most remote places on the globe—the Siberian tundra, the Central African rain forest, and Easter Island in the Pacific Ocean.

Technological development in communications is probably the single most important factor in providing companies greater access to emerging markets. Many telecommunications services previously available only in industrialized countries five years ago have become widespread throughout the entire planet (Table 2.10). In Latin America and Africa, the use of mobile phones is growing at 200% per year—compared to 15% in North America and 27% in Western Europe. Moreover, the widespread availability of television and radio has brought the most distant regions closer together.

The importation process in emerging markets, always an arduous and time-consuming task, has become dramatically easier through the widespread use of the fax machine. Customs authorities all over the world now permit the initiation of the importation process upon presentation of faxed copies of the original documents, while the goods are still in transit. This has saved importers valuable time and money in expediting goods at their arrival in the receiving country.

Although the complexity of the import system has been eased to some extent, it is still quite formidable for unsuspecting and unprepared firms. A U.S. manufacturer of chain saws learned the hard way how difficult the importation process can be when it failed to inspect the goods at its location prior to the loading of the container. The Letter of Credit from their customer in Latvia explicitly required the exporter to arrange a pre-shipment inspection using an independent verification agency. For whatever reason, the U.S. company neglected to carry out this requirement. The end result was a container of their product sitting in

Table 2.8
World Population, Percentages of Youth and Elderly, 2000–2025

	% UNDER AGE 15	% AGED 60 OR OLDER
WORLD TOTAL	30	10
DEVELOPED COUNTRIES	19	19
DEVELOPING COUNTRIES	38	6

Source: Population Division, Department of Economic and Social Affairs, United Nations Secretariat.

the port of Riga for more than six months! "Inside sources" estimate the cost of this oversight, including penalties, payoffs, freight surcharges, and banking fees, to have been in excess of US$250,000.

Nevertheless, the general state of emerging market import regulations is improving. Brazil, once one of the most notorious countries in which to import, requiring more than sixty different documents to be filed, today permits importers to initiate the customs clearing procedures immediately after the shipment departs the originating port and the documents are received by fax. This has reduced the average time to clear goods at a Brazilian port from thirty-five days to three.

Real-time communications has become possible through innovations in electronic commerce via the Internet. The spread of the information superhighway has provided a vanguard informational and marketing tool, especially for small and medium-sized companies. As early as 1996, prospective investors had access to more information about Vietnam than they could digest, from using the World Wide Web. They could read the entire foreign investment law and locate dozens of key business contacts. Foreigners could even tour Vietnam's most remote countryside from their PCs, using the Vietnam Homepage.

In Sub-Saharan Africa, the world's "least-connected" region with only five telephone lines per 1,000, fully forty-seven countries have achieved full Internet connectivity in just the last two years.[2] The percentage of middle-class Africans now with access to the Interest is increasing fourfold every year.[3]

Most important, the cost of telecommunications services has fallen across the board over the past decade. Many of the services previously available only to the rich are now accessible to an ever-larger population as the cost of usage continues to decrease. Yet, despite the fantastic advances in efficiency and cost reduction, companies not properly prepared for the inconsistency of telecommunications service in emerging markets still face an uphill battle.

A Western European producer of pharmaceuticals regularly scheduled a Monday morning teleconference with its distributors in Central Asia. The weekly sessions were designed to provide the manufacturer with the latest news con-

Table 2.9
World's Leading Importers, 1998 (US$ billion)

COUNTRY	VALUE
United States	944.6
European Union	801.4
Japan	280.5
Canada	205.0
China	188.7
Mexico	140.2
Taiwan	128.9
South Korea	93.3
Switzerland	80.0
Australia	64.7
Brazil	61.0
Malaysia	58.5
Singapore	54.9
Poland	48.0
Turkey	46.4
Russia	44.7
India	42.9
Thailand	41.8
Hong Kong	36.2
Norway	36.2
Philippines	32.0
Argentina	31.4
South Africa	29.3
Israel	29.1
Czech Republic	28.2
United Arab Emirates	27.4
Hungary	27.0
Saudi Arabia	25.8
Chile	18.8

Source: Department of Social and Economic Affairs, United Nations.

cerning its products' development in the local markets while also informing the distributors about new research back at headquarters. Unfortunately, the unpredictable local phone service did not allow for a regular series of discussions. The volume of usage on Monday morning seemed particularly high. On certain days, it was impossible to get through. Distributors and headquarters were both

Table 2.10
Communications Access, Selected Countries, 1998

COUNTRY	Televisions Per 100 Persons	Radios Per 100 Persons	Telephones Per 100 Persons
Argentina	4.6	1.5	6.3
Brazil	4.8	2.5	13.0
Chile	4.7	2.9	7.6
Colombia	8.5	5.6	10.0
Mexico	6.1	3.9	10.0
Panama	5.9	4.4	8.8
Venezuela	6.1	2.3	9.0
China	5.3	5.4	30.0
India	25.0	12.0	78.0
Indonesia	16.0	6.8	59.0
Malaysia	6.4	2.3	6.0
Pakistan	53.0	11.0	61.0
Philippines	2.1	6.9	48.0
South Korea	3.1	1.0	2.4
Taiwan	3.0	2.5	2.3
Thailand	8.5	5.3	17.0
Egypt	9.2	3.3	22.0
Greece	4.9	2.4	2.0
Israel	3.6	2.1	2.4
Nigeria	26.0	5.1	275.0
South Africa	9.9	3.2	11.0
Turkey	5.5	6.2	4.7
Zimbabwe	37.0	12.0	71.0
Czech Republic	2.1	1.6	4.2
Hungary	2.3	1.6	5.4
Poland	3.2	2.3	6.7
Romania	5.0	4.9	7.6
Russia	2.7	2.9	5.9
Britain	2.3	0.7	2.0
Japan	1.5	1.1	2.0
United States	1.2	0.5	1.6

Source: Department of Social and Economic Affairs, United Nations, *World Almanac, 1999*.

frustrated. To reschedule the meetings was difficult, and the result was a confused system of communications that set back the sale of the manufacturer's
products.

Samuni, a jewel broker in Congo, maintains a brisk business in his African
nation by staying in touch with the most current prices of gold and platinum on
the London exchange using his IMSAT satellite phone. A lunch with Samuni
in his hometown of Butembo, a city deep in the heart of Africa, will find him
calling his London contact 6,000 miles away every half hour to receive the most
current updates. Such information insures a profitable transaction for Samuni as
he buys and sells the precious metals that are mined from his mineral-rich nation.

GOVERNMENT ACTION

All over the world, governments are moving towards market economies. The
end of the Cold War has left political leaders with really one direction in which
to head their nation's economy—toward free and open markets. The socialist
or controlled model has been relegated to history as a failed ideal. The triumph
of Western values over the forces of communism has compelled the vast ma-

Table 2.11
Rates of GDP Growth, Countries in Transition, 1989–1999

COUNTRY	1989	1990	1991	1992	1993	1994	1995	1996	1997	1998	1999
Albania	-1.5	9.9	-10.1	-28.5	-7.3	9.7	9.4	8.2	9.1	-10.3	2.2
Bulgaria	2.6	-1.9	-9.1	-11.8	-7.2	-1.5	1.8	2.1	-10.9	-5.6	3.6
Czech Republic	N/A	N/A	N/A	N/A	0.5	2.7	4.8	4.1	1.4	3.2	0.3
Slovakia	N/A	N/A	N/A	N/A	-4.0	5.1	6.7	6.9	5.8	5.5	5.0
Hungary	N/A	N/A	-11.7	-3.1	-0.6	2.9	1.5	1.3	3.6	3.7	3.8
Poland	N/A	N/A	4.1	-7.1	2.7	3.8	5.3	6.9	6.2	5.8	3.1
Romania	N/A	N/A	-12.9	-8.8	1.6	3.9	7.1	4.1	-2.2	7.5	2.6
Croatia	N/A	N/A	-7.5	-18.9	-2.0	-2.6	6.0	2.6	5.1	5.7	5.5
Slovenia	N/A	N/A	-8.1	-8.9	-5.5	2.9	5.3	4.2	3.0	4.0	4.0
Macedonia	N/A	N/A	-10.2	-7.0	-7.9	-9.1	-1.9	-1.2	0.7	4.0	4.5
Yugoslavia	-7.9	-11.6	-27.9	-30.8	2.7	3.8	4.4	1.0	2.0	1.5	-1.4
Estonia	N/A	N/A	N/A	-14.1	-8.5	-1.8	4.2	4.1	6.0	6.5	5.7
Latvia	N/A	N/A	N/A	-34.9	-14.9	0.8	-1.0	2.9	3.8	4.5	4.2
Lithuania	N/A	N/A	N/A	-34.0	-30.3	0.8	2.9	3.6	4.5	5.0	4.7
Armenia	N/A	N/A	N/A	-41.7	-8.8	5.4	6.9	5.8	6.0	7.0	5.3
Azerbaijan	N/A	N/A	N/A	-22.6	-23.1	-19.7	-11.7	1.1	5.5	7.0	6.2
Belarus	N/A	N/A	N/A	-9.6	-7.7	-12.6	-10.3	2.5	5.0	4.0	4.7
Georgia	N/A	N/A	N/A	-44.9	-29.3	8.8	3.2	11.3	10.0	9.0	7.8
Kazakstan	N/A	N/A	N/A	-5.3	-9.1	-12.7	-8.2	0.5	2.0	4.0	3.7
Kyrgystan	N/A	N/A	N/A	-13.9	-15.5	-20.1	-5.3	5.6	3.0	7.0	7.0
Moldava	N/A	N/A	N/A	-29.0	-1.2	-31.2	-1.8	-8.1	-2.0	3.0	4.5
Russia	N/A	N/A	N/A	14.5	-8.6	12.8	-4.1	-5.5	0.5	1.5	1.8
Tajikistan	N/A	N/A	N/A	-31.0	-17.4	-12.6	-12.5	-16.8	-4.0	2.0	3.6
Turkmenistan	N/A	N/A	N/A	-35.7	1.4	-17.1	-10.0	0.1	-4.0	4.0	5.6
Ukraine	N/A	N/A	N/A	-9.9	-14.2	-22.8	-12.2	-10.0	-5.1	-1.0	2.8
Uzbekistan	N/A	N/A	N/A	-11.0	-2.3	-5.1	-1.2	1.6	3.2	5.0	5.0

Source: DSEA, ECE, and *World Economic and Social Survey, 1998* (United Nations, No. E.97.II.C.I).

jority of the world's leaders to embark upon the process of "opening up" their economies to the forces of global trade and integration. Even Cuba, widely viewed as one of the last bastions of defiant state control, is looking for solutions outside its borders as a way to meet the rising expectations of the Cuban people. Visiting Canadian businessmen are often treated as VIPs by the communist government as they negotiate trade deals directly with the Castro regime.

Almost all of the emerging markets in Central and Eastern Europe have successfully shifted from centrally planned economies to open, market ones. Although the transition from a command to a market economy began in the late 1980s in some Eastern European economies, political developments following the fall of the Berlin Wall in late 1989 and the breakup of the Soviet Union two years later accelerated this process. The collapse of the previous economic systems and relationships and the ensuing large-scale reorientation and reorganization of production initially sent output and trade into a steep decline and triggered rampant inflation. Since then, however, especially in recent years, the countries of Central and Eastern Europe, the Baltics, and Russia and other countries of the former Soviet Union have made significant progress in transition and in stabilizing output and prices (Table 2.11).[4]

The first phase of this transition consisted of the liberalization of markets and trade, privatization of state enterprises, and withdrawal of government from many activities. In the second phase, now under way in many of these countries, public and private institutions are striving to develop an effective market economy and to ensure that sound business practices become more firmly established.[5] Moreover, in light of the current Decelerated Pro-Activity phase, leaders are being urged to strengthen their financial sectors and maintain a high degree of fiscal integrity.

As governments seek to expand the influence of their country's economy, regional bodies are being formed to allow for a more liberal movement of goods and services across national boundaries. Latin America has emerged from its politically violent and economically volatile past to become a commercial powerhouse in its own right. The last decade has seen integration and growth through the rise of regional trade agreements in Latin America.

MERCOSUR, born in 1988, has achieved a complete and viable free-trade zone throughout Brazil, Argentina, Uruguay, and Paraguay in just eleven years. Chile and Bolivia will soon join. The Andean Pact has brought together Colombia, Peru, Venezuela, Ecuador, and Bolivia. Similarly, Central America established its own common market under the Central American Integration System established in 1993.

The United States, the economic and political leader of the hemisphere, has followed suit with its participation in the North American Free-Trade Agreement (NAFTA) and its support of the Free Trade Agreement of the Americas (FTAA). It is planned that by 2005 a free-trade zone will exist from Tierra del Fuego to Alaska under the FTAA.

When China launched its Economic Reforms and Open Door Policy in 1978, large numbers of foreign investors were immediately attracted to its market of a billion people, the largest in the world. For almost fifteen years after that policy was set into motion, overseas investment was slow to come to China. However, in the last seven years, as the restrictions on foreign firms were dramatically eased, foreign investment and trade has exploded. China is now the third largest exporter in the world. Direct investment from overseas has surpassed US$500 billion since 1993. Though vast areas of the countryside remain backward and poor, many Chinese cities—Beijing, Chongquing, Shanghai, Shenzen, Tienjin, Guangzhou—have now become a match for successful cities throughout the world.[6] It is estimated Shanghai will become the financial and banking center of Asia by 2015, replacing both Tokyo and Hong Kong.

URBANIZATION

As Americans and Europeans continue to flee the cities in favor of the surrounding suburbs, rural residents in developing nations flock to the cities in huge numbers (Table 2.12). According to the World Bank, nearly 50% of all human beings live in urban centers. This number is projected to increase by 29% over the next ten years. Virtually all of this urban growth is in emerging markets.

Table 2.12

Changes in Human Settlements, Urban and Rural, Selected Countries, 1995–2000

COUNTRY	% URBAN 1995	% RURAL 1995	% CHANGE 1995-2000 URBAN	% CHANGE 1995-2000 RURAL
Argentina	88	12	1.62	-1.55
Brazil	78	22	2.04	-1.58
Chile	84	16	1.67	-0.36
Colombia	72	28	2.46	0.33
Mexico	73	27	1.89	0.91
Panama	55	45	2.09	1.07
Venezuela	86	14	2.35	-0.01
China	30	70	2.47	0.22
India	27	73	2.84	1.19
Indonesia	36	64	4.22	0.31
Malaysia	54	46	3.34	0.36
Pakistan	34	66	4.31	1.92
Philippines	54	46	3.74	0.01
South Korea	78	22	1.73	-2.83
Taiwan	84	16	1.87	-0.85
Thailand	20	80	2.51	0.52
Egypt	44	56	2.28	1.59
Greece	59	41	0.58	-0.13
Israel	91	9	2.31	1.21
Nigeria	40	61	4.52	0.86
South Africa	49	51	1.91	1.09
Turkey	69	31	3.35	-2.75
Zimbabwe	32	68	3.53	0.35
Czech Republic	75	26	-0.11	-0.29
Hungary	63	37	-0.07	-0.92
Poland	64	36	0.67	-1.01
Romania	55	45	0.11	-0.93
Russia	76	24	0.31	-1.68
Britain	89	11	0.23	-0.32
Japan	78	22	0.37	-0.44
United States	76	24	1.11	-0.08

Source: Population Division of the UN Secretariat, *World Population Prospects, 1998*.

Latin America is the most urbanized region in the world, with over 65% of its people living in cities. Three of the largest cities in the world—Sao Paulo, Buenos Aires, and Mexico City—dominate their respective countries. "Secondary" cities like Lima, Caracas, Guayaquil, Santiago, and Bogota are each expected to exceed 8 million residents by 2010.

China has seen an explosion in its urban population as poor peasants come to the cities seeking work and better opportunities. Despite stringent resident laws, it is estimated more than 90 million rural Chinese have left their homes and illegally entered urban areas in search of a better way of life.

In Sub-Saharan Africa, still the least urbanized region in the world, Lagos, Kinshasa, Nairobi, and Johannesburg have grown to become regional leaders, affecting events outside their own country's borders.

The rise in the urban population is bringing more and more people in touch with global marketing and advertising campaigns. By 1998, nearly 50% of the residents in developing countries were living in areas where the influences of television, radio, mass advertising, and merchandising were inescapable.

THE RESULTS

The products of shifting demographics, widespread communication, favorable governmental action, and increasing urbanization in emerging markets are the creation of a new consumer class and a need for infrastructure development. Within the next twenty-five years, more than 900 million new consumers with the buying power of an average American household will be created. Well over 90% will come from high-growth emerging markets in Latin America, Southeast Asia, India, Central and Eastern Europe, Russia, Africa, and China.

Ian Menzies, president and CEO of Long-Airdox Company, a Virginia-based designer and manufacturer of coal-mining machinery, speaks for thousands of companies when he says, "The potential in the United States is stable, but the potential in emerging markets is growth, growth, growth!"[7]

For the past decade, many Fortune 500 giants have made less real profits in the United States as compared to the revenues gained from ventures in emerging markets. The meteoric rise in their share values has been due principally to success in new, high-growth emerging markets. Mature markets like the United States, Japan, and Western Europe no longer afford companies the opportunity for explosive expansion.

Recent events in Asia, Latin America, and Russia need to be placed into a proper context. As discussed earlier, Global Manifest Destiny is an unstoppable force. It is, however, not without with shifts and turns. Although the scope of some events like the Asian economic crisis may sometimes overwhelm our emotions for a brief moment, we can never lose sight of the inevitable economic integration of all of humankind. Global Manifest Destiny mandates this. We must look at the long term as "half-full" rather than "half-empty."

Despite all of the bad press, emerging markets still present dramatic growth potential. Leading companies continue to invest heavily in emerging markets while taking full advantage of the new circumstances that now exist. The Decelerated Pro-Activity phase, where we currently find ourselves, is the time to grab market share and prepare for the inevitable growth and profits that will occur in the next Accelerated Re-Activity phase. Smart companies are already leveraging this opportunity to its fullest extent.

Procter and Gamble has instituted "Organization 2005," which is seeking to create business strategies to capture the high-growth markets in the developing world. Procter and Gamble estimates its sales in emerging markets will approach $35 billion and grow by 80% over the next twenty years.[8]

Renault plans to produce its Clio model in plants throughout the developing world, including Russia, Brazil, Argentina, Slovenia, Turkey, and Colombia. Capacity will be 600,000 per year by 2001.[9]

Moreover, there will be 1 billion mobile communication devices worldwide by 2005, versus 600 million devices in 2003. Nearly 80% of the growth in this market will take place in emerging markets.[10]

Table 2.13
Direct Foreign Investment in India, 1993–1998 (US$ millions)

SOURCE	1993	1994	1995	1996	1997	1998
USA	98.8	202.8	192.4	188.6	205.6	245.8
UK	64.1	143.5	70.0	89.4	99.5	109.8
Japan	36.9	95.0	60.9	61.2	75.2	55.7
Netherlands	46.5	44.6	49.2	42.1	45.8	49.2
Germany	35.1	34.6	99.2	78.2	85.4	85.4
Switzerland	22.5	26.2	32.6	33.1	33.8	39.5
Singapore	9.9	24.5	59.8	89.2	78.5	45.7
Hong Kong	6.1	21.4	98.5	96.4	72.5	34.9
France	10.4	14.2	62.7	45.3	55.9	78.9
Others	38.7	265.3	693.1	879.6	558.9	682.1
TOTAL	369.0	872.1	1,418.4	1,603.1	1,311.1	1,427.0

Source: The Times of India, May 13, 1999, p. A9.

Although the current global economic downturn began in Southeast Asia when Thailand devalued the bhat in July 1997, worldwide business leaders are still optimistic on the region's long-term prospects. Eastman Kodak has announced plans to put more emphasis on emerging markets in Asia with the reorganization of its business in the region. According to Carl F. Kohrt, assistant CEO, "Emerging markets are a key for growth area for Kodak. Greater Asia is composed of several emerging and developing markets. Our move to a pan-Asian business model anticipates the future. It will result in a more efficient, customer-focused operation as we leverage growth opportunities in this very important region."[11]

DIC Ink and Chemicals, Inc., Japan's second-largest chemical producer, has announced it will make no basic changes to its business strategy in Asia. The company is pursuing its globalization strategy with emphasis on Asia, particularly in hard-hit Indonesia and Malaysia.[12]

India's GDP of $1.2 trillion makes it the sixth largest economy in the world. Although many of its Asian counterparts have been hit hard by the current downturn, India has held its ground. GDP in India is estimated to grow annually at 4–5% for the next ten years. Further, it is believed India will add between 75 million and 150 million new middle-class consumers within the next twenty-five years, bringing the total middle-class population in India to between 240 and 320 million people. Current market research suggests that there is a middle-class market segment of about 180 million people in India—nearly equal to that of the United States![13]

These consumers will come from India's large and growing pool of educated people who understand a market economy, the importance of customer service, and the challenge of being a global competitor (Table 2.13). India has the third-largest pool of technical and scientific workers in the world. The country reg-

Table 2.14
Direct Foreign Investment in China, 1996–1999 (US$ millions)

	1996	1997	1998	1999
US$ million	6,815,1	5,617.4	6,633.3	5,608.2

Source: China Ministry of Foreign Trade and Economic Cooperation.

ularly launches satellites, runs a sophisticated nuclear energy program, and has created some of the best software engineers on the planet.

Bangalore has become the "Silicon Valley of South Asia." The area has become a magnet for new investors, particularly high-tech companies. The area has strong educational facilities, a well-motivated population, superior software suppliers and contractors, and a developing industrial base.[14]

China has an estimated 70 million consumers with the same buying power as the average American household. This number is expected to quadruple in the next twenty-five years, in spite of current economic events (see Table 2.14). For many, the lunch crowds at the Tony Roma's in Shanghai and the Holiday Inn in Chongqing represent the future of China. Businessmen dressed in Armani suits incessantly scream out orders on their mobile phones between bites. The parking lots are filled with Mercedes Benzes and BMWs.

In Latin America, investment and interest are at record highs, despite recent events in Brazil. As evidence of the U.S. commercial commitment to the Americas, U.S. investment in Latin America in 1998 was US$140 billion. This amount exceeded all U.S. investments in Asia for the same year.

Along the Mexican border with the United States, investment has continued to exceed that of any other region in the world over the last decade. Tijuana, Laredo, Juarez, and Monterrey have become some of the largest manufacturing centers in the world. More television sets and VCRs come from Tijuana than from any other place on the planet.

Throughout the region, U.S. firms are stepping up their expansion efforts, notwithstanding the negative press the Brazilian currency devaluation has created. It has been announced that in the next five years, J.C. Penney will open twenty new stores in Chile and Mexico, Pizza Hut will open 500 new outlets throughout the region, and Blockbuster will open 250 new stores in Brazil—the third largest videocassette franchise market in the world after Japan and the United States. In addition, Wal-Mart, after strong success in Mexico and Puerto Rico, is pushing forward in Argentina and Brazil. And Xerox, the copier leader, has integrated its Brazilian, Mexican, and Argentine operations into its worldwide production system.[15]

European giants are following the U.S. lead and taking advantage of the favorable conditions in Latin America as well. France's Carrefour and the Netherlands' Makro are competing with each other in the supermarket business in Colombia and Brazil. United Colors of Benneton in 1991 purchased a one-million-acre sheep ranch in Argentina to supply wool to fashion apparel producers in South America. These factories have successfully serviced Benneton's 300-plus stores in the region. As a result, Benneton plans to expand its presence in the region by adding an additional 100 new stores over the next five years. Also, Swedish-Swiss multinational Asea-Brown-Boveri (ABB) expects to double its regional revenues by 2001.[16]

A decade into its first venture with free enterprise, Russia is still finding its way. The disparities between the cities and the Russian countryside are stark and in your face. Moscow may very well be one of the world's most expensive cities. Home to fifty casinos and an equal number of discos and theme restaurants, Moscow more closely resembles a major American city than one might think. The city center is the hub for the Russian government and international businesses. Outdoor cafes and restaurants dot the area during the spring and summer. Muscovites proudly proclaim the area is cleaner and safer than any other major city in the industrialized world.

However, once visitors to Russia leave the comforts of Moscow, they are transported some eighty years into the past. Bottled water with gas is everywhere. Bottled water without gas is not easy to find in the Russian countryside; it is called vodka. Antiquated roads, machinery, and thinking dominate the rural landscape. Still, given the tremendous disparities and the recent financial difficulties, companies are looking at the long-term possibilities. Vladimir Marov, director of the Otis Elevator plant in St. Petersburg, speaks for a number of Western multinationals when he says, "The crisis hit us very hard. The question came up among our leadership about whether [we] should continue. And we decided we should, because the potential is so big."[17] Nestle, Lucent Technologies, and others are coping with the current downturn by settling deeper into Russia rather than pulling out.[18]

In Africa, Coca-Cola is doubling its efforts. While its products have long been available in South and West Africa, the company has ignored the continent's underdeveloped markets. Only recently has Africa been given priority status. M. Douglas Ivester, former CEO of Coca-Cola, aimed to double sales in Africa within five years, from 712 million cases in 1997. Although it is currently only 3% of the company's global total, Coke's strategy includes strengthening the bottler network, increasing the number of outlets and intensifying the marketing to consumers.[19]

Central and Eastern Europe are also experiencing heightened demands for consumer goods. In response, General Motors via Opel is planning to offer a micro-van, dubbed the "O-Car," which is being developed with Suzuki for sale in Central and Eastern Europe. In Poland, GM will build the Astra Classic for at least the next five years, beginning this year. It will add an all-new small micro-van to compete with the Polish produced Fiat Seicento. The GM minicar will be based on a Suzuki model that Suzuki will build in Hungary.[20]

Corresponding to the rise in personal consumption, the governments of emerging markets continue to spend billions of dollars on infrastructure projects and improvements. The World Bank estimates that more than US$2 trillion will continue to be spent on infrastructure in emerging markets over the next ten years. Energy exploration and generation, airports and air traffic control systems, telecommunications and satellite-ready technology, hospitals and health care services, automotive and spare parts production, banking and insurance, and environmental cleanup will all absorb billions of dollars as emerging markets seek to move into the first world.

Danzas, the world's second-largest freight forwarder, is opening its own offices in Latin America, Eastern and Central Europe, and Asia. This is a great leap forward for the transportation/logistics industry in the developing world. This marks a fundamental shift in the traditional model of using local agents to provide import/export services.

In Latin America, vast projects are upgrading airports, roads, and ocean ports. Communications and new patterns in consumer life styles are redefining markets. Tenneco has joined with Australian and British companies to build a 2,000-mile pipeline to take Bolivian gas into Brazil for more than US$2 billion. Hughes Communications, the world's largest private satellite operator, plans to join forces with three Latin American companies to establish Direct-TV Latin America—an estimated joint venture for more than US$3 billion.[21]

As a further example of the need and subsequent investment that comes with infrastructure development, it would be worthwhile to look at India's recent programs. In 1994, the government ended its monopoly on telecommunications and allowed private investors to set up telephone companies. Advanced communication services such as fax, data transmission, and leased circuits are becoming increasingly common. The total amount to be spent was estimated at US$7.36 billion over the next ten years.[22]

The power situation in India is poor, to say the least. Of the forty-nine proposed private sector power projects in India, nineteen involve U.S. firms. Another twenty projects are under consideration. These projects will increase India's current capacity from 66,000 megawatts to over 100,000. The total amount to be spent will be well over US$16.5 billion.[23]

The Indian government is now offering new incentives to private foreign firms in twenty-seven projects to construct, maintain, and operate bypass roads, bridges, and expressways. The total amount already allocated for these projects is over US$4.7 billion. Over the next few years, U.S. networking major 3Com will set up a wholly owned subsidiary in India before mid-2000 and make India a logistics hub for its operations on the subcontinent. Atul Kunwar, Country Manager, says, "We plan to make Indian operations the hub for our business in Nepal, Sri Lanka, and Bangladesh once the subsidiary is announced."[24]

Federal Express has opened its fourth World Service Center (WSC) in Delhi and has announced plans to open three more in the country to strengthen its presence in the subcontinent. Fedex is planning to open two more WSCs in the national capital of New Delhi and the other in Calcutta in the eastern state of West Bengal, according to the Fedex managing director for the Indian subcontinent, Arun Kuma. "The WSC is a reflection of our strategy of being close to our customers and providing them with innovative, value-added services."[25]

In 1996, China announced its plans to bring electricity to three hundred counties and increase its rural hydroelectric capacity by 300% by the end of the century. It was announced in early 1999 that while the goal had been achieved another US$3.5 billion was being allocated to the construction of fifty-two hydropower and water supply projects.[26]

Evidently, despite the well-publicized "crisis" in emerging markets, industry leaders continue to seize the opportunity. During this current Decelerated Pro-Activity Phase, investment and strategic planning for some of the world's smartest companies are still focusing on emerging markets. Global Manifest Destiny has provided the moment; it is now our opportunity to seize it.

NOTES

1. "A Changing World Population," *U.S. News & World Report*, March 1, 1999.

2. Gumisai Mutume, "Communications—Africa," *Interpress Service*, June 10, 1998.

3. Ibid.

4. Julian Exeter and Steven Fries, "The Post-Communist Transition: Patterns and Prospects," *Finance & Development*, 35, September 1998.

5. Ibid.

6. Yim Yu Wong and Thomas E. Maher, "New Key Success Factors for China's Growing Market," *Business Horizons*, May–June 1998.

7. "Virginia Mining Manufacturer Looks Overseas for Customers," *Roanoke Times*, June 12, 1998.

8. Greg Jacobson, "P & G Is Putting on a Global Face," *MMR*, March 8, 1999.

9. Hugh Hunston, "Renault Positions Clio as Global Car," *Automotive Industries*, 31, June 1998.

10. "Global Number of Mobile Communications Devices Will Reach 600 million in 2003 and 1 Billion by 2005," *Computing*, March 18, 1999.

11. "Eastman Kodak Plans to Redouble Its Efforts in Asia," *Newsbytes News Network*, March 15, 1999.

12. *Japan Chemical Week*, 11, May 14, 1998.

13. Philip Banks and Ganesh Natarajan, "India: The Next Asian Tiger?" "DIC Keeps to Asia Strategy," *Business Horizons*, May–June 1995.

14. Ibid.

15. John S. Hill and Giles D'Souza, "Tapping the Americas Market," *Journal of Business Strategy*, July–August 1998.

16. Ibid.

17. Neela Banjerjee, "Hoping Bear Will Awaken," *New York Times*, May 1, 1999.

18. Ibid.

19. "Putting Africa on Coke's Map," *New York Times*, May 26, 1998, p. 32.

20. Diana Kurylko, "Makers Develop Hybrids for Emerging Markets," *Automotive News Europe*, 3, June 22, 1998.

21. Hill and D'Souza, "Tapping the Americas Market."

22. Raj G. Javalgi and Vijay S. Talluri, "The Emerging Role of India in International Business," *Business Horizons*, September–October 1996.

23. Ibid.

24. "3COM to Set Up Wholly-Owned Subsidiary in India," *Asia Pulse*, March 23, 1999.

25. "Federal Express Opens its 4th World Service Center in Delhi," *Asia Pulse*, March 22, 1999.

26. "China Plans Overseas Financing for Hydro Projects," *International Water Power & Dam Construction*, 50, July 1998.

3

Perils: The Inherent Realities of Emerging Markets

The tree with the sweetest fruits is guarded by demons.

Swahili Proverb

Thomas had just arrived into the strange, French-style hotel in Niamey. His journey earlier that day had taken him from N'djamena via Air Chad to the capital of Niger. The normally two-hour flight had taken ten, and all he wanted was a bed and a shower. He filled out the customary forms and turned over his passport. The person behind the counter collected the documents and disappeared. Ten minutes later, the hotel manager came out and gave Thomas the key to his room, his passport, and one electric lightbulb.

"There are no bulbs in your room, sir. They keep being stolen. This is *the* bulb for your room."

"Thank you very much."

"By the way, sir, I'll need 15,000 CFA."

"For what?"

"Deposit on the lightbulb."

The commercial environment in the United States allows for a substantial amount of flexibility for the businessperson. The phones work. The federal government guarantees depositors' bank accounts. The transportation network is one of the most developed in the world. In a dispute between parties, juries, not soldiers with guns, are likely to resolve the issue.

However, the atmosphere in emerging markets is not nearly as accommodating and can be downright hostile. In order to take advantage of the phenomenal opportunities that exist in high-growth emerging markets, it is critical to identify the inherent realities of those nations. All that glitters isn't gold. A failure to realize this can result in terribly expensive and even dangerous consequences.

Just traveling to emerging markets can be considered "on the edge." In many countries, air travel delays can last up to days for no apparent reason. One morning, while waiting for our return flight on Air Madagascar from Mahanjanga to Antananarivo, our three co-passengers and we were told there would be a "slight delay." Eight hours later, we were instructed to take all of our luggage and wait for the arriving plane on the tarmac. As the approaching aircraft came into view, it descended to about 3,000 meters, but then quickly reversed itself and flew off into the setting sun. The airline representative came out, announced that the flight was canceled, and—incredibly—stated that the next departure would be in three days. He then quietly slipped away.

Our American psyches demanded an explanation. After scouring the airport for nearly an hour for someone to speak with, we finally found an "airport official" who looked as if he knew what he was talking about. We explained the situation:

"We saw the plane!"

"How many were there on the tarmac?" he asked.

"Five."

"Well, there's your problem," he quipped. "They won't land unless there are seven passengers. However, there is good news. The bus ride over the mountains to Antananarivo is only forty-eight hours. You'll actually arrive a whole day earlier than if you wait for the plane."

Police, customs officials, and other pseudo-authorities always seem to be shaking down visitors as a way to supplement their meager salaries. From the moment you leave your plane in Lagos until the moment you arrive at a downtown hotel, the number of occasions on which you are asked for "a little more" than the usual and customary fees is around five. If, by bad luck, your flight is delayed and you arrive at night into the Nigerian capital, it can easily cost an extra US$100 simply to have your yellow fever card approved, customs clearance of your baggage facilitated, and your passport stamped.

When you finally arrive at your hotel room in most emerging markets, you quickly discover that basic services like lightbulbs and warm water are never in great supply, even in the most "deluxe" of accommodations. In Russia, the difference between visiting Moscow and the rest of the country is like that between night and day. Moscow is home to several five-star hotels that are quite comfortable, although very expensive. On the other hand, throughout the vast Russian countryside, clean sheets and hot running water at a hotel are often considered extra amenities. It is quite common for foreigners to have their incoming faxes pilfered and hotel rooms bugged by competitors, current or potential distributors, or even local business partners seeking to gain valuable information. Across West Africa, a hot shower typically consists of three buckets of lukewarm water left in front of your door in the morning.

Doing business in emerging markets can be equally frustrating. A few years ago, one of the largest candy and ice cream makers in the world decided to provide portable freezers to small grocery stores throughout Kazakhstan in order to keep its products fresh. This global manufacturer believed that such a large investment would bury the competition and give it a virtual monopoly in the country of 17 million. However, management failed to realize a fundamental reality of daily life in Kazakhstan.

Neighboring Uzbekistan, which provides much of the electricity to Kazakhstan, periodically turns off the power during the middle of the night without any notice. The availability of electricity in Kazakhstan is a function of the daily political situation between the two countries and the amount of money the Kazaks owe the Uzbeks on their electric bill. Needless to say, the morning after the first "blackout" provided quite a lesson for the management of this worldwide confectioner.

In the Ukraine, a Fortune 500 company was asked to provide the funding for a new fiber-optic system for the government offices in Kiev in order to acquire "a special tax relief" for its products. The "investment" of more than $5 million secured the desired result.

Recently, R.J. Reynolds International purchased an already-existing factory in Hyderabad, India. After the sale of the facility, it was discovered that the availability of electricity from the neighboring city was at best sporadic. It was necessary to make additional, sizable investments in a power plant in order to ensure a continuous and reliable supply of energy on the factory floor.

Such stories are commonplace. Without recognizing the realities inherent to emerging markets and being able to navigate the minefields these realities create, firms are doomed to lose money and never realize their full potential.

The realities presented here are not value judgments or moral assessments from the Western point of view as to what emerging markets are not. When leaving the comfort and security of North America or Western Europe to travel to emerging markets, it is best to leave your beliefs and mores at home. Emerging markets pose a tremendous threat to the Western businessperson who vigilantly holds to his or her particular standards of right and wrong. Too many Westerners have been robbed, imprisoned, or even killed for fighting against what they felt was immorality or corruption in a particular emerging market.

In the former Zaire, now Congo, three Western businesspeople were incarcerated in 1998 because they failed to pay the "necessary amounts" to "relevant government offices" in order to secure their mining contracts. The Westerners claimed they would not pay on "moral grounds." They were promptly arrested and put in jail for conspiracy and sedition against the state. They were eventually released six weeks later—with dysentery, dehydration, and malaria—when the "relevant departments" were finally paid in full.

In Colombia, a Western businessman had rented a motorcycle and a helmet for the day to explore the beautiful beach outside of Barranquilla. As he was leaving the rental shop, he was promptly pulled over by the police and placed under arrest. When asked why he was arrested, the police officer told him it was because he was wearing a motorcycle helmet. It seems in Colombia it is against the law to wear a motorcycle helmet because they are often used as cover for the *saccarios* who work as paid assassins from the backs of their bikes.

Emerging markets and their customs, traditions, and ways of doing things just are what they are—not good or bad, not right or wrong. The sooner Western businesspeople accept this fact of life, the better off they will be in doing business in emerging markets.

REALITY #1—CURRENCY ISSUES

A fundamental question is, Can you get your money out? For those doing business in emerging markets, this is a valid concern. Stringent government controls and uncertain banking practices make the process difficult. Along the same line is the question, How can you protect the real value of your currency? Hyperinflation is a real issue. If the exporter is not prepared, hyperinflation can easily wipe out any profits as well as all of the start-up costs.

Before the economic implosion of Russia in August of 1998, the ruble was one of the most stable currencies in all of Europe, trading securely between 5.7 and 6.2 to the U.S. dollar. For most of 1998, analysts both inside and outside of Russia knew a correction was inevitable, at somewhere around 12–13 rubles to the dollar. However, as events spun out of control, nobody could have imagined that by early 1999, the ruble would be trading as high as 32 to 1!

Like Russia, Turkey, Brazil, Hungary, and Venezuela have all recently experienced heavy devaluations of their currencies against the U.S. dollar (Table 3.1).[1]

Moreover, the 1999 inflation rates for some of the highest growth emerging markets are projected to be as shown in Table 3.2.[2] The realities of sudden currency and inflation-rate shocks within emerging markets makes it critical for business leaders to develop their strategic planning accordingly (Table 3.3).

Another major concern is the availability of hard currency. Many of the fastest-growing emerging markets are still based upon local, "soft" currency—money traded only in that particular country. During the runaway inflation in Argentina during the late 1980s and early 1990s, the Buenos Aires government decided to institute a new currency—the peso. The new money was targeted for a 1:1 exchange rate with the U.S. dollar. To substantiate its value, one U.S. dollar was placed into reserve for each new peso released into circulation. In theory, one Argentine peso became worth one U.S. dollar. When paying for dinner in Mendoza or Rosario, it is possible to pay the check in dollars or in pesos and receive change in either currency. The success of this new concept is evidenced by the fact that several years later, neighboring Brazil implemented the same formula in establishing the real. Both nations, through the creation of

Table 3.1
Currency Fluctuations, Selected Countries, 1999

COUNTRY	CURRENCY UNITS 1998 (per $)	CURRENCY UNITS 1999 (per $)	% CHANGE
Argentina	1.00	1.00	nil
Brazil	1.19	1.94	63.0%
Chile	463.00	541.00	17.0%
Colombia	1,566.00	1,942.00	24.0%
Panama	1.00	1.00	nil
Venezuela	569.00	634.00	11.0%
China	8.28	8.28	nil
India	42.50	43.40	0.2%
Malaysia	3.80	3.80	nil
Pakistan	49.80	51.85	0.4%
Philippines	39.90	40.30	0.1%
Thailand	36.30	38.70	0.7%
Egypt	3.42	3.42	nil
Greece	280.00	317.00	13.6%
Israel	4.13	4.21	0.2%
Nigeria	88.85	96.50	0.9%
South Africa	5.68	6.15	8.0%
Turkey	296,095.00	499,550.00	69.0%
Zimbabwe	37.16	38.17	0.3%
Czech Republic	29.80	34.90	17.0%
Hungary	217.00	246.00	13.0%
Poland	3.45	4.19	21.0%
Romania	10,950.00	17,860.00	63.0%
Russia	18.57	26.40	42.0%

Source: The Economist.

new currencies pegged to the U.S. dollar, have halted the 2,000% inflation that defined their countries throughout the last decade.

However, banks throughout South America and the United States refuse to give the bearer of Argentine pesos the equivalent number in U.S. dollars. While trying to change Argentine pesos for Peruvian soles at the Banco Nacional del Peru, it is common to receive the equivalent of 42 U.S. cents to the peso. The highest exchange rate the authors have been able to find is 78 U.S. cents to the peso—22% less than the value in Argentina.

The CFA franc used throughout the Francophone countries of Africa is tied directly to the French franc. In hotels, banks, and Bureaus de Change in Abidjan, for example, it is quite easy to receive the official rate of 100 French francs for 550 CFA. However, upon arrival at Charles de Gaulle Airport in Paris, the exchange rate falls to about 75 French francs for the same 550 CFA. At change houses in downtown Paris, the exchange rate is even worse—about 50 French francs for 550 CFA.

The Chinese yuan in China is pegged at about 8.3 to the U.S. dollar. However, because of the strict currency controls in China, any yuan outside of China is practically worthless. Many Americans have left China with a pocket full of yuan only later to realize the money was literally worth less than the paper it was printed on.

Additionally, the vast majority of emerging markets always seem to be short

Table 3.2
Inflation Rates, Selected Countries, 1999

COUNTRY	Inflation Rate
Argentina	-1.7
Brazil	6.9
Chile	2.5
Colombia	9.3
Mexico	14.9
Panama	4.1
Venezuela	20.2
China	-0.6
India	2.1
Indonesia	1.6
Malaysia	2.1
Pakistan	9.7
Philippines	5.4
South Korea	1.2
Taiwan	0.4
Thailand	-0.5
Egypt	2.4
Greece	2.2
Israel	2.9
Nigeria	8.9
South Africa	1.7
Turkey	64.7
Zimbabwe	26.7
Czech Republic	1.4
Hungary	10.5
Poland	8.9
Romania	8.7
Russia	62.0
Britain	1.2
Japan	-0.2
United States	2.6

Source: The Economist.

Table 3.3
Emerging Markets: Consumer Price Inflation, 1989–1999 (Annual % Change)

	1989	1990	1991	1992	1993	1994	1995	1996	1997	1998	1999
All Emerging Markets	126.9	370.6	534.4	81.6	132.9	254.1	134.6	20.9	16.6	15.1	10.5
Latin America	363.6	1128.6	1679.6	210.7	354.1	757.8	326.4	23.4	19.5	12	8.25
Africa	18.3	19.8	16.1	96.1	172.3	112.5	244.7	40.6	34.2	47.2	8.25
Western Asia	33.1	27.7	23.9	27.9	27,5	41.6	40.7	32.9	35.6	38.5	26.7
Eastern & Southern Asia	6.3	5.9	14.8	9.5	7.2	5.7	7.1	6.8	6.2	5.7	6.75
China	18.8	18.5	3.2	3.3	6.4	14.7	24.1	17.1	8.3	4.3	5.5

Source: UN/DSEA, based on IMF, *International Financial Statistics*, 1999.

on hard currency because of the need to cover their foreign obligations. Therefore, generating hard currency is invariably a challenge. In our work with some of Europe's and North America's most successful firms, we have discovered several creative ways to manage this difficulty, as follows.

1. Finance other local businesses that allow you to get some hard cash offshore. One creative firm financed a coffee plantation in a market where it was selling a completely separate product. The funds gained from the export sale of the coffee compensated for the lack of hard currency generated from the other business.

2. Locate an international agency or company that is setting up operations in the country and needs local currency. It may be possible to supply its local currency needs in exchange for hard currency paid to your offshore account.

3. Sell as much as possible in hard currency, even at discounted prices. Many firms fail to realize that the most important goal is to enter the marketplace. Once the product is well known, it is possible to raise the sale price. However, a desire to keep pricing high from the onset may prohibit the introduction of the product and cause much higher costs in the future.

4. Find a local company that has a large amount of local currency. It is quite possible to cut a deal whereby you would pay that firm in hard currency from an offshore account and receive local currency at a better exchange rate. The difference in the exchange rate would justify the transaction.

5. Minimize the amount of any hard currency brought into the country. It is much easier to bring hard currency in than to get it out.

6. Negotiate with the local government for at least a guaranteed amount of hard currency to be available when you "change back" your locally earned currency.

7. Consider barter or countertrade. Many would-be importing countries lack the capacity to buy goods overseas. These nations seek to use locally produced goods as a means of payment. If the conditions are favorable, countertrade will increase the amount of potential sales and new markets. India, Brazil, Iran, and Mexico are some of the largest "countertraders" in the world. For example, in the cash-strapped former Soviet Union

in the early days after the fall of communism, PepsiCo sometimes swapped Stolichanaya vodka for soft drinks. PepsiCo then sold the vodka in the United States, which allowed it to earn a hard-currency profit.

In addition to these strategies, some emerging market companies seek to overcome the currency issues through parallel invoicing schemes. That is, the amount declared to customs in the receiving country is less than the actual value of the goods purchased. This activity covers two major areas of interest for the importer. First, the amount of hard currency to be sent from the receiving country is minimized and therefore is less costly. Normally, the difference in the value of the two invoices is made up through the transfer of funds from offshore bank accounts. Second, the lower declared value reduces the amount of import duties the importer will pay to the local customs authorities.

The parallel invoice method is commonly used in international trade, especially in those countries with excessively high import duties. However, we would be remiss if we didn't point out that it is still illegal in virtually every country in the world and contrary to every international trade agreement currently in use.

REALITY #2—INFRASTRUCTURE

The wonders of efficient, modern distribution systems are only fully appreciated in their absence. Many countries in the world are "logistically challenged." In other words, things simply don't work very well. Transportation, communication, and energy deficiencies all affect cost and effectiveness when doing business in emerging markets. Firms therefore must adapt their operations to the infrastructure constraints.

Transport is the worst infrastructure failing in emerging markets. Throughout most of Asia and Latin America, the capacity to move goods is highly inadequate. Hot climates, poor roads, and a general lack of modern facilities limit the possibilities of efficient distribution. Delivery of goods from Shanghai to Beijing—a distance of 650 miles—can take up to three weeks. Within this environment, perishable goods face great difficulties. Conversely, products with long shelf-lives have natural advantages in the quest for distribution.

As a way to evaluate the emerging markets with the greatest opportunities, many successful firms have analyzed the percentage of gross domestic product being spent or budgeted for infrastructure improvements. In the early 1990s, South Korea, Brazil, and India were spending on average 2.5% of GDP on transportation-related projects. Interestingly, despite the recent downturns in their economies, both South Korea and Brazil have increased their allocations for infrastructure projects, while India's has remained steady.

Communication infrastructure is becoming a key priority within many emerging markets. China is seeking to triple its switching capacity from less than 40 million lines in 1995 to 100 million lines by the year 2000. The estimated cost of this project alone is more than US$10 billion. India is hoping to match the Chinese example.

The potential for communication growth is fantastic. This is evident by looking at the number of telephone lines per person in various countries in 1998 (Table 3.4).[3]

Energy capacity is a major issue when looking at infrastructure concerns for emerging markets. Repeated power outages affect not only consumer products like television sets and garage-door openers, but also the course of daily business. Security systems, modems, and air conditioning do not function very well without electricity. As anyone who sends fax messages overseas can attest, one of the most frustrating moments in global business occurs when the receiving machine cannot respond due to a power outage. All business seems to come to a screeching halt.

In Guayaquil, Ecuador's largest city and commercial center, the 4.5 million residents of this tropical city are constantly subjected to roaming blackouts. It is a daily occurrence that in one part of the city the electricity is working while another neighborhood has none. As the hours change, so do the places where is electricity is made available. Unfortunately, the blackouts are random and completely unpredictable. There is no way to tell which section of town on a particular day at a specific moment will have or will not have electrical service. Because of the constant uncertainty, things like planning, scheduling, and preparation are done more as courtesies than as serious attempts to accomplish something.

Less than 20% of the world's population has access to safe water and safe sanitation (Table 3.5). At a recent conference in South Africa of the nonaligned nations, the attendees almost unanimously agreed that the number-one environmental issue facing their countries was not air pollution, the loss of the rain forest, or the destruction of particular species, but the processing of human waste.

The deficient infrastructure in emerging markets directly impacts product development. It compels the businessperson to look at several key issues regarding the product.

1. Is barter or countertrade needed? Letters of credit and bank transfers are sometimes so costly they become prohibitive. In many emerging markets the cost of a letter of credit is a percentage of the total amount of the shipment. In some countries, it can be as high as 4% of the value of the credit. The cost of a bank transfer in countries that have strict currency requirements can be exorbitant as well. To wire transfer any amount from a typical African country can easily cost upward of US$500 per US$5,000 sent.

2. What is the degree of the product's standardization? Simple things like electrical outlets and voltage requirements can render products unusable. Anyone who has tried

Table 3.4
Telephone Lines per 100 Persons, Selected Countries, 1998

COUNTRY	Telephone Lines
Argentina	6.3
Brazil	13.0
Chile	7.6
Colombia	10.0
Mexico	10.0
Panama	8.8
Venezuela	9.0
China	30.0
India	78.0
Indonesia	59.0
Malaysia	6.0
Pakistan	61.0
Philippines	48.0
South Korea	2.4
Taiwan	2.3
Thailand	17.0
Egypt	22.0
Greece	2.0
Israel	2.4
Nigeria	275.0
South Africa	11.0
Turkey	4.7
Zimbabwe	71.0
Czech Republic	4.2
Hungary	5.4
Poland	6.7
Romania	7.6
Russia	5.9
Britain	2.0
Japan	2.0
United States	1.6

Source: Department of Social and Economic Affairs, United Nations, *World Almanac, 1999*.

to plug his U.S. electric shaver into a hotel room outlet in Argentina or South Africa will have quite a time before realizing the plug simply doesn't fit the outlet.

3. What is the complexity of the product? If it breaks, can somebody locally fix it? The resourcefulness of mechanics in emerging markets is a tribute to the creative aspects of the human mind. We have seen the complete overhaul of a bus engine in forty

Table 3.5
Water Supply and Sanitation, Selected Countries, 1998

COUNTRY	% ACCESS TO SAFE WATER		% ACCESS TO SAFE SANITATION	
	URBAN	RURAL	URBAN	RURAL
Argentina	71	24	80	42
Brazil	80	28	74	43
Chile	99	47	95	45
Colombia	90	32	70	27
Mexico	90	66	93	29
Panama	99	73	99	81
Venezuela	79	79	74	60
China	65	32	68	16
India	49	82	58	4
Indonesia	87	57	88	61
Malaysia	100	89	94	66
Pakistan	85	56	75	24
Philippines	94	24	88	22
South Korea	93	73	100	100
Thailand	94	88	98	95
Egypt	95	74	95	49
Greece	100	94	100	94
Israel	100	95	100	99
Nigeria	80	39	82	48
South Africa	90	33	78	12
Turkey	72	63	99	90
Zimbabwe	99	64	99	48
Poland	89	80	100	100
Romania	70	10	81	36

Source: White Paper, "Monitoring and Evaluation of the Health for All Strategy" (World Health Organization, 1997).

minutes on an Andean highway with nothing more than three guys, a screwdriver, and a crescent wrench. However, there do exist circumstances when specialized tools or knowledge of a particular product are required, regardless of the abilities of the mechanic or service technician.

4. What is the bulk or size of the product? How will the product be transported? The poor transport system in most emerging markets mandates that products must be easily moved from one transport form to another. As most of the transport industry in emerging markets is still done via human labor, a crate with a gross weight of 350 kg may have to wait weeks before a forklift can be located to move the box. A much lighter object can be moved more quickly, even if by human hands. Further, if the product has a tendency to perish quickly, it may be difficult to maintain its shelf-life, given the inherent delays that transport systems in emerging markets encounter.

5. What are the after-sales service requirements of the product? Where would service centers and spare parts inventories be located? The geographic diversity that characterizes many emerging markets is a challenge for companies looking to establish after-service centers. In Mexico, the mountainous terrain means that separate service centers should be set up in Mexico City, Guadalajara, the U.S. frontier zone, the coastal regions of Yucatan, and in the south along the Guatemalan border.

6. What is the unit price? If it is high, then the local sales per transaction will be low— primarily due to the limited amount of money. Most people and businesses in emerging markets do not have a lot of money. The more expensive your product is, the fewer the people who will buy it.

7. What is the competitiveness of the product? Does a possible substitute for the product exist? There is normally a competitive environment for any product introduced into an emerging market. Rigidity is not a useful characteristic in doing business there. The ability to easily replace a product at a given moment helps in "going with the flow."

Although it may seem that the weak infrastructure in emerging markets is a great hindrance, many firms have actually profited from the poor conditions. Governments are eager to negotiate lucrative deals with companies that offer to improve their infrastructure in some way.

In Vietnam, the raising of capital for infrastructure is even more overt. After witnessing the failure of many of the economic development plans in Thailand, the Vietnamese government desperately wanted to avoid the mistakes of its neighbor's wild, unstructured, and erratic economic growth of the 1980s and 1990s. Therefore, in order to finance their long-range economic goals, the Vietnamese government initiated a system of moderate taxation levied on all foreign companies doing business in their country. These taxes are set aside specifically for such infrastructure improvements as road and bridge systems; water, electricity, and other utilities projects; improvements to telecommunications; and increases in postal efficiency.

REALITY #3—STAFFING

Emerging markets are chronically short on experienced managers. An alarmingly large portion of multinational corporations readily admit that the shortage of competent white-collar personnel restricts growth. Further, expatriates are often required for key management positions, even though their services are incredibly expensive. Housing in Beijing or Moscow can easily cost more than US$25,000 per month for a two-bedroom apartment. It is normal to pay the lease two years in advance—in cash! In many cases, companies have paid as much as US$100,000–US$200,000 additionally to refurbish apartments in order to bring them up to Western standards.

For generations, the best and brightest in Africa and Latin America forsook careers in private enterprise in exchange for jobs in the pubic sector. The potential to acquire wealth was much greater in working for the government than in any other place in society. Young people graduating from universities either at home or abroad invariably entered the bureaucracy because "that's where the money is." It was much easier to take 10% off the top on a government project than to work for almost slave wages in small, inefficient private firms.

In the former Soviet Union, centralized governments trained people in the pure sciences and in applications for the production of military hardware, not in market-oriented practices. As a result, in the former Soviet Union as well as many other emerging markets, there is a shortage of experienced, well-trained workers at both the white-collar and the blue-collar levels. Moreover, for the relatively few trained and experienced personnel, particularly in the white-collar ranks, Western companies entering these markets fiercely compete for the scarce qualified and competent workers. For example, an American manufacturer of telecommunications equipment was forced to pay a local Russian engineer more than US$50,000 as a signing bonus to leave his present employer and sign up with it because so few Russian engineers could grasp Western-style business methods.

Consequently, employee retention is a critical issue confronting many firms doing business in emerging markets. Companies are often forced to bid up pay scales to attract and retain local nationals. Competitors are always seeking to lure employees away because of their knowledge and experience. In short, staffing is a tough, expensive reality in emerging markets.

During the most recent Accelerated Re-Activity phase, it was quite common to witness white-collar nationals enter a new job, only to depart three months later to a competitor for a 10–20% increase in salary and benefits. Stories of local nationals working for five or six different companies in a single year, increasing their salary each time, were quite common during the Accelerated Re-Activity phase.

A Western manufacturer of generators decided to enter India through the establishment of an office staffed primarily by local managers. When word got out of the company's plan for this important market, even before any official announcements were made, the headquarters was inundated with resumes from Indians who were currently employed as managers at its competitor's local office.

It goes without saying that employee loyalty among local nationals has been a fundamental concern with many Western companies. Although difficult to insure, some effective actions have been taken to increase the levels of employee retention and loyalty, such as the following.

- Training and periodic visits to European or U.S. operations provide local nationals with the perspective that they are part of something much greater. The feeling of isolation in an emerging market often leads to a strong sense of self-preservation at all costs. Linking local nationals with the corporate culture at a global level elevates their sense of worth and purpose. A Spanish company provides its South American managers and their wives with biannual trips to its corporate headquarters in Barcelona.

- Provide incentives that may include overseas assignments for local nationals, giving them the opportunity to stake their claim as key players in the long-term goals of the company. After three years of service, the same Spanish company also promises its managers relocation to another South American country or, in some cases, to its headquarters in Spain.

- Offer placement assistance and/or funding for their children in secondary boarding schools or universities outside of their home country. A British pharmaceutical firm has established an internal department that provides its local managers with information and makes arrangements for their children to visit prospective prep schools and colleges in England.

• Arrange for special medical treatment or other related assistance for employees or family members in Western Europe or the United States when advanced care cannot be obtained locally. As part of its compensation package, an American financial services firm provides its local managers with an annual, all-expense-paid physical evaluation at San Francisco General Medical Center.

Only recently have multinationals begun to recruit directly from local universities of high educational standards. The most sought-after graduates are those specializing in languages and engineering. Business programs have also been established, but employers still find they must invest heavily in training to install modern business practices and attitudes.

Blue-collar workers are also in need of constant training, especially where higher technologies are concerned. Cultural factors become more important because of the lack of formal education on the part of most employees. Many companies have threatened to fire workers in their Chinese facilities if they don't stop spitting on the floor, a popular Chinese habit.

REALITY #4—GOVERNMENTS

More often than not, governments play a major role in sales and distribution within emerging markets. Protectionist import duties, state control of public distribution systems, and state-run companies are all used by national governments to control product development within its borders.

Although free trade and antiprotectionism are the stated policies of most governments in the world, high import taxes are still placed selectively on products to protect local industries. Antidumping laws in the United States, the world's most vocal supporter of free trade, still place a 45% tax on certain goods like ball bearings and textiles to protect American jobs. Brazil, in order to protect its local automobile manufacturers, levies a 125% import tax on all non-Brazilian models. As a result, less than 1% of Brazil's 250,000 annual automotive sales are from imported units.

The control of the Indian government over the distribution of alcoholic beverages is a classic case of state authority. In a country of nearly one billion people, it is remarkable that only 22,500 licensed shops and 10,000 other outlets are permitted to sell liquor. All points of sale must be licensed—including wholesalers, retailers, bars, restaurants, and bonded warehouses. Further, licenses from both the central government and an individual state are required. To complicate the process, controls on distribution vary from state to state and enforcement rights are either held by the government or auctioned to private companies. A simple change in the product such as the alteration of the size of the bottle can result in never-ending bureaucratic hassles.

Given the different laws and taxes applied by the various entities, marketers spend much of their time trying to figure out the rules. Import duties, export taxes, excise charges, and vendor fees are applied in various ways at any given moment. On top of the official regulations for alcohol distribution, a Mafia syndicate in Russia with strong political connections has emerged to "shake down" alcohol marketers and take a piece of the action. The combination of these factors discourages innovation and reinforces the status quo. To do any business in Russia, a company needs to have a roof, or *kriesha*, that provides cover from the harsh elements of the new, free-market system there. There are essentially two kinds of *kriesha*: government-sponsored or criminal-sponsored. Each of these provides shelter against the other; both are constantly trying to muscle their way into a given enterprise. For a percentage of the profits, a *kriesha* will use its influence to protect the company from either the local political authorities or the Mafia syndicate.

In China, foreign companies are forced to use the state network and find their marketing approaches severely restricted. Within the major cities, Chinese state systems, not independents, distribute Coca-Cola and Procter and Gamble products. Control over distribution, therefore, tends to remain in the hands of communist bureaucrats.

As we all learned in elementary school, it is better to work together than against one another. Creating partnerships with the government can be a preferred way in which to overcome the obstacles to conducting business in emerging markets. A leading soft-drink maker partnered with the Moscow Metropolitan System by providing mobile carts and kiosks to offer soft drinks and snacks. The Moscow Metro, the largest underground transportation system in the world, viewed the protocol with the Western firm as a way to expand customer service. The end result was a joint venture between the two and the establishment of the "Metro Express."

It goes without saying that the bribing of local officials is another way in which to influence the distribution process. A recent World Bank survey of 3,600 firms in sixty-nine countries showed 40% of businesses paying bribes. The figure in industrial countries was 15%, and in the former Soviet Union it had climbed to more than 60%.

The lobby of the Sheraton in Caracas is one of the world's great meeting centers for foreign businesspeople interested in providing "gifts" to the right person. Venezuelan officials, seemingly unconcerned about the public atmosphere of the hotel, collect plain brown envelopes from foreigners in between shots of whiskey and bottles of Polar beer. On more than one occasion, so many "meetings" have been arranged at the same time that it has been necessary for the foreign businessperson to pay a little extra something to the hotel staff in order to insure a couple of seats in the lobby.

When evaluating the amount of political risk in emerging markets, stability, not form, is the most important characteristic to consider. Capitalism has thrived

in countries like Taiwan, Korea, and China where a history of stable dictator-
ships has dominated the political scene. On the other hand, most of Latin America represents a greater risk, even in light of widespread democracy.

In order to develop a formula for better understanding political risk, many
firms use the following economic, political, and social criteria.

*Economic Criteria—GDP, capital flight, foreign debt, and commodity depen-
dence*

- GDP, or Gross Domestic Product, needs to be looked at from both a past and a present
  point of view. Any tendency toward a steady fall in GDP should alert businesses to a
  greater chance for economic uncertainty and political instability.

- As discussed previously, emerging markets for the most part horde their hard currency.
  When it becomes evident that hard currency is leaving the country, the potential for
  economic downturn and political crisis is enhanced.

- Foreign debt has burdened the economies of many emerging markets for more than a
  generation. It is crucial to understand the amount of foreign debt the market in question
  holds and, moreover, the structures and timetables in place for its repayment.

- Commodity dependence is a common thread that runs through all nations. Emerging
  markets, however, seem always to have a much more profound dependence on particular commodities than their industrialized counterparts. In many emerging markets in
  Latin America and Africa, for example, there is a constant need to import agricultural
  products, even when more than 80% of the population is engaged in farming.

*Political Criteria—Bad neighbors; level of authoritarianism, stability, and
legitimacy; potential for internal violence; and threat of war*

- As in a residential neighborhood, bad neighbors can dramatically affect the peace and
  tranquility of the surrounding area. Bad neighbors can act as bullies or cause migratory
  upheaval if their domestic politics get out of hand. The thirty-five-year civil war in
  Guatemala was a cause of many problems for neighboring Mexico, El Salvador, and
  Honduras. Millions of Guatemalans fled to the surrounding countries, further burdening
  their already overworked systems. In addition, both sides in the struggle used safe areas
  outside of Guatemala to mount incursions back into the country.

- In the post–Cold War era, populations are less likely to tolerate a high level of authoritarianism on the part of their government. Events in Indonesia in 1998, following
  the near collapse of the economy, revealed the quick and bloody manner by which an
  authoritarian regime was disposed of when it could no longer meet the basic expectations of the people. Although their economies were hit equally hard by the Asian
  economic crisis, less authoritarian countries like Malaysia, Thailand, and the Philippines experienced hardly any domestic political manifestations.

- The stability and legitimacy a regime enjoys from the people it governs is fundamental
  in evaluating political risk. Countries that have strong institutions and traditions tend
  to be more stable than those that don't. India, the world's largest democracy, has a
  system, even with all of its faults, that maintains a relatively high level of legitimacy

in the eyes of the population. Neighboring Pakistan, with its checkered history of military coups, offers more political risk because of the lack of confidence with which the people view the government.

- Some nations are more prone to political violence than others. Historically, nations in Latin America are much more apt to solve political disputes out of the barrel of a gun than their counterparts in Southeast Asia. The culture and makeup of the society often are key determinants in the amount and manner in which political violence rears its head.

- The threat of war is greater today than at any other time in human history. Although wars are now smaller in scope and size than in the early twentieth century, regional conflicts based on regional factors are happening with much more frequency and intensity.

Social Criteria—Urbanization, corruption, ethnic tension, religious extremism

- Urbanization is one of the most important transformers of any society. The amount of growth a country experiences in its urban areas places new expectations and demands on governments. If a government cannot meet basic levels of water supply, sewage treatment, electricity, and waste removal, the country is more likely to experience stresses and strains on the political front.

- Corruption is unfortunately a way of life in far too many countries in the world. Corruption erodes the very fiber of the necessary trust and confidence constituencies must have in their leaders. The greater the level of corruption, the more likely that political stability is fluid and therefore the greater the possibility of uncertainty.

- The strains placed on governments at the beginning of the century come from many sources. One of the most powerful is ethnic tension. Deep-seated hatreds for one's neighbors have manifested themselves all over the globe. From Turkey, to South Asia, to Colombia and the Balkans, ethnic conflicts are dominating the lives of an increasing number of the planet's inhabitants. The stronger the level of ethnic tension, the more likely that political instability will dominate.

- Religious extremism is the ugly brother to ethnic tension. Intolerance for others' beliefs is on the rise in a number of places in the world. The presence of religious extremism insures a precarious environment in which to conduct business.

The combination of all these criteria—economic, political, and social—provides a much clearer and realistic perspective as to the level of political risk and governmental stability of a given emerging market.

REALITY #5—TAX-FREE MARKETS

Throughout the developing world, many high-end goods are readily available through thriving contraband markets. Ask any world traveler which city is the largest center for commercial goods and you'll get several educated guesses: Hong Kong, Miami, Dubai. Each is a good try, but not even close. It is Ciudad del Este in eastern Paraguay. More than US$20 billion a year in consumer goods move in and out of this city of 45,000 people.

The reason is simple: corruption. Every morning, the two bridges that connect Ciudad del Este with Iguazu, Brazil, are filled with buses of Brazilians coming to shop. Upon arrival into Ciudad del Este, each bus is met not by Paraguayan immigration or customs officials but by eight-year-old children selling duffel bags. The Brazilian shoppers dismount from the buses, buy the duffel bags, and spend the next six hours filling the bags with every item they can buy—Chinese radios, Japanese VCRs, American handguns, Korean television sets, French champagne, and Italian suits. After the shopping spree is over, the buses are reloaded and visited by Paraguayan officials who wish the departing Brazilians well and extract their daily salary through the collection of "export duties." Once back home on the other side of the bridge, Brazilian customs officials replicate the work of their Paraguayan counterparts by demanding "import duties." Of course, each shopper's tax bills are only a minuscule fraction of what the official taxes would be in Paraguay and Brazil.

Tax-free markets like Ciudad del Este have been used extensively by companies to build product and brand awareness. One of the largest automobile manufacturers in the world reports that 20% of its total earnings in Latin America comes from its spare-parts center in Ciudad del Este. Remembering that the fundamental goal is to get the product into the marketplace, a great majority of firms have viewed the underground economy as a necessity.

In China not too long ago, the global market leader in a particular industry, a United States–based Fortune 500 company; the number-two player worldwide, a United Kingdom–based firm; and the fourth-largest competitor, another United States–based Fortune 500 company, were deciding how best to sell their products there.

After each company evaluated the realities of the marketplace, two distinct strategies emerged. The number-one and number-two market leaders decided to establish a "token" presence with a series of small offices throughout China to provide the necessary "cover" for their marketing and merchandising activities. These local offices were never intended to serve any real purpose except to assure local authorities that they were conducting normal and customary business.

Unknown to the local Chinese authorities, however, the vast majority of real business for both companies was being done vis-à-vis tax-free markets. Instead of importing the goods through a joint-venture partner, most of the commercial activity for these two firms took place through the porous border with Russia. Goods crossed with little or no interference and, therefore, much less in customs duties.

The number-four market leader had decided to take the more traditional approach by working directly with the Chinese government and entering into a joint-venture purchase of an existing factory.

The differences in revenues are truly unbelievable. The market leader earns about US$500 million in annual revenues from its back-door operation in China. The second-leading firm, using the same approach, earns about US$425 million each year. The more traditional competitor has never made more than US$5 million in any of the four years it has been in China. Who's right, who's wrong? You make the call yourself.

However, high growth in many emerging markets is compelling nations to behave in more responsible ways. Stronger regulations and legal action taken against black marketers are on the rise throughout the world. Pockets of the black market remain, but economists agree that as the formal market expands, the black market diminishes.

On the other hand, the gray market is still a strong issue facing global manufacturers and distributors. The unauthorized import and sale of products intended for sale in another, high-priced market is generally defined as gray marketing. Gray markets tend to occur when the consumer price differential between countries causes people to shop for the same product in a country with lower prices.

Honda motorcycles—built in Japan and intended for sale in the United States—are purchased by Argentine importers from dealers in Los Angeles and sold in Buenos Aires at a lower price than that of the official Honda distributor for Argentina. Omega revealed that 37% of Indians buy their Omega watches in Singapore or Hong Kong. Where such situations exist, established distributors lose motivation to sell the product as they see their margins eroded by low-overhead gray marketers. Whatever the reasons or causes for tax-free markets, they are certain to be around as long as governments seek to raise revenues through the collection of high import tariffs. A failure on the part of Western companies to recognize the importance of tax-free markets and, more important, to take advantage of them when possible will more than likely lead to a weakened position and lost profits in emerging markets.

REALITY #6—MARKET INFORMATION

Whatever the market in question, it is necessary to make critical decisions based upon such factors as market size, local competition, transportation costs, buyer behavior, distribution channels, and media practices. Most emerging markets still do not have available, accurate, or accessible market information. Even if the information is accessible, it is rarely accurate. In the rare case that the data is accurate, it may be so closely guarded that it is impossible to secure it. How, then, does one acquire this invaluable information?

Traditional methods implemented in the United States for the collection of data include survey research by mail or telephone. In most emerging markets, the high level of illiteracy and poor postal service discourage this practice. As revealed earlier in this chapter, telephone service is still a luxury for the privileged few in many emerging markets.

One possible alternative is to conduct personal interviews. Many countries with large rural populations have poor roads that make reaching the people quite difficult. In response to this, research firms have been locally established and can provide such services.

Some other unconventional or improvised methods of getting the needed market information have included:

- Contacting local import organizations. For example, almost every country in Sub-Saharan Africa has a national association of motorcycle importers.
- Participating in trade shows and exhibitions.
- Establishing a local office to get "on-site intelligence."
- Engaging in intergovernmental working parties or trade missions.
- Gathering data by simple observation at the local market square or by going to a public institution to see building supplies, office equipment, cement, and so on.
- Test-marketing your product by contacting an importer and simply selling it. Then, conduct follow-up research as to the time it took to sell the product, who purchased it, at what price, and in which geographic areas.
- Working with your international bank's local office is another excellent source for gathering information. Western banks are usually one of the first entrants to a new emerging country and have had the time to foster the relationships essential to entering the marketplace.
- Looking up local affiliates of business associations like Rotary International and Lion's Clubs International. Such groups tend to form up in new markets and grant a social setting in which to network effectively with local decision makers.
- Establishing a small local office prior to your company's entrance into the marketplace can initiate contact with the most important individuals and organizations.
- The U.S. Chamber of Commerce maintains affiliations with many chambers of commerce across the globe. They can provide key information and contacts for companies looking to expand into emerging markets.
- Retaining a lawyer in each local market. Lawyers tend to be very well connected and can oftentimes help establish the most effective government and business contacts. Also, legal representation will be necessary to navigate your way through the thicket of legal bureaucracy that invariably characterizes emerging markets. You will need this attorney throughout your days of doing business in these markets. It is advisable, immediately upon your arrival into a new market, that you secure a "well-connected" lawyer and put him or her on a retainer fee basis, even if you have not yet established an office or shipped your first product to the market. It may cost just a few hundred dollars each month to have a tremendously valuable resource available to answer any questions you may have and access critical information for you even when you are thousands of miles or kilometers away from that market.
- Developing a close relationship with a local employment recruiting firm in each emerging market. Such firms many times have a keen understanding of the local market conditions. They can assist you in obtaining the necessary information and developing the crucial contacts needed for doing business there. You will be surprised how much free and valuable information and insight you can receive in exchange for a mere offer

to utilize the employment agency's services at such time as you may need them. If you conduct the proper due diligence and find that the market is the right one for your company, you'll probably need to use their services anyway. Why not leverage them now rather than later?

- Developing a close relationship with managers of Western hotel chains and airlines. These individuals are similar to banks in their ability to cultivate important local connections. They often have their fingers on the pulse of who is coming and going with regard to international business. As many emerging markets are served by only a few Western hotels or airlines, it is likely that any contact with the outside world has been processed through one or both of them. They may very well know who the key players are and what they have been up to over the past months.

Beyond the potential sources of information discussed here, we have included in the appendix a resource guide that may provide additional sources of information to assist you in analyzing the current market situation.

In light of the present climate, one might view the combination of these inherent realities with the current business slowdown as too much to deal with. However, the inexorable forces of Global Manifest Destiny compel us to look deeper to discover the fantastic possibilities that exist right now for the astute businessperson in emerging markets.

The present phase of Decelerated Pro-Activity, as opposed to the Accelerated Re-Activity phase that existed a few years ago, is the time to build market share. By first recognizing the challenges inherent in emerging markets and then properly navigating the minefields, the capture of a bigger percentage of customers in the Decelerated Pro-Activity phase moves closer to being achieved.

4

Seizing the Advantage: Defining Your Company's Role in Emerging Markets

The will to win is meaningless without the will to prepare.
                                                      Sir Winston Churchill

The Russians are one of the world's most suffering and enduring people. History, the frigid climate, and an unrelenting series of dispassionate governments have exacted a seemingly infinite toll on the people. Yet average Russians continue on, appearing oblivious to the cruel, nasty, and brutish world around them. How do they do it? How do they persist in such a harsh and relentless environment? Vodka.

After four cities in five days across Russia, Caslione was ready to go home. The evening before was the fourth time on this trip when he had been eating and drinking with a different distributor until three in the morning. Although Caslione was an old Russia hand by this time, he still was amazed by the ingenious method the Russians had devised to permit them to consume huge quantities of vodka in one night without experiencing any kind of hangover the next day. Nonetheless, his hosts at the last night's dinner were truly remarkable. The four of them together, with Caslione not even attempting to keep pace, were able to consume over twelve liters of vodka—over three gallons—in less than six hours.

"The System" as Russians call it, is, like many other aspects of daily life in Russia, the individual's way of fighting back and even, sometimes, triumphing over the immutable laws of nature. Over the course of an evening, specific types of food are consumed at a particular moment in time, each portion accompanied of course by precisely calculated swigs of vodka, then followed by deeply inhaling the heavy aromas of Russian brown bread before it is eaten. The goal is to defeat the body's own natural defenses to stop the overflow of alcohol into its system—in other words, to get as drunk as possible without suffering the typical hangover the following morning. To their credit, the Russians have done it. They have been able to figure out how to trick their bodies and drink liters of vodka at one time without suffering immediate retribution. As with the endless, inhuman winters, Russians have somehow overcome the impossible and in many cases thrived.

As Caslione walked out of the terminal at Arkhangelsk, a desperate Russian city near the Arctic Circle, to board Aeroflot for his flight to the Russian city of Chelyabinsk in the Urals—naturally via Moscow—he casually passed by a man fueling the plane with a lit cigarette dangling from his mouth. When he boarded, the smell of jet fuel nearly overwhelmed him. The aircraft was an old Soviet cargo plane; a thirty-year-plus old Tupolev 134 converted to carry passengers by putting plywood on the cabin floor and rolling in unattached rows of seats. While Caslione was taking his seat, he noticed several wet spots on the plywood floor around him. Upon further investigation, he realized they were the source of the jet fuel smell. It seemed the plane was leaking fuel all over, and the plywood was laid to down to act as a sponge. None of the other passengers seemed either to notice or to care. A quick survey of his immediate seating area found seven of eight passengers already smoking or in the process of lighting up. After his initial amazement, Caslione decided it wasn't worth the effort and reclined his badly worn seat to fall asleep. Four cities in five days across Russia will do that to you.

Beyond recognizing the realities inherent in doing business in emerging markets, companies need to constantly examine what their expectations and tolerance levels should be. Each company must address three fundamental questions before determining its business involvement in emerging markets:

1. What is the level of risk the company is willing to accept in light of the inherent volatility of emerging markets?
2. What level of investment is the firm willing to make to succeed in high-growth emerging markets?
3. What level of control is the company seeking for its emerging market operations?

Of course, every company will respond to each question differently, depending on its corporate culture and the market in question. However, before embarking on any venture into emerging markets, these answers need to be quantified and agreed upon on a per market basis. Enlightened companies address these critical issues being completely aware of the inherent realities and "minefields" characteristic of doing business in emerging markets. Further, leading firms design and implement a primary strategy that guides them in their emerging market activities.

Coca-Cola's emerging market program, for example, is directed by the primary strategy of acquiring an equity stake in its bottlers. Whether as a majority or a minority partner, Coca-Cola knows its emerging market success is tied to its ability to maintain a sufficient level of control by taking an equity stake in its local representatives. For Coca-Cola, the primary strategy of an equity position is how this enlightened film deals with the fluid and complex situations emerging markets offer.

Clearly, the equity position approach in emerging markets that Coca-Cola embraces effectively melds with its corporate culture and has done so for many years. Nevertheless, such an emerging market strategy may prove disastrous for another company if it does not best reflect that company's organizational structure and culture, long-term goals, and management capacities. Recently, a major U.S. maker of snack foods tried to formulate its primary strategy based upon the Coca-Cola model. However, unlike Coca-Cola, which places strong emphasis on local market knowledge and defers to its own local "in-market" management, this widely respected market leader sought to run its local emerging market operations from afar, in its international headquarters located in the comfortable confines of Western Europe. The equity stake the U.S. company acquired in a key Central European market, albeit quite small, seemingly gave its European and U.S. headquarters staff personnel a greater feeling of empowerment at the expense of its local in-market management—even though the majority of the headquarters staff knew incredibly little about the particulars of each emerging market situation. Very few individuals, if any, from the headquarters support-staff departments had ever been to the market in question. Even more remarkable, several interoffice memos revealed that the name of the capital city was chronically confused with the capital city of another Central European nation, Bucharest replaced Budapest! The faulty decisions made by headquarters lacked the flexibility and responsiveness that characterize those organizations that pay particular attention to the local aspects of their emerging market operations.

The recognition of the critical value of a local presence dramatically helps companies better deal with the inherent realities faced in emerging markets. Further, it allows companies to develop the agility required in managing an emerging market operation. In the case of the European snack-food maker, the complete lack of attention paid to the situation on the ground resulted in an interdepartmental war over the firm's control of its emerging market operations between the well-informed locals and the nearly blind higher echelons and headquarters staff personnel.

Enlightened companies, in deciding upon their primary emerging market strategy, build their foundation on a few key strategies that naturally flow with their corporate culture. In short, the primary strategy is customized to each market with a single thrust. Once the primary strategy is in place, the issues of risk tolerance, the amount of investment to be made, and the level of control desired can be placed into proper perspective for each market being considered.

Simply stated, ascertained risk is manageable risk. Certain undeniable risks come with pursuing commercial activities in emerging markets. Notwithstanding this truth, there are proven ways in which to minimize the level of risk and make it palatable for your firm's emerging market appetites. These methods are concerned with the level of investment to be made and the level of control your company desires. Therefore, if your company has a high tolerance for risk, there are methods available by which to build upon this factor and seek to maximize the opportunities emerging markets have to offer. On the other hand, if there exists a low tolerance for risk, there are techniques that can still bring profits and market share to your company, although in lesser amounts.

The evaluation of risk and your company's tolerance of it must be determined within the normal constructs of business. There do exist particular circumstances unique to given markets at given moments in time. For example, certain industries in Brazil, India, and China have typically required a joint venture first to be established with a local entity before a foreign company can enter that market, although this requirement is beginning to change in selected industries within some markets. Nonetheless, for purposes here, the factors that influence evaluation of risk as well as your company's expectations for emerging markets will be discussed within the natural framework and scope of normal business events.

To best evaluate risk, the expectations of your company in an emerging market, and moreover the realistic objectives for that market, it is crucial to analyze both the external and internal factors (Figure 4.1). Setting your company's realistic objectives is the net result of several varying and conflicting forces. The scope of these forces, the determination of their importance, and the need to anticipate their direction all combine to give your company a greater sense of the amount of risk involved and serve to guide the establishment of your genuine expectations.

EXTERNAL FACTORS TO CONSIDER IN SETTING REALISTIC OBJECTIVES

Factors that lie beyond the control of your company and its sphere of influence are labeled as external factors. They include the target country's market, environmental, and distribution factors, as well as certain home country factors.

Target Country Market Factors

The present and projected size of the market in question is an important determinant with regard to "break-even" sales volumes. Small markets usually favor low break-even sales volumes, while larger markets tend to justify entry modes with higher break-even sales volumes.

It is necessary here to determine the total market potential. In many instances,

Figure 4.1
Factors to Consider in Setting Realistic Objectives

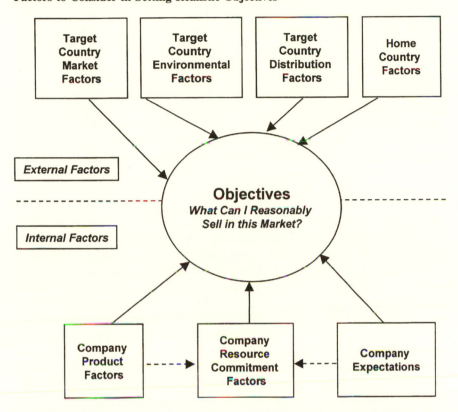

depending upon the amount of market research data available, it is possible to conduct a market segmentation analysis in order to better understand the likely response to your product or service in the targeted market. For this kind of study, three variable groups—demographic, geographic, and psychographic—might be analyzed to provide a clearer picture.

Within the demographic variable group, population characteristics such as age, gender, racial mix, income, educational attainment, family sizes, social stratification, and religion should be looked at.

As previously shown, the median age in most emerging markets is well below that in industrial countries. Further, most young people today are living outside of developed nations. Fifty-two percent of all Asians are under the age of 25, while only 35% of Americans and 28% of Germans are as young. A visit to Latin America, India, or Africa is memorable if only for the number of children and young people seen out and about in the streets. Children and teenagers seem to be everywhere.

The status of women in many developing nations is not nearly so advanced as it is in the industrial world. Property rights and social respect for women lag far behind. The relegation of half of the population in many emerging markets to a secondary status is a key factor that retards the economic and social growth of these countries. Unfortunately, for far too many women, the only real status they derive in too many emerging markets comes from their ability to produce children. The ability to care for those children is ancillary. In Ecuador and Pakistan, it is only too common to observe that poor women sell their newborns for around US$500 and, dishearteningly, several months later, to find the same women pregnant again.

Income distribution is generally poor in most emerging markets. The vast majority of the wealth is usually held in the hands of a few super-rich families. Brazil, one of the largest countries in the world, also has one of the greatest disparities between rich and poor. Any visitor to Rio de Janeiro can quite easily distinguish between the fabulous homes found in the suburbs and the shanty-towns that dominate the hills overlooking Copacabana Beach.

Educational attainment varies from country to country. In some cases, there is a generally high level of educational achievement on the part of a population that yet does not lead to economic prosperity. Russia has a large sector of its population highly educated in the hard sciences, that is, physics, chemistry, and biology. Nevertheless, for more than seventy years of Soviet rule, the education and skills attained by the Russian people were not directed toward the commercial applications needed in a free-market system. Rather, the focus was based upon the needs of a centrally controlled economy where military demands superseded all other aspects of development. As a result, the country remains relatively poor because it lacks educated individuals who understand how to operate in free and open markets. Taiwan, on the other hand, has fewer college-educated persons per capita than Russia. Nevertheless, Taiwan is relatively wealthier than Russia, in part because of the focus of its educational system on the development of capitalism and business.

Family size in many emerging markets is much larger than in the industrial world, often twice that found in industrialized countries. In a number of circumstances, families are always producing children because the most difficult thing for a child in Africa, South Asia, or Latin America is to make it to five years of age. Disease and malnutrition kill more children than any other factors. In some parts of West Africa and the interior of India, the mortality rate is so high that children do not receive names until they reach three years of age. The predominant thinking in many of these countries is, "Why would you give a name to something that is going to die? If 'it' gets to three, we'll give 'it' a name." The exception is China, which still maintains its "one-child per family" rule in the overcrowded urban areas.

Social stratification based upon race, class, and economic attainment dominate most emerging markets. The infamous "untouchable" system in India is still alive and well. In Latin America, race and skin color are still strong determinants of social class. Tribal affiliation preoccupies the lives of the vast majority of Africans.

The influence of religion, although steadily on the decline in the industrialized world, is on the rise throughout most emerging markets. Africa is experiencing the largest growth in the number of Muslims and Christians in the world. Also, the sway of religion—Hinduism in India, Islam in Indonesia and Pakistan, and Catholicism in Latin America—is increasing rapidly. For many countries, the variable of religion directly influences government policy and how the society looks at business, especially with foreigners.

The analysis of groups that vary by geography should take into consideration the influence of regions, cities, urban areas, rural sectors, and climate within the targeted market. For many emerging markets, the area surrounding the capital city is the center of financial and political power. In Argentina, for example, half the population of the entire country lives in and around Buenos Aires. The result is essentially two countries with their own distinct culture and business traits: greater Buenos Aires and the rest of the country. An acknowledgment of this dual business climate is crucial when determining strategy for a potential market.

Throughout the developing world, megacities dominate the landscape. Sao Paulo, Chongqing, Mexico City, Lagos, Shanghai, Moscow, and Almaty are dominant cities both inside and outside their respective nations. Urban areas like these serve as the seat of capital and business. Rural sectors tend to play secondary roles in most emerging markets. The result in many emerging markets is like the following Argentine example. In Argentina, the heat of the afternoon moves rural residents indoors for their siesta, whereas workers in bustling Buenos Aires never seem to rest, regardless of the temperature. Attention to such differences between rural and urban should be paid when preparing emerging market entry strategy.

Climate plays a key role in the determination of expectations for a given market. In the tropics, most people do not venture outside after 8 P.M. for fear of contact with malaria and dengue-carrying mosquitoes. Monsoons, annual floods, and dry seasons are all critical in evaluating the impact of climate within a given market. Trying to transport product during the rainy season in Panama, for example, can result in rotten perishables and rusted metal components.

Psychographic-variable typologies seek to explain and predict consumer behavior for the country in question. Variables in this category of data may include consumer personality, attitudes, lifestyles, brand loyalty, amount of product benefits accepted, volume usage, and price sensitivity. The sophistication of the marketplace is necessary to understand when appraising entry strategies. Although not always the case, countries with a long history of free markets more frequently demonstrate a sophisticated consumer class than countries that are newer to capitalism.

The consumer personality of a given country reflects the culture of its people. The collective background, experience, and viewpoints of the nation's residents are unique to that particular place and moment in time. Like an individual, markets will develop unique noticeable traits and behavior patterns that set them apart from all others. A staunch Muslim nation such as Iran will certainly demonstrate a much different consumer personality than a formerly socialist country like Hungary.

Functions of the collective background, experience, and viewpoints of a nation's residents are its attitudes and lifestyles. Global advertising campaigns are full of examples where tremendous success in one market is overshadowed by a more noteworthy failure in another because of a failure to recognize specific aspects of a people's attitudes and lifestyles. The use of sexual images, sarcastic humor, and violence in advertising may play very well in one nation while meeting stiff resistance in another. Throughout Africa and the Middle East, the depiction of women in advertising is more likely to be that of mother, friend, or caregiver. In Latin America, on the other hand, women are portrayed with a sexual or flirtatious nature, more often than not.

Brand loyalty is a result of the success or failure of previous ventures into a given market. Although European colonialism was effectively over in the 1960s, a visit to a former Francophone or Anglophone colony will reveal the continued presence and often dominance of French or British products. Peugeot, for example, still holds the vast majority of market share in its former Southeast Asian and African colonies. In Southern Africa and India, Walker Biscuits are eaten by millions of Southern Africans and Indians.

The amount of product benefits accepted is a further extension of the consumer personality of a market. After losing millions in China, Amway Corporation eventually discovered that the 100% money-back guarantee that worked so well in Japan and the United States was not at all suited to the nature of the Chinese consumer. For more than forty years, Amway prided itself on its policy of a complete return in exchange for the container and a sample of the product. Such an approach was extremely effective in the United States and Japan, where consumers looked at the "no questions asked" policy as a guarantor of quality. In China, however, the consumers looked at Amway's return policy as way to get something for nothing from a rich Western company. For nearly six months, Amway's management could not understand why so many customers were returning its products in unprecedented quantities. It was only when Amway's warehouses were completely filled with returns that management realized that the amount of product benefits accepted by Chinese consumers was very different from that of Japanese and American consumers.

Volume usage is determined by a wide variety of factors, including product demand, population size, climate, and price sensitivity. Clearly, luxury products like yachts and nonessentials will probably not experience high-volume usage when compared to products necessary for the sustenance of the population or the infrastructure, especially in emerging markets. Most Ugandans, for example, are much more interested in the price of a secondhand Toyota Price than a new Land Rover. Sensitivity plays a key role in this determination, as emerging markets and their consumers simply have less money to spend than their counterparts in industrialized nations.

It may be impossible to glean all of this research from the target market because of the natural difficulty of attaining information about emerging markets. Nevertheless, any information gathered will certainly assist in evaluating the impact of target country market factors in setting your company's objectives there.

Target Country Environmental Factors

The political, economic, and social character of the target country can have a decisive influence on the amount of risk as well as the expectation level for that market. Particularly in the developing world, the politics of a nation are a major factor in the determination of who gets what. As most emerging markets are undergoing democratic transformations, election results directly influence the direction of business. Most business transactions grind to a halt some forty-five days prior to an election while people "wait and see." Not until the results are clear do emerging market businesspeople begin to plan for their future. Perhaps the most crucial elements for us are government policies and regulations pertaining to the conduct of international business. It is important to realize that political control over business in most emerging markets is much stronger than in the industrialized world.

The geographical distance of the target market from the home country needs to be recognized. A U.S. firm trying to manage its CIS operations from London—the typical, although usually not the best, headquarters city for U.S. operations in Europe—will find it difficult to exert authority, simply because of the large distance between the two places. Further, the availability of ocean ports and the strength of neighboring countries need to be added to the evaluation process. Bolivia is inherently a difficult place to do business because of its lack of ocean ports. Most merchandise is shipped to the Chilean port of Arica and transported over the Andes by truck to La Paz, Cochabamba, or Santa Cruz. Although Arica is a greater distance away, Bolivian importers prefer the Chilean system to its Peruvian counterpart because of its efficiency and organization.

Target Country Distribution Factors

Once the size and the environment of the country are determined, it is incumbent to then ascertain the competitive atmosphere of the marketplace. Places like Ciudad del Este reveal that, in today's world, people will always deliver product to a demand point. Identification of informal, underground sales and distribution channels should be a top priority. The distribution infrastructure should be of concern when evaluating the target market. Road systems, warehouse space and access, railroads, and airports are important factors in evaluating the capacity of the nation's infrastructure to handle your product. A perishable or any temperature-sensitive product must be shipped to Siberia prior to November. In India, the typical method of transporting goods is by road, that is, by truck, which presents its own set of logistical issues. Within China, goods are typically transported by train.

Subsequently, an analysis of the availability of competitive or complementary products needs to be undertaken. If there are competitive or complementary goods already in the marketplace, it is a minimum prerequisite to understand who is distributing these goods and by what means. As basic as it may seem, it is surprising how many companies fail to engage sufficiently in such an analysis.

Finally, it is quite helpful to have a handle on the skill, experience, and sophistication level of acceptable distributors within the target country. Are these distributors capable of developing a brand and building value-adding services around it? What is the ability of distributors to engineer or fabricate accessories or add-ons to your product? How much more do they need than they have right now? Answering these questions will provide you a clearer sense of how much training and support will be required when your product is introduced by a new distributor.

Malaysian heavy equipment distributors, for example, are incredibly sophisticated when it comes to the application of the latest technologies for their sales and service departments. Indian computer distributors are exceptional when it comes to bundling value-adding services around the purchase of a network. South African distributors are at the forefront of e-business and web-based services. Whatever the product or market in question, it is critical to recognize the strengths and weaknesses of potential distributors in target countries.

Home Country Factors

Market, production, and environment factors in the home country also play key roles in how a company will set its objectives and evaluate risk as it seeks to penetrate a target country. The relationship, or lack of one, between the home country and the target market is related to many aspects of the commercial relationship. Banking regulations, for example, can make it impossible to receive money from the target market. Portugal's relationship with Brazil is an example of a strong relationship. The United States–China relationship, although one of the most important in the world, is always fluid and subject to change. The European Community's interaction with the former Yugoslavia is tenuous at best.

Trade agreements can ease the difficulties in the importation process. NAFTA, consisting of the United States, Mexico, and Canada, and MERCOSUR, whose members include Brazil, Argentina, Paraguay, and Uruguay, have both made business easier in the Western Hemisphere. On the other hand, volatile trade relations between the home country and the target market can seriously threaten any long-term goals, like the longstanding embargo between the United States and Cuba.

Ease of travel between the two markets is crucial to understand, as personnel from both countries will need to visit each other on a regular basis. The ability to get there needs to placed into perspective. South Africa, for example, is seemingly a long way from anywhere. As a result, it needs to be recognized that any South African operations will more likely be characterized by a lower degree of control merely because of the distance, compared to geographically closer ones.

INTERNAL FACTORS TO CONSIDER IN SETTING REALISTIC OBJECTIVES

Within the domain of your company lie several factors that can be directly affected by decisions or actions within the corporate structure.

Company Product Factors

The degree of differentiation within the product line is proportional to the amount of pricing discretion and the ability to control transportation costs. The higher the degree of differentiation that exists, the more likely it is that the products can absorb higher costs and remain competitive. Conversely, weakly differentiated products must compete on a price basis in a target market and always face the prospect of being undercut by a scrupulous competitor. Ball bearings are more likely to be price sensitive than, say, computer hardware.

Further, the degree of product standardization varies for each potential market. Packaging and the need for after-sales service need to be taken into account. The language requirements for the product may vary from country to country. The ability of technical products to be engineered and serviced is critical in the proper application of after-sales service. The adaptability of consumer products to the climate and infrastructure constraints as well as their shelf-life and perishability should be understood.

The competitiveness of the product, including the unit price and the availability of other product substitutes, also needs to be looked at. A strong capacity for the product to compete will tend to lead to a higher unit price. Flexibility in product offering and the availability of substitutes should be considered when trying to best manage the realities of emerging markets. The Japanese auto industry is an excellent example of how the flexibility and availability of substitute products can flourish in emerging markets. By offering both right-side and left-side steering in the 1980s, Japan's automakers were able to capture a much larger segment of the world's automobile market in the early days in many emerging markets than the slow-to-react Americans, fixated on left-side steering. For years, large markets in East Africa, South Asia, Japan, Hong Kong, and Nigeria were closed to American manufacturers because they refused to build right-side-steering vehicles for these markets. The substantial market share of the Japanese in these and other places is striking to the first-time visitor.

Company Resource Factors

The financial capacity of a company to enter an emerging market and implement its primary strategy is obviously fundamental in setting realistic objectives. The formula for determining the level of resource commitment is an in-depth analysis of the relationships among the following:

• Management
• Capital
• Technology
• Production

The sum total of these relationships is the demonstrated level of resource commitment on the part of the manufacturer.

The issue of management regarding the level of resource commitment is a delicate one. How many of us know a senior executive who claims to have an understanding of doing business in an emerging market when, only after further discussion, we learn that on that person's only visit to the country the only exposure to the market was the airport, the inside of a taxi, a five-star hotel room, and a Western-style business center inside the hotel for meetings over two days?

For far too many companies, decisions are made by individuals who are terribly misinformed about the market they are taking under consideration. They have relatively little, if any, knowledge of the markets about which they are making key decisions. Poorly understood demands from the market are conveyed to middle managers, who must somehow relate the issues to office-bound upper management. To achieve real success in emerging markets, it is critical for managers at all levels to understand to the best of their ability all they can about the market they are entering. Executives from enlightened companies take the time and make the effort to learn all they can. One leading European firm mandates that all its executives spend one week per quarter in a given market visiting at least three different cities in the country. The holistic perspective this experience has provided senior management allows for better decisions at all levels of the corporate structure.

As a guide, the company may want to consider the capital resources required and available for each market. All markets are not equal. Brazil is not the same as Chile or Peru, although they all sit in South America. Also, it is important to note that the investment requirements, including the amount of capital required, will vary dramatically based upon the chosen method of entry. Unless your company is the market leader, the issue of capturing market share needs to be framed within the context of your ability to dominate a distributor's product category. An inability to exert the needed influence over a distributor—sometimes referred to as "share of mind"—will almost certainly lead to a secondary or tertiary position of importance in the distributor's thinking. Later in this book, strategies and processes will be shared as to how to capture that "share of mind" for your product category within the distributor's portfolio.

Information systems and information technology resources available for commitment need to be placed into the proper context in regard to the strategic competitive advantage your company can gain by deploying these resources in selected emerging markets. The absorption rate that most, not all, emerging markets have for new technology can be startling. Where it took over one hundred years for North America and Western Europe to progress from "two tin cans and a string" to the modern telephone, wireless communications such as "mobiles" have been firmly established as the preferred or even exclusive means of communication in most emerging markets.

On the flip side, a company seeking to leverage these technologies must also recognize the tremendous amount of effort and investment that often must be made to utilize such technology to its competitive advantage. Also, in some emerging markets, the local market's capacity to embrace and integrate these resources may be challenged. Just because your sales staff in North America can communicate in real time via e-mail, voice, and data lines to headquarters in Chicago doesn't mean that the same technology will work as easily in Islamabad or Karachi. Again, realistic objectives and expectations must be considered and appropriate plans for investments need to be made, including substantially more local, in-market investments in training than you've planned.

Production needs to be looked at in the same way as technology. In Muslim countries, the need for regular prayer causes all activity to cease. The afternoon siesta in Africa and Latin America also changes production schedules as compared to the home country. It is very strange for many Westerners to walk down the street of a Latin city around 14.00h (2 P.M.) on a normal workday and see virtually no one. On the other hand, offices and businesses are full of workers at 09.30h (9:30 A.M.). A U.S. manufacturer of auto accessories runs two shifts at its plant outside Mexico City: one before siesta from 08.00h (8 A.M.) to 13.30h (1:30 P.M.) and one after siesta from 16.30h (4:30 P.M.) to 22.00h (10 P.M.).

Lastly, imperative to working in emerging markets, and in fact all markets outside North America, is the adoption of military time within a company's business, as it is the global language of communicating time—standard for all markets and people outside of North America.

Company Expectations

After a complete assessment of all of the preceding factors, a self-analysis of the company's expectations needs to take place. Unrealistic expectations can lead to failure more quickly than any other circumstance. It is at this point that the three fundamental questions introduced earlier need to be answered:

1. What level of risk is the company willing to accept in light of the inherent volatility emerging markets present?

Figure 4.2
Emerging Markets Tolerances and Expectations Map

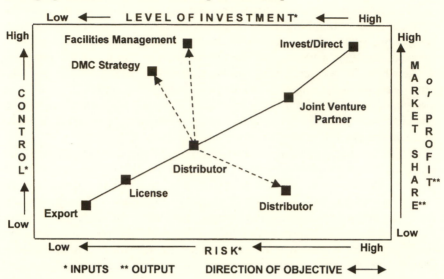

2. What level of investment is the firm willing to make to succeed in high-growth emerging markets?

3. What level of control is the company seeking for its emerging market operations?

The recognition of a primary strategy compatible with the corporate culture and the combination of these factors—external and internal—now provides a blueprint from which a company can realistically determine its emerging market objectives. Once in place, this framework can be built around the company's desire for profits, revenues/sales, and market share in the chosen market—otherwise known as outputs. The following chart is the model by which the relationships between levels of risk tolerance, investment, and control are shown in relation to the outputs. The result, or outcome, is demonstrated as a particular entry strategy or a combination thereof.

Figure 4.2 evaluates the normal emerging market entry strategies of direct exporting, licensing, direct sales/local manufacturing, and distribution. When a manufacturer is debating whether to sell its product abroad, the simplest and least risky way to do so is through exporting. Nevertheless, limited control of what happens to the manufacturer's products once they are "in country" needs to be accepted. The trade-off for the low levels of investment, risk, and investment characteristic of exporting is ordinarily a low level of control (Figure 4.3).

A manufacturer who chooses to enter a new market through the exportation process typically can pursue three avenues:

Figure 4.3
Degree of Control Varies

1. Manufacturers' agents

2. Wholesale importers

3. Trading companies

Manufacturers' agents represent a number of noncompeting foreign suppliers in a particular market. The agents are typically residents of the country in which they are doing business and operate on a commission rather than take title to the goods. Some agents do maintain inventories of the products they represent, although most of the orders they take are in the name of the manufacturer. In most cases, emerging market manufacturer's agents are similar in nature to those of their industrialized world counterparts. American Home Products, a United States–based producer of prescription drugs, household goods, food, and candy, uses manufacturers' agents in selling to Europe and Latin America. Nearly 30% of American Home Product's revenues comes from this method of entry. This method for entering new markets is a reflection of America Home's strategy as it relates to their company's inputs (level of risk, level of investment, level of control). The resulting outputs (market share, revenue, profits) are directly impacted by American Home's inputs or, in other words, their corporate culture.

Wholesale importers are another way in which manufacturers can enter a new market using direct exporting. They import goods that are stocked for resale. Most wholesale importers are specialists in a particular field, such as chemicals or processed foods. Quite a number may have exclusive territories and, in return, agree not to handle competing brands. In this scenario, exclusivity is not a one-way street. Exclusivity works both ways and must be understood accordingly. Further, importers may have their own sales forces to cover their territories and assist dealers. Wholesale importers generally purchase through manufacturers' agents when the exporter uses them or directly from the manufacturer itself. One of the clearest examples is the relationships some wholesaler importers have with select governments in the Middle East. There often exists a virtual monopoly in the importation and market distribution of some products.

Trading companies are important product outlets in many nations, especially those that tend to be underdeveloped. These import firms commonly own and operate grocery stores, department stores, automobile distributorships and dealerships, and farm machinery distributorships. Throughout Africa, for example, many French, German, Danish, and British companies that acquire product all over the world use their local trading centers to distribute it.

Licensing is another thoroughfare available to manufacturers looking to enter emerging markets. While the level of risk and investment required using the licensing strategy is usually higher than for exporting, the amount of profitability and control over one's product is frequently greater. Licensing is the agreement between a manufacturer and a foreign firm to make and sell the manufacturer's products abroad. Within such an agreement, the profits are shared between the two companies. The normal arrangement is for the manufacturer (the licenser) to supply technical assistance to the licensee in such a way as to insure sufficient management strength and capital. The licensee receives the right to use the production processes, marketing strategies, and the licenser's trademarks. In Eastern Europe, L&M Tobacco Company grants licenses to local licensees to produce and distribute its products there. Although the overall level of investment is relatively low under the licensing strategy, the level of control may still not be suitable for a particular manufacturer. It is sometimes difficult to impose strong authority over a licensee's operation. Further, the licensee may eventually break the agreement and become a competitor.

Direct sales/local manufacturing is an additional option available to manufacturers looking to break in to emerging markets. The direct approach allows the manufacturer to acquire a high degree of control over foreign marketing, with larger profits to be reasonably expected. Union Carbide, the manufacturer of batteries, antifreeze products, chemicals, and pesticides, has manufacturing facilities in Europe, Africa, Asia, the Middle East, and Latin America. These operations provide approximately 60% of the company's total revenues.

As a rule, the level of investment required is quite substantial and the level of risk is also very high. In addition, the direct approach requires that the manufacturer acquire specific skills in doing business abroad that other entry strategies do not demand, further increasing the level of investment.

For the vast majority of companies seeking to take advantage of the tremendous opportunities emerging markets have to offer, a narrow range of distribution strategies that are best suited to each corporate philosophy, the corporation's ability to invest in these markets, the amount of control desired, and the level of acceptable risk must be developed on a market-by-market basis. Furthermore, the strategies chosen by each company will require each company to develop appropriate functions and operations to adequately support those strategies. For example, if a company decides that a key input is a high level of control over a distributor's operation, then the appropriate resources must be dedicated to integrate selected key functions of the distributor's business into its own, that is, direct or indirect management of the distributor's sales, service, or manufacturing departments. This is a key distinction, as the direction of the integration activity tremendously impacts the degree of monitoring and control that the manufacturer has within the distributor's business. Such a high degree of monitoring and control is usually achieved only when a manufacturer's effective direct management of the distributor's sales, service, or manufacturing departments is undertaken—otherwise known as the Distributor Monitoring & Control (DMC) Strategy©.[1]

The remainder of this book focuses on the processes needed to ensure the proper placement or distribution of your product or service in targeted high-growth emerging markets. The march of Global Manifest Destiny has led us to its current phase, Decelerated Pro-Activity, in which there may exist new opportunities to establish more effective sales and distribution strategies in targeted markets. Paramount to the success or failure of an increasingly larger number of foreign ventures, the criticality of sales and distribution has become widely recognized. Throughout the world, manufacturers are realizing the inescapable truth that proper sales and distribution are essential in achieving long-term profits, revenues, and market share. Again, the difference between industrialized markets and emerging ones is that within emerging markets, manufacturers normally have more opportunities to affect and influence the evolution and development of sales and distribution structures.

Unfortunately, in the industrialized world, manufacturers have historically failed to recognize their role in distribution and have eventually abdicated significant control in key areas over the sales and distribution of their products to their distributors. In too many cases, distributors have become more important than manufacturers in the supply chain. In some industries, distributors are now bigger and more powerful than the companies that produce the products they sell. The "corporate DNA" of a manufacturer—those characteristics that often make up the personality and behavior of a company and define its corporate culture—is many times left out of the sales and distribution of its products. In industrialized markets, Wal-Mart and Home Depot are really not retailers as much as they are distributors. Any manufacturer who deals with Wal-Mart's purchasing department in Bentonville, Arkansas, will say the same thing: You will play on their terms or you do not play at all. Dealing with this new breed of megadistributor is similar to what an industry gadfly once mused about doing business with AT&T in the early 1980s, before deregulation. He aptly stated that "doing business with AT&T was like having sex with a gorilla." In other, less explicit words, if you choose to do business with AT&T, you play by their rules, on their turf, and by their clock. In too many cases in the industrialized world, this is the situation. Moreover, the "corporate DNA" of the manufacturer is simply pushed aside and replaced with the corporate culture, strategies, and goals of the distributor.

Some in the industrialized world firmly believe that such manufacturer-distributor relationships have become dysfunctional. Over the last several decades, manufacturers have, for the most part, abrogated the responsibility for the distribution of their products. In fear of alienating their distributors, too many manufacturers have relinquished control to their distributors. Furthermore, it was easier to do so than to pursue strategies that proactively monitored and controlled key aspects of the distributor's business essential to successful sales and distribution.

Many distributors, therefore, have over the years been able to "self-develop" based on the needs of their own self-interest, sometimes to the direct benefit of the manufacturer, but more often only to the gain of the distributor. This has been especially true in those cases where the manufacturers are not dominant market leaders within their respective industries. This self-development has tended to be unresponsive and, at moments, downright hostile to the needs of the manufacturers. Over time, "gorillas" have been created in a number of industries; for the most part, they substantially dictate success or failure for the manufacturer, as in permitting or not permitting the manufacturer to cost-effectively offer its products to the consumer.

Throughout the industrialized world, national and global strategic account programs are under increasing pressure from their end-user customers to bypass distributors. Ironically, many of the same manufacturers who have complaints from their end-users have failed to properly control their distribution channels. Admittedly, there are cases when forward-thinking and like-minded manufacturers and distributors act in concert to develop productive, non-adversarial strategic alliances that seek to leverage the best that both have to offer the relationship. Nevertheless, such a mutually beneficial relationship is an aberration among the adversarial manufacturer-distributor relationships that dominate most industries.

In industrialized markets and even in some emerging ones, it may be too late to change this out-of-balance scenario. It is extremely difficult to change set patterns of behavior when this is viewed as limiting someone's freedom. The powerful distributors who do not seek mutually beneficial relationships, but rather blatant self-interest in the industrialized world may find it unnecessary to change their behavior.

Fortunately, emerging markets are unlike industrialized ones in this respect. Emerging markets are more malleable, only because they are new. Because of this malleability and newness, distributors still exist in emerging markets who are more receptive to the guidance and direction of foreign companies in the implementation of a mutually beneficial relationship between manufacturer and distributor. In many circumstances, the adversarial nature of the manufacturer/distributor relationship has not yet come to fruition. It is still possible for the "corporate DNA" of the manufacturer to be internalized within the responsive emerging market distributor. The current phase of Decelerated Pro-Activity in emerging markets provides manufacturers with a window of opportunity not to repeat the mistakes of the past, that is, by abrogating the manufacturer's role to proactively affect the evolution of distribution networks and distribution structures in a given market. Further, public sector entities are more apt to engage in the absorption of the manufacturer's "organizational DNA" in light of the present Decelerated Pro-Activity phase. However, proper strategies need to be implemented in order to seize the initiative and gain greater control of the distribution of the manufacturer's product or service. It is at this point that the manufacturer can influence or model the behavior of its distributor.

If a manufacturer has pursued the "old model" and already created an overly dominant distributor, it may be necessary to make the difficult decision to get a new distributor and grow the relationship with it, employing new strategies. Although this may seem an unpleasant, time-consuming, and expensive task, it may be a necessary one. Decelerated Pro-Activity offers the manufacturer a second chance to get it right. Those who seize the moment today will be the leaders of tomorrow.

DISTRIBUTOR MONITOR & CONTROL (DMC) STRATEGY

The vast majority of the time, it is in a manufacturer's interest to better monitor and control the sales and distribution of its products. For most companies, properly monitoring and controlling critical aspects of a distributor's business rather than "owing" the local business may be a much better approach to developing business in emerging markets. This is the basis of the Distributor Monitoring and Control Strategy (DMC). The DMC approach provides greater leverage and better leads to the appropriate allocation of resources so as to maximize the effectiveness of the relationship. Solid distribution also encourages the development of a more constructive and balanced relationship built upon "mutual self-interest." By better monitoring and controlling those activities within the distributor's business that are essential to successful sales and distribution, the distributor is more effectively managing its resources—its own money, staff, and other resources—for the manufacturer's direct benefit as well as its own. This frees up scarce resources that might be better spent someplace else.

The same resources and people employed by the manufacturer cost much less if employed by the local emerging market distributor. Whereas the foreign manufacturer must pay all social costs and taxes for its employees, the local emerging market distributor is often able to creatively avoid payment of such costs. Moreover, the wage and salary levels for comparable jobs are much lower in the local distributor's business than in the foreign manufacturer's business.

The underlying presumption here is that the manufacturer recognizes its role in dealing fairly and reasonably with its selected distributors. As often as distributors operate in a purely "self-interested" mode, so do most manufacturers.

The collective goal of both manufacturer and distributor should be the development of constructive, mutually beneficial, long-term relationships.

The key elements of the DMC Strategy are:

- Manufacturer-Exclusive or Manufacturer-Dominant Distributor Relationships.
- Manufacturer-Exclusive or Manufacturer-Preferred Territories.
- Distributor Sales/Service Supervisor (DSS) is on-site within the distributor's business to monitor and control critical activities of the distributor's business that are essential to the manufacturer's success in that market. DSS is the manufacturer's employee. A DSS might manage the distributor's
    - Sales and service people.
    - Sales, service, installation, and technical management.
    - Inventory safety stocks and delivery logistics.
    - Marketing, advertising, and merchandising of manufacturer's products.

The DSS, an employee of the manufacturer, can be on-site full time or spend one day a week with the distributor. The DSS performs an operations checklist to ensure that the distributor is fulfilling every aspect of the distribution function in accordance with the performance standards set by the manufacturer. At its essence, this checklist is a monitoring and controlling function of the distributor's operation that surrounds the manufacturer's products. If your company decides to install full-time staff at the distributor's location, two individuals should be sent from your company. Even the most well-intentioned employee, if alone, can fall prey to an unscrupulous distributor who might offer a "gift" to have the employee help the distributor get more control over the relationship. Further, your office inside the distributor's facilities should have its own separate computer system and a secured area for all documents, files, correspondence, and the like.

The DSS may manage the manufacturer's interest within the distributor's business by placing orders on behalf of the distributor, monitoring the credit of the distributor, ensuring product remains within the distributor's territory, and keeping levels of pricing and distributor credit to its customers in accordance with pre-set agreements with the manufacturer. In well-developed DMC applications, the DSS can also have budgetary responsibilities for the manufacturer within the distributor's business. However, in no circumstance should the DSS have direct access to managing the distributor's money.

A United States–based major fast-moving consumer goods (FMCG) company in a key Central European market implemented a full DMC Strategy beginning in 1996. This manufacturer is the fourth largest company in its industry on a global market share basis. Yet, in this Central European market, they are number one, with almost 30% market share. The next closest competitor, the global market leader, has less than half of the market share captured by this innovative and aggressive FMCG manufacturer.

A DSS was deployed to each county in this market—almost forty in total. For strategic reasons, the consumer goods company pursued a direct sales and distribution approach with their employees in control of the operations in the four largest cities in the country. This was done to demonstrate to the then unconvinced national wholesalers that this manufacturer was quite serious about pursuing the DMC Strategy. As soon as these four major cities were taken from local distributors, they immediately changed their attitudes and became much more flexible and willing to work with the foreign company.

To demonstrate the tremendous benefits a manufacturer can receive through the implementation of a DMC approach, the manufacturer's return-on-investment (ROI) in its own business in the four cities was 97%. The return-on-investment using the DMC Strategy vis-a-vis local distributors was nearly 500%—almost a five-fold leverage of the DMC Strategy over the manufacturer-owned one.

Within the last year, three of the four manufacturer-controlled cities were turned over to distributors to operate. The manufacturer, to maintain the necessary equilibrium in the marketplace, has strategically retained the capital city, representing nearly 20% of the entire market share in this market. This has been explicitly done so as not to disturb the delicate balance that currently exists between the manufacturer and its many regional distributors within this market. To allow any existing or new distributor to take over operations in this very desirable market in the capital city would create tremendous upheaval with the current distributors in the marketplace. Despite the promise of a much higher ROI arguing to extend the DMC Strategy to this capital city, the manufacturer is astute enough to know when "non-financial" factors outweigh financial ones.

A United Kingdom–based electronic measurements equipment manufacturer has very successfully implemented the DMC Strategy in Brazil. Not currently having sufficient revenues generated from this market or the resources to dedicate a full-time, on-site DSS within each of four distributors, the manufacturer has modified the DMC Strategy to meet its specific needs. Their Distributor Operations Director (DOD) once a week visits each of the four distributors that the DOD manages. A comprehensive distributor operations plan has been developed for each distributor to ensure that the manufacturer's business "within the distributor's business" is managed as best as it can be.

For a full day each week, the DOD meets with the distributor's owners, managers, and employees to review achievement of the daily and weekly operational performance objectives as well as to actively develop and nurture more and deeper relationships with key people within each distributor's business. After just eighteen months implementing this variation of the DMC Strategy, the U.K. manufacturer has already doubled its market share in this market and is on target to possibly double its business again, despite economic problems in this market.

Nevertheless, at times it may be necessary for a manufacturer to "own" its distribution channels, usually by implementing its own direct sales and distribution strategies utilizing its employees and all of its own resources. This situation typically arises when the complexity of product, customization of product, support required, or level of expertise needed are beyond the abilities of the local distributor.

When seeking to monitor and control distribution, it is clear that some of the old paradigms of distribution is flawed. Antiquated thinking about distribution fails to fully recognize the inherent conflict between manufacturer and distributor. The paradigm simply resigns itself to the conflict or simply ignores it, or both. In addition, the paradigm fails to recognize the distinct role manufacturers need to have in the distribution process. Manufacturers lack information, and in many cases the old paradigm dictates that such a lack of information on the market, the end-user, or the consumer is the distributor's best security.

A new paradigm of distribution needs to be created. It needs to step away from the failed thinking of the past and acknowledge the dynamics of distribution, especially with regard to emerging markets. Further, it needs to place these dynamics into a suitable context in terms of the manufacturer/distributor relationship. At its core, the new paradigm must include operational integration between manufacturer and distributor and, to the largest extent possible, cultural or organizational factors. In other words, the "corporate DNA" of the two companies should meld. Those dynamics are essentially:

1. Distributors' markets are fluid and always changing. The enlightened manufacturer has to affect and effect those changes and make a commitment to the notion that it, too, can play a critical role in the evolution of the distribution networks and structures in a given market. The manufacturer must also make the necessary commitments and investments to that end that are commensurate with both phases of Global Manifest Destiny—Accelerated Re-Activity and Decelerated Pro-Activity.

2. Manufacturers and distributors have historically had opposite and often adversarial goals. In many cases, this is true for the majority of the cases in emerging markets. The old thinking that the manufacturer's lack of information is the distributor's best security needs to be reconsidered. However, there still exists an opportunity in emerging markets, given their malleability. It is incumbent upon the manufacturer to proactively develop strategies to minimize and harmonize such goal conflict. The manufacturer must acknowledge its pro-active role in the ongoing monitoring and control process of its distributors. Although it may be a formidable task in some markets, it is still possible. The authors have always been able to identify right-thinking distributors even in some of the most difficult markets on the planet.

3. Manufacturers are always competing for their distributors' time, especially when the distributors carry competing products. For manufactures, the commitments should be made to dominate the product category and mindset of their right-thinking distributors. The manufacturers should dedicate themselves to building their distributors' business. Even for small or medium-sized firms, it is quite possible to dominate a niche or subcategory via the distributor if the appropriate commitments and investments are undertaken. All too often, manufacturers attempt to take finite resources and spread them too thin across a wide number of markets. Instead, the new paradigm of distribution mandates that manufacturers dedicate their resources in a more specific

and targeted manner, where they can best affect and effect the evolution of the distribution structures in a particular market.

There is hope. The relationships between manufacturers and distributors in emerging markets don't have to be adversarial. However, it is incumbent upon the manufacturer to take the initiative. Distributors in emerging markets are more often likely to see any passivity or compassion on the part of the manufacturer as a sign of weakness and may very well seek to wrestle control away. This is at the core of the adversarial relationship between manufacturer and distributor.

For emerging markets, the distribution strategies and models to be built have to be more similar to an all-terrain vehicle than to a sports car that works well in an industrialized market. Successful distribution in emerging markets needs to be simple in its sophistication and quickly and easily adaptable for a variety of conditions. Like an all-terrain vehicle, a manufacturer's well-managed emerging market distribution strategy needs to take into account sudden turns in the road and deep potholes along the way. Oftentimes, it can be a bold and aggressive strategy that seeks to get the attention of distributors in the market. In industrialized markets, precise fine-tuning of current distribution networks and structures are needed to attain any small efficiencies that may be possible or to gain a slight competitive advantage in the marketplace.

In essence, the most effective emerging market distribution strategies are multi-year and developed with strategic forethought. The planning cycle for emerging markets sometimes needs to be month by month and quarter to quarter for a period of between two and six quarters—depending on the market and the present situation—as compared to a yearly analysis in an industrialized market. It is necessary to plan for many potential adjustments because of the realities emerging markets offer, especially in light of the current Decelerated Pro-Activity phase. Flexibility and adaptability must reign!

For the manufacturer, always building for the future while attending to daily needs is fundamental in maintaining the critical balance that a constructive manufacturer/distributor relationship needs. To better achieve this goal, the manufacturer must take it upon itself to develop a keen understanding of the core competencies regarding the logistics, in-market sales, and distribution of its product within the marketplace and apply these competencies to evolve both its distributor's business and the emerging market's overall sales and distribution networks. Doing so reinforces the distributor's recognition of the manufacturer's commitment to a successful relationship as well as positively contributes to the success of the distributor's business. Further, it reaffirms the role of the manufacturer as mentor as it seeks to integrate the manufacturer's knowledge and experience within the distributor's business.

Finally, the most effective sales and distribution strategies seek to enable the manufacturer to maximize its critical monitoring and control over critical activities within the distributor's business and seeks to minimize the manufacturer's overall risk. Manufacturers must reassert themselves and overcome the flawed

Figure 4.4a
Sales and Distribution Strategy Development Flowchart (1)

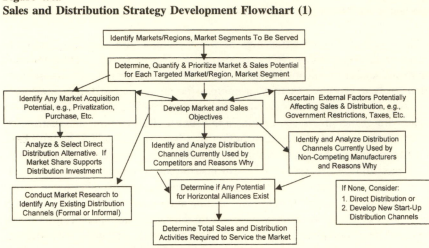

thinking of the past. Global Manifest Destiny has provided the moment. It is now time to seize the advantage.

THE PROCESS FOR DEVELOPING EMERGING MARKETS DISTRIBUTION STRATEGIES

The following steps are intended to illustrate the process by which enlightened manufacturers begin to formulate their entry sales and distribution strategies for emerging markets (Figs. 4.4a, 4.4b, and 4.4c). In determining your company's distribution strategy, the following steps should be carefully considered:

1. Identify the markets, regions, and market segments to be served. This objective determines which customers the company is looking to approach. As with the P&G example, it is necessary to look at particular emerging markets within a larger framework. Regardless of the framework chosen, it is necessary to determine where customer groups are concentrated. They normally tend to be located primarily in either specific geographic, cultural, or industry segments. In some cases, however, customer groups can be widely dispersed.

2. Identify markets to be reached. This is really an objective of the company—which customer groups to approach. Determine whether these groups are concentrated in specific geographic or industry segments or dispersed. Determine the market segments to be reached by customer groups. This follows from the previous step. Further, determine the market and sales potential for each market segment. How many customers are there? How much will each customer buy, on average? Use government, trade association, and publication research sources or conduct your own studies to obtain this information.

3. Determine relative importance of each market, industry, and geographic

Figure 4.4b
Sales and Distribution Strategy Development Flowchart (2)

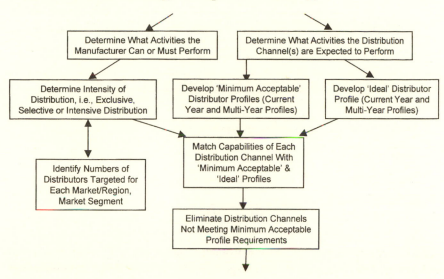

segment. This can be a mere priority ranking or a sophisticated approach weighing a variety of factors to determine ranking. Include expected market share in the analysis.

4. Ascertain external factors and internal factors potentially restricting development, that is, government policies, monopolies, tax issues. Use all secondary and primary research sources available to you to study the industry for possible long-range market changes that affect channel decisions.

5. Determine, quantify, and prioritize the market and sales potential for each emerging market. As stated previously, all markets are not equal. It is critical to be realistic here.

6. Identify any market acquisition potential such as privatization or purchase of an already-existing company. Most products have distribution channels, many of them informal. Ciudad del Este in South America or Soweto in South Africa, for example, are some of the best avenues manufacturers have found to capture regional market share in these parts of the world; at the same time, formalized distribution networks are not readily identifiable.

7. List the channels or networks currently used by competitors or "complementors" in your industry to contact end-users or consumers (including alternatives not currently employed) to bridge the gap between customer and company and the reasons why these channels are being used.

8. Gather insights and opinions on the markets and channels from sales and marketing executives in your company, from noncompetitors in the same industry, from middlemen, and from customers. Ask related trade associations and trade publications for information on channels customarily employed. The sea-

Figure 4.4c
Sales and Distribution Strategy Development Flowchart (3)

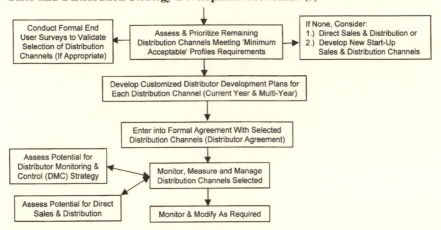

soned emerging markets traveler will readily agree that it is much easier and quicker to meet with most businesspeople and governmental representatives within most emerging markets than it is within most industrialized markets. Further, the willingness to share information in these markets is also much greater than in industrialized markets.

9. Determine the level of intensity of distribution and quantity of distributors needed, whether intensive, selective, or exclusive (Figure 4.5). Intensive distribution centers upon making product available at all locations where a customer or consumer might be expected to find it. This level of distribution is widely used for consumer and convenience goods, such as soft drinks and snacks, as well as for some manufacturing supplies, such as fasteners, bolts, and screws, especially in the early entry stage in most emerging markets. Intensive distribution is most appropriate when the customer's brand loyalty is low. The highest need for the customer concerning product at the intensive distribution level is convenience of purchase. A widespread availability of locations that carry the particular product is fundamental to its success or failure. As a result, intensive distribution requires large numbers of outlets and many individual distributors with which to place the product. The distributors involved vary widely in size, scope, and capacity. With widespread placement of the product as the primary or sole objective, a manufacturer will deal with essentially anyone who can "get the product into the market and/or onto the shelves." A consequence of this process is that many foreign companies are forced to do business with firms that may fail to pay their bills on time, do not promote the products aggressively, or demand excessive levels of service. In intensive distribution, there typically exists no exclusive relationship in either direction between manufacturer and distributor.

Selective distribution as an emerging market entry strategy is used for both consumer and industrial products. Consumer goods are often products like household

Figure 4.5
Determining the Intensity of Distribution

appliances, jewelry, and some types of liquor. Industrial goods include accessories, parts, and processed materials. For such products, the number of distributors at the selective level is limited to a smaller quantity than at the intensive level. Accordingly, foreign manufacturers can focus their energies on distributors who are believed to have the best potential for achieving success and forgo those distributors who may be problematic in the future. Although still not exclusive in their dealings, distributors are now very often required to make additional investments in the sales and distribution of the manufacturer's products. Likewise, the manufacturer is now limiting its distribution channel options.

Manufacturers who follow an exclusive distribution strategy use only one distributor for each geographical area to be served. The manufacturer can secure the advantages of low cost and high sales to a greater degree than with selective distribution. Management can restrict the distribution channel to low-cost distributors who are willing to stock large inventories and furnish strong promotional support or to distributors that possess special skills, resources or "special" relationships in an emerging market. Exclusive distribution is common for specialty goods that require more sophisticated pre-sale and/or post-sale resources. IBM computers and Komatsu tractors are sold through a network of exclusive distributors throughout the developing world.

Many times in emerging markets, as the market evolves, so must the strategy. Whereas it was wholly appropriate to enter the market employing an intensive or selective distribution approach, for all types of goods, both industrial and consumer, it becomes increasingly more important that value-adding services be employed by the distributor. Most often, the motivation for the distributor to dedicate greater resources to the sales and distribution of a manufacturer's product line lies in the manufacturer's grant of exclusivity to the distributor for the sales and distribution of the manufacturer's products within the specific geographic territory in which the distributor conducts business.

Remember that exclusivity is bipolar in that, while the manufacturer may offer a distributor its products on an exclusive basis, the distributor may or may not reciprocate such exclusivity in its dealings with the manufacturer's competitors. Also be mindful that it may not be in the manufacturer's best interest that a distributor sell and distribute only the manufacturer's products to the exclusion of the manufacturer's competitors. Many times, it is much more effective for the manufacturer to engage in a "manufacturer-dominant" relationship with some distributors rather than a "manufacturer-exclusive" relationship if the distributor is perceived by its customers to be less desirable to do business with because the distributor carries a less robust and less attractive product portfolio. Many manufacturers very often miss this point, which typically creates needless and counterproductive friction between manufacturer and distributor.

10. Determine total marketing, sales and distribution, and servicing activities required in the market. List all activities the distribution channel is expected to do (i.e., those they must do and those you would like them to do such as sell, stock, promote, frequency of calls, number of people needed). List those activities that your company can or *must* perform either because some other company or channel won't do them or because they will achieve the desired level of control, market share, and so on. Match the capabilities and resources of each channel identified and analyzed against the requirements dictated by overall company and marketing objectives. Eliminate those channels that cannot or will not fulfill essential activities. Then, rank the remaining channels according to ability to accomplish assigned tasks and to best satisfy end-users' needs. Calculate estimated total costs to the company per unit of sales through alternative channels (covering expected volume ranges over a period of at least three years). Include average frequency, size, and profit per sales or service call to each end-user. Include all costs: inventory control, shipping, sales expense, supervision, advertising, billing, carrying accounts receivable, and so on. Use break-even analysis to evaluate each alternative channel considered. Eliminate channels the company clearly cannot afford because of internal company-imposed return-on-investment standards. Then, rank the remaining channels according to

- Estimated profitability.
- Ability to fulfill essential and desirable activities.
- Effectiveness in reaching marketing goals.
- Advantages and disadvantages.
- An overall comparison of the costs of operating your own direct sales and distribution force and the like and providing the associated services required.

11. Analyze the top two to five channel mixes to determine whether and to what extent all desired goals and activities are achieved (Tables 4.1, 4.2, and 4.3). Select the channel or channels that offer the best balance of serving target markets and returning profits for the company.

Throughout this process, an understanding of distribution channel effective-

Table 4.1
Channel Analysis (Economic Analysis)

1.   Determine manufacturer's FIXED costs of sales in terms of:

     a.   Salaries

     b.   Employee benefits, accrued and non-accrued

     c.   Sales expenses

     d.   Allocations of non-sales overhead for which manufacturer is charged; e.g., secretarial, finance, etc.

     e.   Other fixed costs

2.   Determine manufacturer's VARIABLE costs of sales applied to each distributor.

3.   Determine the sales revenue volume for each channel of distribution and the time required to achieve such volume (or potential to estimate future investment).

4.   Calculate the total profit contribution available to manufacturer from each distributor.

5.   Divide manufacturer's estimate of total profit contribution by manufacturer's estimated total manufacturer's costs to support the channel and calculate the Return-On-Investment (ROI) for each channel (or anticipated ROI).

Definitions:
Fixed costs - all costs of operations not directly related to the costs of product sales and which occur independent of generated sales revenues.

Variable costs - all costs of selling, distributing, advertising, and promoting products which are directly proportional to the sale of product.

Costs of goods sold - all costs directly related to the manufacture of goods, including cost of raw materials, purchased products, labor, value-added and quality control, etc.

Profit contribution - total sales revenue less the costs of goods sold, less the variable costs of sales.

Pretax margin - profit contribution less the fixed costs of sales.

Return-on-investment - pretax margin divided by total costs to support each channel.

Table 4.2
Distribution Channel Analysis (Cost Analysis)

Cost Item	Direct Sales	Distributor #1	Distributor #2	
Fixed Costs:				
Salaries				
Benefits				
Employment Taxes				
Travel Expenses				
Auto Expense				
G&A Allocation				
Total Fixed Costs				
Variable Costs:				
Inquiry, Sales Lead & Quotation				
Processing				
Order Entry & Scheduling				
Billing & Invoicing				
Receivables				
Sales Accounting				
Handling & Freight				
Inventory Possession				
Advertising & Promotion				
Training				
Relocation				
Other				
Total Variable Costs				
Total Costs				

88

Table 4.3
Distribution Channel Analysis (ROI Analysis)

	Direct Sales	Distributor #1	Distributor #2
1. Sales Revenue/Volume			
2. Cost of Goods Sold			
3. Variable Costs			
4. Fixed Costs			
5. Profit Contribution (1 - (2 + 3))			
6. Total Costs (3 + 4)			
7. Pretax Margin (5 - 4)			
8. Return-On-Investment (7 ÷ 6)			

Definitions:

Fixed Costs - all costs of operations not directly related to the costs of product sales and which occur independent of generated sales revenues for each channel.

Variable Costs - all costs of selling, distributing, advertising, and promoting products which are directly proportional to the sale of product for each channel.

Cost of Goods Sold - all costs directly related to the manufacture of goods, including cost of raw materials, purchased products, labor, quality control, etc. for each channel.

Profit Contribution - total sales revenue less the costs of goods sold, less the variable costs of sales for each channel.

Pretax Margin - profit contribution less the fixed costs of sales for each channel.

Return-On-Investment - pretax margin divided by total costs to support each channel.

ness in emerging markets from a financial perspective needs to be undertaken. It never ceases to amaze us that normally successful companies will run a return-on-investment (ROI) when purchasing capital equipment or venturing into new domestic businesses. But, when making the equal or larger investments required to enter emerging markets, these same companies come up short on continually monitoring the returns on investments that they make with their emerging market distributors. The logic and need are inescapable. At the same time, the ROIs for emerging markets business cannot be keyed to industrialized markets because of the unique realties inherent to emerging markets. The ROIs in emerging markets must be analyzed over a longer investment period than their industrialized market counterparts.

For properly determining channel analysis for emerging markets, both the cost and ROI analysis should be done. Nevertheless, nonfinancials can be at least as important as financial factors in determining ROIs. Distributor reputation, distributor market share, distributor future potential, availability of distributors, or other key distributor strengths or assets may all play decisive roles beyond the numbers in determining true emerging market ROIs.

A U.S. manufacturer of go-karts maintained its strong relationship with its Hungarian distributor for two years despite low ROIs because of the strong dedication each party had to the other. In the third year, the ROIs began to rise, and by the fifth year, all expectations had been exceeded.

Once this process is completed, it is then possible to embark upon the next step in the implementation of successful sales and distribution in emerging markets, the recruitment and selection of an effective distributor.

NOTE

1. The Distributor Monitor & Control (DMC) Strategy is a copyright of John A. Caslione and Andrew-Ward International, Inc.

5

The Local Presence: Selecting and Recruiting Emerging Market Distributors

A man's true worth is measured by the people who enter his tent.
Ancient Arabic Proverb

In many situations, the best distributor to represent your product in an emerging market does not always appear on the surface to be the best candidate. While visiting his distributor in Nairobi a few years ago, Thomas was introduced to a man from eastern Zaire who came in to discuss buying some motorcycles. Thomas had been eager for the meeting because he had no representation there. His enthusiasm evaporated when he first saw the man from Zaire, who looked as if he had arrived right out of the bush, wearing old plastic sandals, a stained, torn and dirty shirt, a ripped pair of pants. Most obvious of all, he could be smelled from two kilometers away. Meeting this man defied the logic of the timeless expression, "You never get a second chance to make a good first impression."

When Thomas and the Zairian businessman were formally introduced and exchanged the traditional three-kiss, French greeting, Thomas proceeded to do the most typical of American business practices and offered the African his business card. The Zairian asked for a sheet of paper and wrote his name and country on the paper and presented it as his.

After the formalities, Thomas began his standard sales pitch, not wanting to offend this poor man, who obviously did not have the resources to do business with him. As one of the motorcycles was sitting on the showroom floor, they started the unit, discussed all its wonderful features, and then took a spin around the block. Upon their return to the office, Thomas gave the Zairian a baseball cap and key chain. A smile covered his entire face and he gave Thomas the three-kiss, French greeting.

After three hours, boredom was beginning to set in. Still, Thomas did not want to offend this "wanna-be" businessman. He thought, "When in Africa, do what the Africans do. If he wants to play big shot, go along with him." When the Zairian began to ask more seemingly irrelevant questions, Thomas suggested they get a Coke. The caffeine rush would permit him to stay awake long enough to make the poor African feel important. After another hour, the most important questions finally came:

"What is the unit price?"

"$1,500 delivered to Nairobi."

The Zairian asked for another sheet of paper and wrote down $1,500.

"How many motorcycles could be loaded into a twenty-foot ocean container?"

"Forty."

For the next ten minutes the Zairian proceeded to multiply, in longhand, fifteen hundred by forty. Thomas was tempted to offer his calculator but reckoned it might be better to let the man play big shot for a little longer. After he successfully completed the equation, the Zairian stared at nowhere in particular for ten minutes.

Finally he announced, "I'll take forty units."

Thomas wasn't shocked. He was certain the Zairian believed Thomas would ship the motorcycles and let him pay later. Still trying not to offend him, Thomas told him as politely as possible that it would be necessary to pay the entire amount prior to shipment. Thomas figured this would quietly end the meeting so they could get on to the more pressing matter of lunch.

Without saying a word, the Zairian reached behind the desk and pulled out an old cardboard box wrapped in worn-out tape that smelled almost as bad as he did. The African then opened up the box and proceeded to count out US$60,000 in one hundred dollar bills. As he counted, Thomas peered unbelievingly into the box and roughly calculated there was at least three million dollars inside, all in U.S. currency. At that moment, this poor, wanna-be businessman was transformed into Thomas' new distributor for eastern Zaire and his new best friend.

Any astute international business traveler will tell you that it is not smart to ask someone from where they have accumulated their wealth. In any airport waiting lounge in the world it is possible to find an American who will tell you his or her life story in twenty minutes. An African, Latin, Asian, or Russian, however, will never *tell* you how he got rich. If you have his confidence, he will *show* you. With local distributors and other businessmen in emerging markets, the expression "You can ask me how I made my millions, but do not ask me how I made my *first* million" applies almost universally.

Some months later, Thomas ventured to eastern Zaire to see his new best friend—call him Samuni. Zaire, now the Democratic Republic of the Congo, is one of the great paradoxes of the world. Underneath its soil are some of the largest gold, diamond, copper, and platinum deposits on earth. If they were properly exploited, Congo's forty-four million people could live healthy and prosperous lives. Instead, because of rampant corruption and perennial governmental mismanagement of these assets, the average life expectancy for both men and women is less than fifty years and the average annual income is less than $250. It is in this environment, however, that some tremendous personal fortunes have been amassed. Everyone knows of the US$5 billion that Mobutu Sese Seko, the former president, accumulated during the reign of his kleptocracy for over thirty years. What people may not know is how Samuni and many like him also became rich. They did not steal from the government. They did it the old-fashioned way: they *earned* it. Admittedly, favorable relationships with key government officials usually serve as an essential "enabler" for the owners of such successful businesses.

Because of the severe lack of infrastructure, many of the minerals in Congo are being extracted by individuals in search of instant wealth—like the forty-niners of California's gold rush in the nineteenth century. The gold or diamonds are sold for the most universal of currencies, the U.S. dollar. It was recently concluded by the Federal Reserve that over 70% of all U.S. currency bills in the world are held outside the United States. A significant portion it seems is in eastern Congo. Dollars are everywhere, as they are in almost all emerging markets. In a former Belgian colony where French is the official language and English is rarely spoken, the universal communicator is the U.S. dollar.

Samuni goes into the mining areas with his old box and buys gold and diamonds with his U.S. Dollars—at a high margin for himself, of course. Next he travels to Nairobi or Kampala, where he exchanges the metals for consumer goods like cups, plates, knives, clothes, radios, Coca-Cola, televisions, and spare parts with Asian middlemen—again at a high margin for himself.

Using his connections in customs—connections that are supported as just another cost of doing his business—Samuni transports the goods from Kenya or Uganda to eastern Congo as imports with little or no duties. He then sells the goods back to the miners in exchange for the same U.S. dollars that started the process—at a high margin for himself.

The goods are sold from two tractor-trailers that move slowly down the road like a portable shopping mall. Whenever the trucks approach a small village, people come from miles around to see the latest goods: Indian kitchen utensils, American soft drinks, Korean television sets, Chinese radios. It is the Central African version of a suburban shopping center.

It is hard to calculate the net worth of Samuni's business since there are no bankers, accountants, lawyers, insurance brokers, tax collectors, or dry cleaners for hundreds of miles. A close friend estimates it is at least US$300 million. Thomas' business with Samuni alone has averaged over US$2.4 million each year for more than four years, especially high for such a small, impoverished market such as Zaire.

Samuni's business empire was built in the middle of the worst genocide since the killing fields of Cambodia. The conflict between the Hutu majority and the Tutsi minority in Central Africa has led to untold atrocities throughout the region. In April of 1994, Rwanda, Burundi, and Eastern Zaire erupted into a tribal bloodbath that has claimed the lives of at least 1.5 million men, women, and children. The violence continues unabated today, with no end in sight.

On Thomas' last visit to the region in May of 1997, he found Samuni operating near Goma, the site of the largest refugee camp, where more than 200,000 Hutu were living under the pseudo-protection of the United Nations. After the traditional three-kiss French greeting, Samuni took Thomas and one of his brothers by foot deep into the bush. They walked for almost an hour until they came upon a clearing where a forty-foot ocean container was resting. The box belonged in the middle of the African rain forest as much as Thomas did. As they approached, an overwhelming smell caused Thomas to vomit. To the right of the container were two local men throwing lime on the newly dug ground. After regaining his composure, Thomas approached one of the men and asked him what was going on:

"Two days ago, a local bushman discovered the container. The doors were locked and it smelled real bad. The bushman opened the doors and discovered, piled up at the entrance to the container, the corpses of several small children."

Right before Thomas vomited for the second time he asked, "How many bodies were in the container?"

"We counted two-hundred and six," he said calmly. "There wasn't a child over the age of five inside."

Thomas vomited again and then began to cry. The man with the shovel continued to throw down the lime as if he wasn't even there. As Thomas tried to recompose himself and began to stagger away, the man whispered to him, "God has left here."

When Thomas rejoined Samuni and his brother on the other end of the clearing, he found them talking on their IMSAT satellite phone to a London commodity house. They were asking for the closing price of gold on the London Exchange, completely oblivious to the massacre of the children. When he asked them their feelings about what had happened here, they brightly smiled and exclaimed, "Gold is up US$2 per ounce," and started back to the trail.

The best way for many companies to prosper in emerging markets is through the proper application of new and different distribution strategies quite different from those used in mature, industrialized markets, including passing or affixing Western value judgments upon the businesses and businesspeople in emerging markets. Such atrocities as mass genocide can never be accepted by any of us; at the same time, to consider Samuni an evil or dispassionate man is merely to acknowledge our own naiveté and our ignorance of the lives of these people. Simply put, there are a lot of men in the world like Samuni who would make wonderful distributors for Western manufacturers and their products who have been either ignored or rejected by the typical Western businessperson.

Unfortunately, many firms fail in emerging markets because they do not acknowledge the need to properly select and recruit the appropriate emerging market distributors or fail to develop suitable strategies that best reflect their company in a particular market. Neglecting to implement what may be new methods for this vital endeavor almost certainly guarantees failure in the sales and distribution of their products. The stories of manufacturers who have been deceived and exploited in emerging markets by unscrupulous importers and distributors are numerous and compelling. Years ago, a Fortune 500 client of Caslione's, unknown to him, gave the exclusive distribution of its product line to the younger brother of a competitor's representative in India. Only after the contracts were signed was it discovered that "family ties" were going to prohibit the company from doing business in this very important market. The result was a six-year battle and over US$6 million in legal costs. Even a rather perfunctory assessment of the market, vis-à-vis some of the processes presented in this book, would have revealed such family ties, alerting the Fortune 500 manufacturer that all was not as it appeared.

Many of America's and Europe's most successful companies have initially sold their products into new markets with great expectations, only later to realize that they were blocked either entirely or severely from doing the intended business because of unknown local factors. Undisclosed family relationships, unknown representation of competitive products in other companies set up by the distributor for the sole purpose of deceiving the foreign manufacturer, and unstated real intentions are all ways in which unsuspecting companies have been blindsided in emerging markets.

The "black hole syndrome" of distribution is an all too common occurrence for those aspiring to succeed in emerging markets. Orders are filled and shipped to a foreign customer, only to have the product disappear into the proverbial "black hole" of distribution where, after a few months, their products cannot even be located or are sold differently at prices never intended by the manufacturer. Stories abound of companies selling their products with all the right intentions to a customer only to discover later that their units were being used for completely different purposes. After months of absolutely no communication with its new "exclusive distributor," a Japanese manufacturer of machine tools was shocked to discover that its highly respected product was being used only to provide spare parts to the cousin of its distributor, an unauthorized gray marketer of the same Japanese company's products and an authorized importer of the manufacturer's most fierce and threatening competitor.

Fortunately, help may be available to allow us to avoid such hazards. Setting up the right distribution channels with the right distributor is one of the biggest challenges facing foreign companies entering an emerging market. New entrants often find themselves competing against multinational and local companies with well-established distribution networks. Moreover, companies are increasingly spending more on improving distribution, inventory management, and merchandising as they strive to maintain or gain a marketing advantage.

Although its critical importance cannot be overstated, distribution is generally the most globally differentiated and least understood of all marketing mix components. It is also the component most likely to hinder success in foreign markets for small to mid-sized companies. Proper distribution planning aims to ensure that the best available channels and physical distribution methods are in place to efficiently and economically get the right products and services to the right customers at the right time and right place and in the right form. In the global marketplace, where channels lengthen and materials handling problems multiply sometimes exponentially, effective sales and distribution strategies coupled with efficient channel and physical distribution systems can help offset high costs and help level the competitive playing field.

The level of involvement of a manufacturer in selling its product to foreign markets is usually delineated by one of the following typologies:

- Simple Exportation. This is the most basic and least involved level for the manufacturer in selling its product to a foreign market. The focus here is the processing of purchase orders and the expediting of the payment process.
- Reactive Distribution. This concerns itself with the development of a distribution relationship typically characterized by two or three personal visits per year to the market by an employee of the manufacturer.
- Low Active Distribution. It is generally characterized by the establishment of a small, local office within the market.
- High Active Distribution. It is usually marked by the integration of the manufacturer's employees into the distributor's company.
- The most complete involvement in a new market is the establishment of a complete operation, with the manufacturer totally in control of the production, personnel, and distribution process.

The most common typology is Reactive Distribution. Simply stated, the vast majority of manufacturers in the United States and Europe have neither the resources nor the desire to establish a local office or complete operation in a foreign market. For a great number of companies, the building of a relationship with a local distributor who needs to be visited two to three times per year is the best use of their available resources.

Addressing the fundamental importance of the distributor is critical to understanding the necessity for proper techniques used in distributor recruitment and selection. The distributor is the direct link between the manufacturer and customer or consumer. When a distributor is selected to sell a manufacturer's products in a particular market, the name, brands, and reputation of that manufacturer are being placed into the hands of somebody else. It goes without saying that such an action needs to be monitored closely.

Choosing the wrong distributor can be costly, time consuming, and damaging to your company's good name. Unfortunately, in many cases, a manufacturer does not realize it has made an error in distributor selection until many months after the beginning of the relationship. For those companies that have a level of involvement described as Lower Reactive Distribution, there is typically a "honeymoon period" for the six months of the kinship in which any problems that may arise are chalked up to the newness of the situation. However, in a large number of circumstances, after the honeymoon wears off, the problems between manufacturer and distributor usually persist and often increase. The end result is commonly a lost year, which in the rapidly changing environment of emerging markets is the equivalent of three to four years in the industrial world.

Before looking at the techniques for selecting and recruiting an emerging market distributor, it would be worthwhile to evaluate the impact a third-party advocate can add to the process. In many emerging markets, there is a small group of well-connected individuals who maintain strong relationships with both the business community and the government. As discussed in Chapter 3, these type of individuals can assist manufacturers in conducting primary and secondary research about the business climate in the local marketplace. In-market local lawyers, general managers of the major hotels, and personnel agencies, as well as other key individuals, are wonderful sources of information about what is happening and who the players really are. When it comes to offering advice as to which distributors to approach, individuals like these can prove invaluable in both the short term and the long term.

Shrewd companies usually develop relationships and may even retain one or more of these individuals to work as their "eyes and ears" in the market that they desire to enter. The cost is usually quite nominal, while the return-on-investment can be fantastic. The reality that nobody is really your friend needs to stand at the forefront of any entry strategy. Until a manufacturer is able to grasp the big picture in the local marketplace, it is always better to maintain a low profile.

Seemingly normal day-to-day activities such as applying for a visa to visit the country under consideration can have far-reaching ramifications. Because most potential distributors come from wealthy and influential families, they have access to information normally restricted to similar individuals in the industrialized world. For example, in order to monitor what is going on, several South American and African nations put out to a select group of businessmen a weekly list of those foreigners who had applied for a visa from their U.S., European, and other key countries' embassies and consulates. All visa forms require the particulars of the individual who will be traveling as well as the company they work for and, more important, the persons they will be visiting once in the country. Such information is then disseminated to the business elite, who are now fully aware of any plans or activities of foreign companies. The right third party on retainer in a market may help to mitigate some of these potentially debilitating issues and make the initial steps into an emerging market much smoother and less risky.

Once a foreign company feels that it has a handle on the situation in the marketplace, it is necessary to embark upon the eleven steps that leading firms use to recruit and select an emerging market distributor. The goal in this process is to establish a relationship that is forthright, mutually beneficial, and built upon a strong foundation. Although some of the steps may appear less relevant than others in light of a given situation, the proper application of these comprehensive steps will minimize the likelihood of choosing the wrong distributor.

Before starting the process, it is important to note that the first three steps need to take place prior to ever speaking with or meeting a prospective distributor. The ability to perform these crucial functions can be greatly enhanced by the third-party advocate described earlier. Throughout this entire procedure, but especially in the initial stages, discretion and low visibility should direct the manufacturer's actions. Remember, the nature of emerging markets dictates that hardly anyone is truly looking out for your best interests. Also remember that the following is as much a learned set of skills and processes as it is personal intuition and "street-smarts." This book can provide you with the former; only you will know if you have the latter.

STEP 1: IDENTIFY ALL POTENTIAL END-USERS OR CUSTOMERS

For any new market, leaders in their industry develop a profile of potential customers and existing end-users and create a database for each. In this step, it is vital to estimate sales revenue potential for each targeted market as well as to segment the market accordingly, that is, geographically, linguistically, and politically.

In order to acquire this information, it is necessary to develop a profile of potential and existing accounts by class-of-trade or industry, within the distributor's marketing area. Then, once this is accomplished, estimate the sales dollar potential available within the distributor's marketing area, again by industry or class-of-trade.

Using your existing knowledge of the market, make a list of product specifies (those functional titles who would normally specify or purchase your type of product) for each industry or class-of-trade. Finally, develop a calling list of the names of specifies from a cross section of your list of potential customers or end-users (approximately 15% of the potential: large accounts, small accounts, and geographically diverse). In this step, be certain to exclude all "direct" and/or "key" accounts from your list.

A manufacturer of contact lenses looking to enter Egypt might distinguish between their customers and consumers as follows: potential customers might be distributors or importers of pharmaceuticals, medical supplies, or hospital equipment. Consumers would also likely be optical stores, pharmacies, or eye doctors. Once determined, a database of both potential customers and consumers needs to be created.

Although Egypt is geographically a large country inhabited by a relatively homogeneous people, a significant portion of the population is located in a relatively small area. The contact lens manufacturer would probably focus on the few key urban areas, which would probably contain a substantial percentage of customers and consumers—Alexandria, Cairo, and Luxor. After these primary target markets are identified, an estimate of the revenue potential for each metropolitan area needs to be done.

In many situations, the analysis that comes with this undertaking provides critical information that was not known before. In the case of contact lenses, Egyptians were reluctant to use them because of the unsupported fear that they might damage the eyes in a sandstorm. By learning this, the manufacturer was aware that an education of the marketplace was necessary in order to sell its product there.

STEP 2: PERFORM A CUSTOMER OR END-USER SURVEY

A customer survey needs to be done by someone in your company, a trusted associate in the local market, or the home country's local consulate—not by a potential distributor! During its implementation, the names and the number of times each potential distributor is mentioned needs to be recorded. Further, using the new information, develop a list of sales skills and distribution resources needed for your product.

Although still not possible in a few places, the explosion of telecommunications across the globe has allowed such surveys to be completed more frequently using the telephone. Telephone surveys may be the most effective in markets where the foreign manufacturer may engage the services of a local, in-market research company. However, it is much more effective to meet personally with the potential buyer or customer. Also, determine on a case-by-case basis if it is suitable to specifically describe your product or identify your company; usually it is in your company's best interest to do so. The key areas that you as a manufacturer will need to explore relating to potential distributors in a given market are as follows:

- Product Knowledge
- Technical Expertise
- Market Knowledge
- Call Frequency and Availability
- After-Sales Service
- Billing and Credit Practices
- Product Mix
- Responsiveness
- Sales Professionalism

Be certain to record the name of each distributor mentioned next to each checklist category and then rank each distributor in terms of the number of times its name was mentioned. Those distributors most often mentioned are in many cases those with whom you may want to do business.

In the case of the contact lens manufacturer seeking to enter Egypt, in-person visits should be made to a suitable number of optical stores, pharmacies, and eye doctors in the segmented markets of Alexandria, Cairo, and Luxor to achieve a credible and sufficiently broad base of responses (in this case, somewhere between ten and twenty customers).

For those markets where a telephone survey is not feasible, other techniques need to be used. We have gone to the local bazaars in India or the "Mercato" in Addis Ababa and spoken directly with the retailers in these locations to solicit their feedback. In China, Hong Kong traders many times serve as a valuable resource. In South America, local customs officials quite often have their finger on the local pulse and always seem willing to share normally confidential information for the right price. Whatever the methodology, it is crucial to gather this information in order to make the right choice in determining who will represent your products.

STEP 3: DEVELOP PROFILES OF "IDEAL" AND "MINIMAL" DISTRIBUTORS

Before undertaking the distributor search, it is important to decide upon the attributes of an ideal or minimally acceptable distributor—and to stick to them. The creation of a methodology that qualifies and quantifies each attribute is the best way to provide perspective.

Based upon your company's outputs as derived in Chapter 4, describe the attributes of the "Ideal" distributor. Next, establish the "Minimally Acceptable" attributes of a distributor. The "Ideal" and "Minimally Acceptable" attributes of a distributor need to be customized for each market. The "Ideal" distributor should be one that is thought to exist for a specific market given the current state of market conditions as well as the present state of your company. The "Minimally Acceptable" distributor should conform to the most basic requirements of your company and in the market specifically targeted (Table 5.1).

Remember, it is important to "check your Western mores at the door." In many emerging markets, the individual who would be your best representative may not appear as such on the surface. When establishing the "Ideal" and "Minimally Acceptable" criteria, it is critical to view them as a function of the local marketplace.

A U.S. manufacturer of cookies believed a "minimally acceptable" criteria for its distributor in the Philippines should be a fleet of delivery vehicles, which could serve both as transport and as moving billboards. When the final choice was between two prospective local companies, the U.S. firm chose the firm with the best-looking fleet—more than seventy brand-new Toyota Maximas. The losing company was disqualified because its delivery fleet contained only twenty-two 1985 Mitsubishi pick-up trucks. Unfortunately, the decision turned out to

Table 5.1
Distributor Profile Evaluation Worksheet

Distributor Name: _____   Date of Evaluation:_____
Address:_____   Evaluated by (Name): _____

Phone: _____   Key Contact: _____
Fax: _____   Title: _____

Distributor Attributes	Ideal	Good	Minimal	Less than minimal	Does Not Exist
1. Knowledge of the Market	5	4	3	2	1
2. Knowledge of Importing/Distribution	5	4	3	2	1
3. No/Acceptable Involvement with Directly Competitive Products	5	4	3	2	1
4. Ability to Cover Assigned Market - Sales - Physical Distribution	5	4	3	2	1
5. Prompt Payment	5	4	3	2	1
6. Access to the Sales Organization	5	4	3	2	1
7. Administrative Support	5	4	3	2	1
8. Adequate Inventory Stocks Maintained	5	4	3	2	1
9. Sales Records Maintained	5	4	3	2	1
10. Forecasts of Purchases (Accuracy)	5	4	3	2	1
11. Marketing Plans Developed	5	4	3	2	1
12. Competitive Information Collected	5	4	3	2	1
13. Market Research	5	4	3	2	1
14. Advertising/Sales Support	5	4	3	2	1
15. Successful Manufacturer Relationships	5	4	3	2	1
16.	5	4	3	2	1
17.	5	4	3	2	1
18.	5	4	3	2	1
19.	5	4	3	2	1
20.	5	4	3	2	1
Total Each Column	+		+	+	+	
Evaluation Score:	(Total All Columns) =				

be a bad one. The Toyota Maximas could not handle the treacherous roads outside of Manila, especially during the rainy season. As a result, the cookies were never properly distributed in a consistent manner, and the venture eventually failed.

The criteria mentioned in Table 5.1 need to be quantified against the company's "Ideal" and "Minimally Acceptable" attributes. A leading global motor oil manufacturer looking to establish a presence in Vietnam, for example, would want to describe the characteristics of an "Ideal" distributor in Ho Chi

Minh City. After completing the checklist, the "Ideal" attributes might be described as follows: Two offices—one on each side of town; a sales force of ten salespersons, each equipped with a company-supplied pickup truck; an administrative staff of three individuals, two of whom speak English; and a warehouse space of more than 5,000 square meters. The "Minimally Acceptable" distributor may have only one office, four to six salespeople who use their own scooters, one English-speaking administrator, and a storage facility of at least 2,500 square meters.

A word of caution: Whatever the "Ideal" and "Minimally Acceptable" attributes are that your company agrees upon, do not change them. Far too many companies lower the bar after creating their criteria simply in order to enter the market. The thinking goes like this: "Once we get in, it will be much easier to fix any problems later." This mindset should be avoided at all costs. In most cases, your first instinct is your best one. Remember, there are times when not having a distributor at all is much better than having a distributor who does not meet even the most basic standards. Your company's reputation, brands, and good name are all at stake!

STEP 4: PERFORM A SURVEY OF POTENTIAL DISTRIBUTORS

Now, once the potential customers and end-users have been identified, a customer and end-user survey performed, and the "Ideal" and "Minimally Acceptable" attributes established, all from a far distance, it is necessary to perform a survey of potential distributors.

During this step, manufacturer and potential distributor should speak for the first time. In preparation for this initial encounter, a survey checklist should be used to ask questions of the potential distributor and determine its knowledge of the marketplace as well as its compatibility with your company and its product line.

With the checklist at the ready, contact each potential distributor principal and identify yourself, your company, and your specific product line. Unlike industrialized markets, where it may take several phone calls and weeks to coordinate a first business meeting, a surprising and refreshing dynamic of emerging markets is how quickly and easily you can arrange meetings. Be sure to advise the potential distributor that you are calling as a direct result of the findings of your end-user survey. At this point, do not attempt to convince the potential distributor to take on your product line. The sole purpose of this discussion is to establish contact, glean whatever information possible, and set the personal interview.

As each potential distributor responds to your questions, rank your impression on each element on a nominal scale from 1 to 10 (1 being lowest, 10 being highest). This data will become fundamental in the final selection. Finally, when the conversation seems to come to its natural conclusion, thank the potential distributor and request a time and place where you can meet in person.

STEP 5: PERSONALLY INTERVIEW PROSPECTIVE DISTRIBUTORS

Having successfully accomplished Steps 1, 2, 3, and 4, you will be much more informed and better prepared than the vast majority of Western companies seeking to recruit and select the right emerging market distributor. With all of the information collected at your disposal, you will be ready to present your company and yourself in a confident and professional manner. Many emerging market distributors have had a lot of experience dealing with Western companies looking to expand into their market. From the potential distributor's point of view, the typical lack of knowledge on the part of Western companies puts it in an immediate position of strength. Although we would never recommend arrogant or elitist behavior, it is important to begin the relationship from a position of mutual respect and understanding.

When you are finally face to face for the first time, your meeting materials should include your annual report or other relevant information, applicable product information and samples, a profile of your current business plans for the market, verbal results of your end-user survey, key markets or accounts in the distributor's market area of interest to you, and the list of your current distributors. In addition, depending upon the circumstances, a copy of your distribution agreement might be helpful. In all cases, however, discretion should dictate to what extent you share the more confidential information.

A word of caution regarding providing a blank copy of your company's distributor agreement must be stated here. On the plus side, providing the agreement raises the level of seriousness of the discussion and helps the manufacturer establish its requirements regarding working with distributors very early in the relationship. On the negative side, in some markets, the mere providing of a blank distributor agreement is tantamount to your acceptance of the distributor and "closing the deal." As with other issues in these emerging markets, a previously established relationship with a "trusted," retained local lawyer is invaluable in understanding local business customs and country culture.

The personal interview may take place in a restaurant, a café, a bar, a hotel conference center, or, most likely, the office of the person being interviewed. Regardless of the venue, it is important to be formal, polite, and steady as you try to secure key information from the potential distributor. Notwithstanding interruptions by waiters, mobile phones, urgent-message-bearing secretaries, or bottles of Jack Daniel's, keep the focus and seek to direct the meeting toward the following points:

Credit and Financial Stability

Be prepared to discuss your business with reference to your annual report and other relevant financials. From the potential distributor, request credit references and financial statements, if available. Remember, fundamental information such as financial statements may not be available in emerging markets. It can also prove to be very difficult to check a potential distributor's financial strength and creditworthiness. International distribution companies generally can provide verifiable financial statements, but such information may be difficult to obtain from a local distributor, who may have several companies used to creatively avoid payment of taxes. Such behavior in some emerging markets is a sign of a clever and successful businessperson rather than an untrustworthy and ineffective one.

Many companies believe the most effective way to find out about the financial status of potential distributors is to make inquiries to other suppliers who deal with them. If they are not competitors, suppliers are usually willing to share information. Approach the supplier to ascertain the distributor's payment history. If the potential distributor claims to pay promptly but the other supplier says it has two months of receivables outstanding, you know there is a problem.

Sales Strength

- How large are the potential distributor's field sales and service forces?
- How are the salespeople utilized or allocated in the potential distributor's marketplace and what responsibilities have they been assigned?
- What is their share of market against local competition?
- What has been the turnover rate of the potential distributor's sales force?

Sales and Service Competence

- How knowledgeable are the potential distributor's sales and service personnel in terms of their product lines and manufacturers?
- How often does the potential distributor use manufacturer-sponsored training programs?
- How successful are the potential distributor's sales and service personnel in prospecting, establishing new business, and retaining existing business?
- What type of compensation plan does the potential distributor use for their sales and service force?
    - Straight Commission
    - Salary + Commission
    - Salary + Sales Bonus
    - Salary + Profit Bonus
    - Other

Market Knowledge

- How well does the potential distributor and its sales and service force know the markets and individual accounts to whom you wish to sell and provide service?

Product Mix

- How does the potential distributor position its business to the marketplace, in terms of products and services?

- Does the potential distributor believe that its current product and service mix is sufficient to meet market needs?

- Is the potential distributor's present product and service mix complementary, supplementary, or competitive with your product line?

Sales Performance

- What information is the potential distributor willing to share with you regarding past sales and service performance, by product or service line?

Planned Growth

- How does the potential distributor perceive the potential for growth within your desired market?

Sales and Service Forecasts

- How often does the potential distributor prepare sales and service forecasts and for what purpose?

- What market or business indicators does the potential distributor depend upon, and do they use any formal forecasting method?

Inventory Handling Capabilities

- Is the potential distributor equipped to handle your product line without additional capital investment?

- What does the potential distributor consider as acceptable turnover and sufficient inventory?

- How does the potential distributor finance and control inventory?

Delivery and Transportation Capabilities

- What are the potential distributor's current capabilities to deliver product to customers, end-users, retailers, and so on? Is it sufficient to meet your company's requirements?

- What is the potential distributor's ability to expand delivery and service capacity for your company if necessary?

Total Facilities

- Does the potential distributor have sufficient facilities for storage, modification, and shipping for your product line?
- Does the potential distributor have computer facilities, fax and phone capacity, and the like to sufficiently handle the market requirements for your product?

Overall Management Ability

- How does the potential distributor view the planning and training functions of management?
- What are the potential distributor's practices regarding cash management, cash flow control, credit management, and the like?
- Are there well-established lines of communication between the potential distributor and its current manufacturers?
- To what degree does the potential distributor consider outside training and development of its employees by manufacturers important?

Succession

- Who are the potential distributor's other principals/owners, shareholders, and so on? (Be careful in asking these questions in some markets. In the CIS, for example, the real owners may very likely be members of organized crime and/or government officials.)
- What arrangements have been made to continue the potential distributorship in the event of retirement or death of the principals/owners/shareholders?
- Are the potential distributor's principals/owners/shareholders allowed to sell their shares/ownership to a third party?
- How will your distributor sales agreement change upon a change of ownership of the potential distributor's business or your business?
- Is the potential distributor willing to consider providing your company a first right of refusal to purchase its business in the event that it decides to sell the company?

The information collected here, coupled with the knowledge garnered during the first four steps, now provides the opportunity to make the right decision in distributor selection.

STEP 6: SELECT A DISTRIBUTOR FOR EACH TARGETED MARKET, MARKET SEGMENT, AND GEOGRAPHIC REGION

Rate all potential distributors against the profiles developed in Step 3 and immediately eliminate any that do not meet the "Minimal" profiles, using the Distributor Profile Evaluation Worksheet (see Table 5.1).

Once the survey is completed, begin the negotiation process with those firms that achieved at least a minimally acceptable score. From this point forward, it is appropriate to introduce the contract.

If none of the potential distributors meets the minimal standards, do not in any circumstances accept one of the candidates! As already stated, you are better off with no distributor rather than a bad one. In one nightmare scenario, a Western home appliance manufacturer knowingly selected a "less than minimal" distributor in a Middle Eastern country and gave it exclusive distribution for the entire market, primarily because of the unusually large purchase order the manufacturer received. Even though management readily admitted it was taking a big gamble with this poor selection, it was certain it could manage the situation, especially because of the amount of volume it was going to move to the new distributor.

However, six months after shipping the first order, things began to move quickly and uncontrollably out of control. First, the manufacturer learned that all of its products were being private-labeled by the distributor, completely in breach of the agreement they had just entered into. Second, these private-labeled products were beginning to find their way into the surrounding countries, upsetting the manufacturer's distributors who were already established there and conducting high-quality business. Obviously, this caused a great degree of angst between those distributors and the manufacturer and, not surprisingly, these same distributors placed significant pressure on the manufacturer to quickly correct the situation. Most disheartening, it was learned the prices of the private-labeled products were much less—sometimes by as much as 50%—in these other markets. It seems the "less than minimal" distributor was a former military officer who was able to move product duty free across national borders to his retired army friends throughout the Middle East. The damage done to the relationships between the manufacturer and its distributors in these markets needed a lot of time and effort to heal. The end result was a setback to the manufacturer of several years, loss of market share, millions of dollars of lost sales, and a lot of needless headaches.

The alternative to a "less than minimal" distributor is to look at other ways to introduce new product channels. This is often the best solution for companies that are introducing a new concept into the market or, as in this case, if there exists no capable distributor to handle the product. It is at this point that creativity needs to take over while a company determines what to do next. Many leading companies have created new channels by purchasing an existing business within the market, licensed their product, established a joint venture, or allied with their competitors.

Purchasing an already existing business can provide the highest level of product control as well the assurance that 100% of all profits will remain in the manufacturer's hands. Further, the invariable conflicts of interest inherent between manufacturer and distributor do not exist. On the other hand, such a leap can be overwhelming and quite costly. This is made even more formidable when the lack of local knowledge and contacts that come from a distributor are realized. Nevertheless, for companies committed to entering a new market, this is a viable option.

A West European candy manufacturer was unable to find a worthy distributor to handle its product line in Peru—one of the largest candy-consuming nations per capita in the world. In order to enter this market, which was viewed as vital to its global expansion, the West European firm purchased an already-existing candy business in Lima. Although the final cost was more than expected, the benefits that came as a result of entering this significant market far outweighed the financial investment.

Quite opposite to the large capital resources necessary to buy an existing business, licensing requires little, if any, capital outlays. Also, if the market is monopolized, licensing your product may be the only way to enter. The ease and quickness that characterize licensing are some of its strongest benefits. Finally, by working with a local licensee, the manufacturer immediately gains access to important local market knowledge.

The drawbacks to licensing concern themselves with the nature of the relationship between licenser and licensee. Because of the lack of control inherent in this relationship, it is quite possible for a licensee to establish a competing business. In addition, the returns for the manufacturer will normally be less, as the typical licensee works on a large percentage of sales and profits.

Establishing a joint venture is another entry strategy used by companies when no appropriate distributor is available or the market conditions mandate its necessity. Joint ventures usually afford greater returns than traditional distribution channels while still supplying the local market knowledge so critical in emerging market operations. As a result, the feedback from the market concerning the manufacturer's product or service is much more comprehensive. Also, because of the nature of a joint-venture relationship, the danger of expropriation is less than with the other channel alternatives like licensing. Nevertheless, a larger investment is typically required when undertaking a joint venture than for other options. Moreover, it is normally quite difficult to integrate a synergistic operation between two very different organizations.

Forming a joint venture with a local firm or the government has been the common route for many firms entering emerging markets in recent years. In China, where total foreign investment in the 1990s is believed to have exceeded US$1 trillion, nearly all Western companies entering this important market have established some kind of joint venture, most commonly with the government. In Brazil, high import tariffs usually move American and European companies to seek out a Brazilian firm to establish a joint venture in order to remain competitive. Bombardier, the world's leading manufacturer of personal watercraft, sells more units of its "Sea Doo" line in Brazil than any other market in the world. This is made possible by the joint venture Bombardier undertook with a local Brazilian company to assemble its units in the duty-free zone of Manaus, some 2,000 kilometers up the Amazon River.

Another possibility smart companies use to creating product channels where none exist is through alliancing with competitors. In emerging markets, it is oftentimes a good idea to work with the competition rather than against it. You and the competition are stronger as a team rather than independently, especially when lobbying efforts are needed to help secure concessions from national and/ or local governments. If your company's strategy is to become the dominant player in the market, it may serve you well to engage in such cooperative alliancing. Low cost and risk as well as the ability to exploit new opportunities describe the benefits of such alliancing. In the United States or Europe, a tactic like this might border on antitrust transgression. Further, alliancing with your competition may even help to broaden your offering in the market as it assists in developing and stimulating the need for new product offerings. On the other hand, there are legitimate concerns that come with sharing potentially vital information with your company's competitors, especially as the market in question evolves over time.

Whatever the situation, it is necessary to consider several factors when choosing a new channel if no appropriate distributor exists. The political and economic environment in the market can most certainly influence which strategy is to be used. Also, the fluid nature of emerging markets may cause your strategy to change. As emerging markets change from underdeveloped to partially developed nations, the requirements and demands within the marketplace may change. Finally, the recognition that different strategies might be needed within a market forces companies to look at regional differences, urban versus rural and the like. Again, with creativity as your guide, a hybrid or combination of these alternative channels might best serve your entry strategy when no appropriate distributor exists.

STEP 7: JOINTLY DEVELOP DISTRIBUTOR SALES FORECAST

Enlightened and resourceful manufacturers are able to develop a sales forecast in conjunction with their distributors. A U.S. flooring manufacturer achieves nearly all of its annual sales projections with its emerging market distributors because of the yearly review that takes place at its headquarters. At its own expense, the U.S. firm brings each distributor to its office to discuss the previous year and develop the sales forecast for the next year. The "mini-vacation" for the distributor serves as a way to confirm the existing relationship and instills in the distributor the necessity for planning and preparation for the upcoming year.

Confirm with the distributor which target markets are applicable to its geographic market. Then, jointly agree on sales forecasts for each target market area, including key accounts. Next, detail each of the distributor's roles and responsibilities. Lastly, finalize the forecast and preliminary sales plans together. The importance of getting everything in writing cannot be overstated. Meeting minutes or verbatim transcripts best accomplish this task.

Discuss your "Sales Forecast Analysis" with the distributor and gain its concurrence that your target market segment list is applicable to the market.

Conversationally, compare your annual sales per account with the distributor's estimates of annual sales per similar accounts within the primary market area.

Then, edit your list of account potential within the distributor's area jointly with the distributor and agree upon a target account list for each target market segment. During this process, you may want to develop your forecast based upon products or product lines, such that you would have a "Sales Forecast Analysis" by product. Further, don't get overly detailed or too analytical or try to force your company's estimates of sales potential upon the distributor. Remember, this is a jointly developed forecast, to which the distributor must be committed.

Next, multiply the distributor's estimate of annual sales per account by the agreed-upon number of accounts and establish an estimate of sales (revenue/volume) potential. This is not a forecast; it is an estimate of sales potential to specifically targeted accounts within given industries. Finally, agree with the distributor as to what share of the estimated potential it thinks is practical for the projected sales period (year, quarter, etc.). The finished product is your distributor's forecast.

The last evening of the visit, the U.S. flooring manufacturer goes over the final sales forecast immediately before a fantastic, catered dinner in the distributor's honor. The next day the distributor departs with a clear, concise understanding of the sales forecast.

STEP 8: NEGOTIATE DISTRIBUTOR'S INITIAL INVESTMENT IN PRODUCT INVENTORY

It is critical to mutually agree upon the level of inventory required to support the sales forecast. Once this amount is agreed upon, the negotiation of commercial issues like pricing, credit, and consignment should be initiated. Following the discussion of the commercial topics, it should be mutually determined how the distributor will maintain adequate stock levels and provide installation, as well as other operational servicing support. It is again important to be very specific and avoid the all-too-common "loading of trade," which overstocks your distributor to meet your company's overly ambitious sales forecasts. Trade loading at the initiation of the relationship is the quickest way to sour the relationship between your company and the distributor.

Together with your potential distributor discuss and decide upon the level of inventory required to support the sales forecast (see Tables 5.2 and 5.3). Make certain that what is decided is agreed between you. Prior to meeting with the distributor, do your homework. If, from the analysis of the distributor's business, you know that this distributor tries to maintain a minimum profit contribution of 25%, for example, then you are going to have to adjust inventory requirements to insure that this 25% profit contribution is realistic and attainable.

Negotiate credit and/or consignment terms with the distributor. This should be very clear so that there is no misunderstanding now or in the future as to

Table 5.2
Initial Investment in Inventory Worksheet—Method 1

Line 1.	Cost of Proposed Inventory	$_____
Line 2.	Other Initial Costs of Possession	$_____
	--	
Line 3.	Total Initial Investment	$_____
Line 4.	Estimated Annual Sales	$_____
Line 5.	Distributor's Variable Sales Costs	$_____
	Costs of Goods Sold	$_____
	Direct Selling Expense	$_____
	Commissions	$_____
	Materials	$_____
	Shipping & Handling	$_____
	Other _____	$_____
	Total Variable Costs	$_____
Line 6.	Profit Contribution (Line 4 - Line 5)	$_____
		_____%

Line 7.   Distributor's Allocated Fixed Expense

Warehousing	$_____
Insurance	$_____
Taxes	$_____
Administrative Costs	$_____
Depreciation	$_____
Other _____	$_____
_____	$_____
Total Allocated Expense	$_____

Line 8.	Pre-Tax Profit	$_____
Line 9.	Return-on-Investment (Line 8 divided by Line 3)	_____%
Line 10.	Margin of Safety (Line 8 divided by Line 6)	_____%

how payment will be handled. Credit terms are constantly lengthening in places such as China. The vast majority of distributors in China do not have the resources or banking ties to take title to goods before sales are made, and most will insist on a consignment arrangement. With credit so tight, foreign companies have few options other than to agree to payment terms that are out of line with general practice outside the country. You may have to explain this to your headquarters office. You may have no choice but to finance long-term credit terms extended to distributors.

Table 5.2 (*continued*)

Example:

Line 1. What is the product cost of the proposed inventory?

Assume $100,000

Line 2. What other ancillary costs must the distributor bear in order to take on your line?

(e.g., shelving, file space, handling equipment, etc.) Assume $10,000.

Line 3. What is the total initial investment required of the distributor?

Line 4. From your joint forecast, what is the estimated total annual revenue to the

distributor? Assume $50,000.

Line 5. What are the distributor's variable costs of sales, including the costs of goods

sold? (Assume costs of goods for $500,000 in sales to be $200,000 and sales

expense plus handling to be $50,000.)

Line 6. Line 4 - Line 5 = $250,000 for a profit contribution of 50%.

Line 7. The distributor allocates overhead at a ratio of 8% of sales; thus fixed costs are

$40,000.

Line 8. Line 6 - Line 7 = a pre-tax profit of $210,000. (42.0%)

Line 9. Estimated return-on-investment = Line 8 ($210,000) divided by Line 3

($100,000), or 2.10, which equates to a 110% return-on-investment.

Line 10. Margin of Safety = Line 8 as a percent, divided by Line 6 as a percent.

| Line 8 | = | 42.0% | | |
| Line 6 | | 50.0% | = | 119% |

Note: In this example, an initial inventory investment above $100,000 would be rejected by a knowledgeable distributor, unless they could see additional sales and profit resulting from other lines that could be sold in conjunction with this product inventory at no additional selling expense.

The very nature of international business mandates that much more time is needed to ship, import, receive, and distribute products than in a domestic setting. For many emerging market distributors, the time difference between the payment date for the goods and the receipt of the merchandise into the warehouse can be months. A German spare parts manufacturer lost most of its dis-

Table 5.3
Initial Investment in Inventory Worksheet—Method 2

Line 1. Distributor Sales Objective	$_____	
Line 2. Distributor ROI Objective	_____%	
Line 3. Distributor Discount	$_____	___%
Line 4. Distributor Estimated Costs	$_____	___%
Line 5. Estimated Pre-Tax Profit (Line 3 - Line 4)	$_____	___%
Line 6. Maximum Inventory Investment	$_____	

Example:

Line 1.	$ 400,000	
Line 2.	$ 140%	
Line 3.	$ 140,000	(35%)
Line 4.	$ 72,000	(18%)
Line 5. ($140,000 - $72,000)	$ 68,000	(17%)
Line 6. ($68,000/1.40)	$ 48,750	

tributors in Southeast Asia because it demanded its distributors pay in advance for purchase orders that would normally take 120 days to ship and another 45 days for transport and customs clearance. The distributors simply did not have the necessary capital to be able to finance such a delay and ended up becoming distributors for a competitor.

Note that in the example using Method #1, an initial inventory investment above $50,000 would be rejected by a knowledgeable distributor, unless it could see additional sales and profit resulting from other lines that could be sold in conjunction with this product inventory at no additional selling expense.

In the example using Method #2, the distributor would achieve sales and profit objectives by turning over inventory approximately eight times per year and approximately six times per year to break even. Most distributors will tell you their ROI Objective and Estimated Costs (as a percentage of sales). Once you and the distributor have agreed upon a Sales Objective, it is a simple matter to calculate the Maximum Inventory Investment.

STEP 9: DEVELOP A JOINT SALES AND SERVICE PLAN

At this point it is necessary to work with the distributor to agree on business goals for the coming year. Verbalize strategies and write them down in ranked order according to priority. Detail the tactics that will be employed to implement the sales strategies and negotiate specific clear responsibilities, checkpoints, and contingencies. This is also the time to develop any subdistribution sales estimates and plans. As previously noted, an ever-vigilant attention to specificity is critical here to avoid future surprises or conflicts.

Jointly with the distributor, the manufacturer agrees upon a business goal for the coming calendar year. The goal will probably be in terms of revenues or unit sales volume. Next, verbalize strategies. A strategy says what you want to consider doing, not how you are going to do it. Write down every strategy mentioned. Don't discuss them at this point. After you have completed your list of strategies, discuss each strategy and set priorities on each using the following criteria:

- Top Priority ("A"): Absolutely essential to attain the goal
- High Priority ("B"): Not important in and of itself, but may support a Top ("A") Priority
- Low Priority ("C"): Not important to goal strategy. Forget it.

Once this is accomplished, study and discuss your "A" (Top) priorities and rank them in order of importance, using 1, 2, 3, and so on. On a separate sheet of paper, write your "A1" priority strategy.

List the tactics you and others will physically perform in order to implement this "A1" strategy. Begin as you did before by listing all of the activities that come to mind. Don't discuss them; just list them as they are recited. The priorities should be set by discussing each tactic and using the A, B, C ranking as before. Your discussions should include the following:

- Negotiate responsibility for each tactic.
- Estimate a timeline or schedule for completion of each tactic.
- Negotiate checkpoints, dates, or events at which you will evaluate attainment of the plan.
- Negotiate contingencies. If an "A" priority tactic is not working, what alternative tactic can you bring to bear to insure implementation of the strategy? Study some of your "B" priorities. You may already have defined a contingency.

STEP 10: CONDUCT INITIAL PRODUCT AND SALES SERVICE TRAINING WITH THE DISTRIBUTOR'S STAFF

If the salesperson believes in your product, you are much more likely to achieve success in the market. Therefore, it is incumbent to properly train the distributor's staff in why they should dedicate their valuable time to selling your product.

At an initial training session, the following should be addressed: What are the products and their competitive positioning? What are the product features and attributes? Marketing, sales merchandising, and promotional material need to be reviewed. An explanation of applicable pricing, commercial terms, and the like should be detailed. Basic sales, installation, servicing procedures, and techniques should be discussed. Moreover, additional in-depth follow-up training should be scheduled.

Limit the initial training program to only one or two hours. Remember these salespeople probably had no voice in the agreement to sell your product line. Like most salespeople, they believe that they already have too many products to sell and their time is valuable. As a result, your first meeting with the distributor's sales force could be adversarial. Your job is to make these people feel comfortable with the new line by showing them how the product is sold and how easy it is to sell. Always keep your initial training program generic. Further, the content should address five points:

- What is the product/service line?
- What are the product/service attributes?
- Product/service differentiation.
- Competitive positioning.
- Marketing support material.

Make the opening of this initial program upbeat and motivational. It is designed to gain attention and promote questions.

A French distributor of home electronics holds its initial training session at the finest hotel in the capital city of its distributor's country. The salespeople are treated like royalty and provided with breakfast and lunch. The session is filled with promotional videos of the products, and each salesperson is provided a packet of sample products to be used at home. Such attention to the sales force has made this French company the leader in many of the emerging markets where it does business.

STEP 11: ESTABLISH A DISTRIBUTOR IDENTIFICATION PROGRAM

Through the first ten steps, you have selected and signed up your distributor. The next step is to let the market know of this newly established relationship. On your letterhead and signed by your CEO or Managing Director, write to each person on the distributor's mailing list and to all other potential accounts within the distributor's market advising them that you and the distributor have decided to do business together.

Provide the distributor with the necessary marketing promotional and point-of-sale material to identify the distributor's relationship with the manufacturer and its products and services.

Although the process discussed here may seem basic and unsophisticated, it is necessary to engage in the steps put forth so as to choose the right representative of your products and services.

6

Maximizing Your Assets, Minimizing Your Risk: Training, Communicating with, and Controlling Your Emerging Market Distributors

> The weakest of all things is a relationship that has not been tested under fire.
>
> Mark Twain

A morning meeting in Venezuela can be one of life's great adventures. All offices—government and private—tend to start the workday early, around 7:30 A.M. This is due primarily to the early hour that Venezuelans retreat to their homes for siesta. In the rest of the Spanish-speaking world, a siesta is intended to avoid the intense heat of midday and allow for a recuperative rest after a large lunch. In Venezuela, the siesta seems to have more to do with recovering from a morning drinking binge than anything else.

A typical meeting will commence with the traditional exchange of business cards. In Latin America, you are a nobody unless your name appears on a business card. Then you are offered something to drink. In most places in the world, it would be coffee or tea. In Venezuela, it is beer or whiskey. Not to accept is outside the realm of possibility. After the first round is completed, another is immediately served. Followed by another and another and another. This continues until lunch, where even larger quantities of alcohol are consumed. By siesta time, one is fully loaded and totally inebriated.

We have tried to understand why Venezuelans drink so much. It may have to do with the fact that oil-rich Venezuela should be prosperous, like Saudi Arabia or Bahrain. Instead, because of terrible mismanagement, it is closer to a banana republic than a wealthy Gulf state. You can see the utter frustration in the eyes of the people everywhere you go. They are ashamed and bitter. A recent public opinion poll showed that 84% of all Venezuelans wished they lived somewhere else. It is no wonder that beer or whiskey is preferred over coffee or tea.

Although it is probably impossible to monitor and control the drinking activity of your Venezuelan representative, certain activities must be done in order to ensure the proper representation and distribution of your company's brands and products with all of your company's emerging market distributors.

Before considering how to integrate distributors into your business, it is important to consider what a distributor expects from its relationship with you and vice versa. The relationship between a company and its distributors can be highly complex. Specific responsibilities must be understood between the manufacturer and the distributor as part of the process of training and communicating with the distributor.

DISTRIBUTOR RESPONSIBILITIES

Knowledge of the Market

Knowledge of the specific market is the predominant responsibility of the distributor. No matter how long a person works in international trade, he or she will never come to know the Venezuelan market as well as someone who has lived and worked there for decades; the same is true of Thailand, or Poland, or any other market. The first responsibility of a good distributor is to know the nature, the system, and the methods of the particular market.

In Nigeria, for example, whether a distributor truly understands the marketplace is determined by counting the number of cars it takes to a business meeting. Because of the near anarchy that permeates many aspects of Nigerian society, wise Nigerians will arrive in a convoy of at least two cars for a meeting—one to carry themselves and the other(s) for backup. There are numerous stories of a car breaking down and the passengers not only being robbed but left for dead on the roadside. In such a chaotic environment, the only way to ensure safety and security is by always having a second option available. Hence, the backup car(s).

Knowledge of Importing and/or Selling Manufacturer's Type of Product

A distributor must know all the mechanics of ordering, shipping, insuring, paying duties, obtaining import licenses, and performing other routine tasks of importing. While it may not need specific experience with the manufacturer's type of product, experience with allied products is indeed important. For example, an agricultural importer might have great difficulty successfully importing and selling consumer goods. On the other hand, in very small markets, one will find importers that are, indeed, "general traders," meaning they import and trade in a wide variety of goods such as foodstuffs, auto parts, and perfumes, as in many African countries. The ideal profile is a distributor that has some general knowledge about the manufacturer's particular product, may have complementary but not competitive lines, and does not have so many diverse lines that the manufacturer's products become lost in the crowd. Occasionally, one will find single-line distributors that exist to handle only one product, but these are usually joint ventures between a sourcing company and the importer.

Within the Commonwealth of Independent States (CIS), any importer worth its weight will have some kind of relationship developed with federal and local government officials and will possess key relationships in Odessa, Ukraine—a key port of entry for both duty-paid and non-duty-paid goods. Kallingrad, a very small Russian protectorate in the Baltics, also serves as a major transshipment point for shipment farther into the interior. A CIS importer's ability to manipulate the system in Kallingrad is often as important as its knowledge and contacts in Odessa.

No Involvement with Directly Competitive Products

The distributor should not be involved with directly competitive products. It is generally understood by most distributors that a built-in conflict of interest helps no one. But with many large companies diversifying, a conflict often arises. If you have a very good distributor, you may not want to terminate the relationship because of one or two minor product conflicts. Such cases must be negotiated on an individual basis, depending on the relationship between manufacturer and distributor.

If your company decides to enter with Simple Exportation, Reactive Distribution, or Low Active Distribution, it will probably be best to go with a company who has experience in distributing competitive products. Nevertheless, a distributor's direct experience with your competitors' products can be a double-edged sword. The distributor may believe it possesses the knowledge of how to successfully sell your type of product in its market; however, this past experience may also create a level of arrogance on its part with regard to effectively representing your product. The distributor may be unmanageable and possibly hostile when it comes to the specifics of your products and brands if you try to exert control. A test of wills can easily erupt. Your ability to monitor and control the distributor is likely to be less with companies who have already distributed a product like yours.

If you chose to pursue High Active Distribution, success is more likely to be achieved with a company that sells or has sold a complementary product but still has the business infrastructure, contacts, skills, and other necessary resources to properly sell and distribute.

Most important, whichever level your company decides upon, the distributor's knowledge should be a function of your company's Map of Tolerances and Expectations in emerging markets, not the other way around.

In Thailand, a mid-size European electronic components producer desired a high degree of control in this very strategically important market for it in the region. As a result, the individual finally chosen as the distributor was not experienced in selling the European firm's product line, but was exceptionally well connected to the then Prime Minister and the financial and banking sectors. He was the owner of a disparate number of businesses representing many Fortune 500 companies that were all successful and highly capitalized.

The European producer, in order to ensure a better-run operation than those of its competitors in the same market, installed the Managing Director and the Directors of Information Technology, Marketing, Sales, and Logistics to oversee the distributor's eighty-three employees and essentially took over the business, vis-à-vis a facilities management approach under the DMC Strategy. Over a two-year period of time, steady increases in market and double-digit growth made the distributor and, subsequently, the European producer the number-two player in the marketplace—second only to the global market leader, whose sales are still more than five times theirs on a global sales basis.

Ability to Thoroughly Cover the Assigned Territory

The distributor should have the organizational capability to service thoroughly the entire assigned territory. Some distributors are strong in metropolitan markets but weak in outlying districts. Some are proficient with one channel of distribution and inexperienced in others. The manufacturer has the right to expect its distributor to sell and service the entire geographic territory agreed upon and to sell to all potential customers through all appropriate channels of distribution. If this means adding sales personnel in order to carry a manufacturer's line, so be it. On occasion, a distributor in, say, Colombia will argue that he wants the territory surrounding Bogota but not the coastal region to the north. It is possible to create two distributorships within one market, but this often leads to jurisdictional disputes involving overlapping customers, pricing, or service policies. It is usually best to find one distributor who will be responsible for an entire market, which in some cases may mean an entire country.

If the manufacturer has not yet found a distributor it sufficiently trusts, it may prudently want to wait to assign the entire country until trust is confirmed or it finds another distributor. A small machine manufacturer in Florida was squeezed by its new distributor in Bogota for the exclusive representation for all of Colombia. When the United States–based company refused on the basis of a lack of trust, the Colombian company asked for a meeting at their offices. During the meeting, a narcotic was secretly slipped into the coffee of the international sales director. When he awoke two days later in his hotel room, several compromising pictures of him and others in various states of undress were conveniently placed on the nightstand next to his bed. Upon his return, the international sales director submitted his report, stating that a suitable distributor in Colombia was not found and that the country was "not a high priority market for us at this time." To this day, this company has not done any more business in Colombia.

Prompt Payment

Without question, the manufacturer expects and has the right to be paid promptly. Payment terms should be agreed upon before any appointment letter is signed, and the distributor should honor those terms. Any departure from this arrangement should have the manufacturer's prior approval.

Bluntly put, most distributors do not pay like Samuni the Zairian businessman, with immediate cash. Cash in advance, Letters of Credit confirmed by Western banks, or secured funds in off-shore accounts should always be the preferred methods for insuring prompt payments. In Latin America, far too many exporters have been lulled into a false sense of security when, after three or four shipments paid for by cash in advance, a distributor asks to pay half up front and half after shipment because of "difficult and changing economic situations in the country." In order to be accommodating and maintain the flow of product, the United States–based company obliges and never receives the other half.

Only in very special circumstances should manufacturers consider the unsecured credit option with their emerging market distributors. The key and mitigating factor would be the situation where the manufacturer is already actively monitoring and controlling the day-to-day operations of its distributor's business. In this case, the concern about payment is dramatically eased.

Access to the Sales Organization

Before signing any distributor agreement, the manufacturer should make certain to be thoroughly acquainted with how the distributor intends to generate sales of the product. Will the sales force be part time or full time? Will there be a sales manager? A marketing manager? A customer service manager? How will territories be assigned? While it is important to be flexible and to allow for local customs and methods, the manufacturer should be satisfied that the distributor has a selling organization suited for its product.

The "Minimal" and "Ideal" attributes of the original distributor survey should also guide the evaluation of the distributor's access to a sales organization. Moreover, do not "sell out" your "Minimal" attributes with the hope the distributor will one day develop an adequate sales force. A Swedish office products company was promised big volume by its new Turkish distributor, even though the existing sales force was woefully inadequate. Trusting the projections more than their common sense, the Swedish firm foolishly gave the exclusive distribution of their products and brands to the impotent distributor. To date, after more than four years, sales in Turkey have been a minuscule fraction of the original projections.

Administrative Support

A distributor should provide warehousing of the manufacturer's products, inventory management, order filling, delivery, credit, collection and all the other customary administrative back-up required for the manufacturer's products. Once again, the distributor's administrative staff may not replicate the one possessed by the manufacturer, but the manufacturer should be satisfied that the distributor can do the job. Bear in mind that a distributor usually spreads administrative costs over several or all of its imported lines. The manufacturer's product will be one of many that are stored, inventoried, delivered, and so on. But the manufacturer has the right to receive a fair share of administrative support and service.

Reasonable access to administrative staff should always be a minimum requirement for the manufacturer. Moreover, any changes in relevant personnel should be immediately reported to the manufacturer in order to maintain an uninterrupted flow of communication. For nearly six weeks, a Japanese exporter of home electronics was completely unaware that the person in charge of the logistics for its Mexican distributor had retired. As the shipment got closer to Manzanillo, the Japanese firm did what it thought was its duty and sent all the documentation addressed to the now-retired former logistics director. When a secretary mistakenly placed the original Bill of Lading in another file, the new logistics director was unable to locate the critical document. The Japanese were informed and immediately responded that the document had already been sent. What ensued was a two-week search in both Mexico and Asia and more than US$15,000 in port charges for storage of the "unclearable" container.

Adequate Inventories

The adequacy of inventory is usually a matter of repeated negotiation, because a distributor rarely wishes to carry every product and in the quantity desired by the manufacturer. While the manufacturer must respect the distributor's knowledge of what sells and what does not sell in its market, in turn the distributor must respect the manufacturer's desire to fulfill the needs and demands of the marketplace. The mutual goal is to avoid missing one sale, and the argument is that to achieve this the distributor must carry sufficient stocks of all available products.

An Italian outboard motor manufacturer and its Ugandan distributor lost a tremendous amount of potential business and experienced high opportunity-loss costs when they failed to adequately supply the necessary quantities of spare parts after they were awarded a World Bank tender. When the motors experienced the inevitable breakdowns, they were unserviceable because of the lack of replacement parts. Needless to say, nobody was happy.

Sales Records

The manufacturer has the right to periodically receive and examine the sales data for its own product, although this does not apply to other lines of goods carried by the distributor. Receiving regular data on sales of the manufacturer's product should be a requirement. The distributor must keep some record of outgoing sales, and the manufacturer merely wishes to see copies or extracts of those records. As the manufacturer studies this data and observes the flow of sales, it can suggest that the distributor should increase its minimum inventory of a given item or add new products. This is all part of the patient, friendly negotiation process when dealing with a distributor. Further, the manufacturer is better able to monitor and control the distributor's sales efforts around its products.

Through a review of its Russian distributor's sales records, a Norwegian oil-rigging manufacturer was able to identify an inherent weakness in the sales strategy of its main product line. It seems the distributor's sales force was completely unaware of the product's superior technological advantage over the competition. As a result, there was a re-training of the distributor's sales, service, and administrative staff, with a steady increase in sales based upon the new approach. Also, a number of key relationships were developed between the Norwegian firm's staff and the distributor, who proved to be invaluable in the development of the mutual relationship.

Forecasts of Inventory Purchases

Very few customers like to be pinned down to forecasting what they intend to buy in future months, but as the relationship with a distributor matures, the manufacturer should emphasize that such forecasting is the only way to assure an uninterrupted supply. One unpleasant way for a distributor to learn the role of forecasting is to be suddenly confronted with strong demand for the manufacturer's product when the manufacturer cannot rush shipments because the factory was producing according to old, conservative forecasts. The manufacturer should explain this possible circumstance to the distributor, assuring it that forecasts are not necessarily commitments to buy but are, instead, methods for production planning. One company's policy on forecasting was as follows: The distributor was required to provide a twelve-month rolling forward forecast that was used for production planning only; it was not a firm commitment to buy. Then, the distributor was required to submit firm orders at least three months before shipment with modifications permitted in those orders up until thirty days prior to shipment. When the thirty-day limit was reached, the order became a firm commitment and was shipped accordingly. This is just one way to manage sales and production forecasting with a distributor.

A Marketing Plan

It is perfectly reasonable to ask the distributor to prepare, with the manufacturer's help, an annual marketing plan. Here a forecast of purchases becomes integral. As many distributors in emerging countries may not be accustomed to sophisticated planning, be patient. However, the need for basic planning for advertising, promotions, seasonal campaigns, establishing new channels of sales, and introducing new products is understood almost everywhere. Once the plan is established, the next step is to assure six-month reviews and revisions—and even quarterly reviews, if possible. As more and more distributors are added, the manufacturer will find that these separate marketing plans become essential for the manufacturer's own forecasting and marketing planning within its own company. It is important to reach an understanding early in the relationship about producing periodic marketing plans.

A U.S. carpet manufacturer is able to avoid an interruption in the supply of product to its South American distributors by holding twice-a-year conventions in the city of one of its distributors. New products and designs are displayed and new pricing and sales strategies are discussed. During the conventions, each distributor is required to place its order for the next six months. Such a commitment compels the distributor to look six months forward, to both the next convention and its future sales.

Competitive Information

A basic ingredient of any marketing plan is intelligence about competitor's prices, models, methods of distribution, strengths, and weaknesses. It is reasonable for a manufacturer to ask for and receive periodic reports from its distributor on the activities of the manufacturer's competitors in its market. A good example would be copies of advertising by manufacturer's competitors in that market. These help the manufacturer understand the marketing position of the competition and may also signal new products or new strategies being introduced by the manufacturer's competitor.

A Northern California software company spent hundreds of thousands of dollars in conjunction with its Malaysian distributor on an introductory campaign for what it thought was cutting-edge technology that only it held. Immediately after the commencement of the campaign, a Taiwanese competitor introduced an upgraded version of the same technology. As a result, the United States–based company and its Malaysian distributor ended up throwing a great party to which nobody came.

Reports on Economic Conditions

The distributor may not supply reports on economic conditions regularly without gentle prodding from the manufacturer. Not only are they important to the conduct of the manufacturer's business, but asking for them demonstrates that the manufacturer is just as interested in the sales climate in the distributor's market as is the distributor. Incidentally, it is prudent to verify the distributor's economic forecasts with other sources, if possible.

The rapidly changing environments in emerging markets demand that particular attention be paid to each country's economic conditions. As described in Chapter 3, wild currency fluctuations, rampant inflation, and irrational actions on the part of governmental leaders can seemingly overnight transform the economic conditions of an emerging market. Western companies need to be ever-vigilant in their understanding of what is happening on the ground in the emerging markets where they are doing business. One of the best sources for Western companies is, of course, the local distributor.

When the Mexican peso devalued by nearly 100% in three days in early 1995, thousands of U.S. exporters were caught with their proverbial pants down. As the cost of money had almost doubled in seventy-two hours, existing purchase orders from their Mexican distributors were immediately cancelled. The end result was a backlog of product across the United States and dramatically increased inventory costs for many U.S. manufacturers.

Price Calculations

The manufacturer has the right to receive basic price calculations showing how its distributor marks up the product for resale in the distributor's market. These calculations should show shipping, insurance, duty and other landing charges, inland freight to the warehouse, the gross margin added to cover distributor's costs, local VAT taxes, and retail markup, if any. All of this will be converted into the distributor's currency, of course, and the exchange rate should be clearly indicated. A point of debate may arise over the breakdown of the distributor's gross margin. The distributor may not wish to reveal this percentage of net profit, but the manufacturer may certainly ask what portion of its margin is contributed to advertising and promotion. Some distributors may offer gross margin information freely; others contend that their costs for administration, sales, service, and other expenses, plus net profit, is privileged information. Gross margins, or markups by the distributor, will vary from product line to product line. The manufacturer will have to use its own good judgment on whether or not the distributor is applying unreasonably high or low margins. Within appropriate margins, the distributor charges costs for administration, sales, service, and profit. It may also contribute money to advertising and sales promotion from that margin. Because one leading determinant of pricing in each market will be competitive prices, it is essential that the manufacturer receive periodic updates on what its competition is doing: prices, payment terms to customers, new products, and new marketing strategies.

An Australian pharmaceutical manufacturer was caught off guard in 1998 when its long-time distributor in the Philippines was undercut by a competing brand imported from France. With the devaluation of the French franc against the U.S. dollar in 1998, the French manufacturer passed the savings along to all of its emerging market distributors. In the Philippines, the price advantage once enjoyed by the Australian-made product was completely wiped out and, at the end of the year, the Australian-made products cost 30% more than the competing French brand. After more than twenty years of successful operations in the Philippines, the Australian company was nearly finished there because it failed to anticipate what a change in its competitors' pricing would mean to its business.

Market Research

The distributor may provide empirical information about competitors and market share, but normally the cost of any formal market research is borne by the manufacturer. An alternative is to have the cost for market research shared between the manufacturer and the distributor. No matter who pays, make sure some research is done. It needn't always be expensive—just enough to get a feel for the market and what the end-user or consumer thinks about the product. Everyone wants to avoid big mistakes or surprises.

Through intensive market research, a Japanese motorcycle manufacturer and its Chilean distributor were able to detect a distinctive shift in customer preference from two-stroke to four-stroke motors in 1997. As a result, when the new models were introduced for 1998, the focus was almost exclusively on the benefits of four-stroke technology. The rise in market share for the Chilean representative rose more than 38% that year.

Advertising and Sales Promotion Support

The manufacturer should not assume that the distributor will contribute funds for advertising or sales promotion. As such support will depend on what margins the distributor has at its end, this is a matter for discussion and negotiation. In many cases, the manufacturer provides all advertising and promotion funding. In other cases, the landed cost of your merchandise plus prices among competitors allows the distributor to generate funds for these expenses. In high-duty markets, if the manufacturer includes an allowance for advertising on the invoice, the distributor will have to pay a duty on that allowance. In that circumstance, it is perhaps better to negotiate with the distributor to arrange to omit any unnecessary costs as the manufacturer's end so that duties are levied on the lowest possible invoiced price and to have the distributor provide the necessary advertising and promotion funds from its margin.

A leading U.S. auto manufacturer provides its emerging market distributors with a 3–5% advertising and promotion allowance, or "holdback," for each unit purchased. Similar to the system used with the U.S. dealer network, emerging market distributors can opt for the funds to be held in reserve for use in future shipments or sent to an off-shore bank account of the distributor.

Clear Understanding Regarding Termination

It is essential that the manufacturer and the distributor have a clear understanding concerning how and when termination of their agreement can occur.

Visits to Manufacturer's Home Factory and Offices

The manufacturer has the right to expect its distributor to pay occasional visits to its home headquarters. These visits are extremely useful in developing the feeling of partnership. One reasonable compromise is that the distributor pays travel expenses to the nearest major airport and the manufacturer then picks up all expenses for meals, accommodations, and overland travel.

A United States–based electronics company requires all of its distributors to attend two conferences a year held at its Los Angeles offices. In order to facilitate the travel, the manufacturer pays the airfare and hotel expenses, while the distributor absorbs the rest of the costs. Such regular visits ensure the distributor's understanding of new developments and products within the manufacturer's business.

Language Translations

Distributors should assure that manufacturer's printed materials—from advertising to instruction manuals—are properly translated into the vernacular. The distributor need not provide formal translations for lengthy technical texts, but it should review all materials to assure that they are acceptable for the local market. Keep in mind, too, that usage within one language is often different from country to country. What is common in Mexico may not be proper in, say, Argentina (both Spanish-speaking countries). These best rule is to have the distributor in each country review your proposed translation. Johnson Wax sent some Argentine-developed advertising material for its bug killer product, Raid, to Mexico and Puerto Rico. The Argentine advertising said, "Raid kills bugs dead," which, in Argentine Spanish was *Raid mata bicho*. But, as it happened, in Mexico and Puerto Rice the word *bicho* is a slang term, and there the message meant, "Raid kills the male organ."

MANUFACTURER RESPONSIBILITIES

The responsibilities of the manufacturer are equally important to the development of the business relationship. They include the following items.

Exclusivity

Exclusivity ranks first, understandably. The distributor wants control over the agreed-upon geographic territory. They want no interference from the outside, although this may be impossible to guarantee, and the manufacturer should discuss this problem in advance. For example, the manufacturer may agree to ship directly to others in the distributor's market but only with its prior approval. Indeed, the distributor may even generate orders for the manufacturer to ship directly to such a customer. That process is called "indent" orders, a British term. It means that the manufacturer's appointed distributor may develop an order and send it to the manufacturer for direct shipment to a third party within its assigned territory. In these cases, it is important that the distributor understand that it has "del credere" responsibility, meaning that it bears the final responsibility for payment. One frequent problem with exclusivity is that you cannot guarantee absolute protection. The distributor will want assurances that the manufacturer will exercise every legal method to provide it with exclusivity in its territory. When the manufacturer grants exclusivity to a distributor, the manufacturer is saying, "I will do my utmost not to knowingly sell to any other party in your territory without your permission, but I cannot absolutely guarantee that my goods will not find their way into your market. If and when that happens, I agree to work with you to resolve and remove that problem within the limits of the law."

Patent and Trademark Protection

The distributor may want assurances that the manufacturer's product and brand names will not be legally imitated and that the manufacturer will take appropriate legal action if such counterfeits are brought into its territory. This means that the manufacturer must register its trademarks and patents in advance in that market. The distributor might be able to assist the manufacturer with evidence and other information, but generally a distributor assumes that the final responsibility rests with the manufacturer.

Manufacturers need to be aware that the potential always exists for their products to be counterfeited, especially as their usage becomes more widespread. In order to insure its distributors that it is "on the case," a Japanese manufacturer of consumer electronics has established a department that is responsible solely for the worldwide investigation of counterfeiting claims surrounding its products.

Quality

The distributor will want trouble-free merchandise and will also want the protection of a liberal warrantee agreement. Bear in mind that replacement of defective products is especially costly in international trade because of the distances and tariffs involved. A distributor imports a product, paying shipping and duty costs, and if that product is found to be defective, it is inconvenienced for more than just time. Even if the manufacturer replaces the product at no cost, the distributor must once again pay shipping and duty expenses. A U.S. producer of machine tools failed miserably when over 5,000 units of a particular product were found to be defective. In its ignorance, the U.S. firm offered a credit to its distributors against their next purchase. Needless to say, the tremendous cost involved for the distributor was incredibly more than a mere credit towards future business. No reorders ever followed from any of the twelve emerging market distributors.

Commissions

Depending on the agreement, the distributor may expect to receive a commission on each purchase, or each sale, of the manufacturer's product. The same would apply to rebates, bonuses, or awards if they are negotiated as part of a sales forecast system. Many manufacturers offer commissions as an incentive to increase sales and entice distributors with the opportunity to receive some valuable money in an off-shore account.

Shipping and Delivery Services

A distributor expects the manufacturer to provide efficient export shipping and local delivery services. This means proper packing, labeling, and documentation. The distributor may ask the manufacturer to help arrange for insurance and actual shipment, subject to its approval, and later reimburse the manufacturer for those costs.

Smart manufacturers give choices to their distributors as to which forwarders and shipping lines to use. In many emerging markets, a given worldwide ocean carrier or forwarder is only as good as the local agency that represents it. The availability of choice allows the distributor to choose which local office to work with, based on its needs.

Favorable Prices

The distributor expects that the manufacturer will provide it with the lowest possible prices for three compelling reasons: (1) because it is absorbing some of the manufacturer's normal selling costs, (2) because both want the end price to be as low as possible compared to competition in that market, and (3) because the process of price escalation occurs, meaning the manufacturer's end selling price escalates as it moves through several distribution levels. The distributor will also want to receive advance notification of any price increases. In any market, this is always problematic. A manufacturer is wise to regularly print on its price lists the words "prices subject to change without notice." However, because a distributor is a quasi-partner, a manufacturer might give some short prior notice of a change and accompany it with a degree of leniency such as honoring all orders already "in the house" at old prices or allowing one average-size order before applying the new prices.

Payment Terms

Suffice it to say that the distributor expects leniency as his credit rating is established and proven to be reliable. One way to solve this issue is for the manufacturer to offer payment terms at the regular price by Letter of Credit at 30, 60, 90, 120, or 180 days from Bill of Lading date. In this manner, the distributor is able to finance the amount of the Letter of Credit using interest rates in the Western country, which are almost always dramatically less than in emerging markets.

Advertising, Sales Promotion, and Packaging

Whether or not the manufacturer provides dollars for the purchase of advertising is a negotiable point. However, the distributor has a proper expectation that the manufacturer will provide products in packages suitable to its market. That means packaging in the proper language with colors, symbols, and designs that are suitable and inoffensive in that market. Certain packaging or labeling laws must be heeded, such as bilingual requirements. Other sales promotion materials, such as display cases, banners, streamers, window cards, illuminated signs, customer leaflets, and sales catalogues, are also customary in international trade and a reasonable expectation of any distributor.

New and Modified Products

The distributor will assume the manufacturer wants to fill needs in its market, which may mean modifying the product or introducing new products to suit that market. The manufacturer's actions may be as simple as providing a new color or may introduce a total innovation when compared to competitive offerings. The distributor expects the manufacturer to stay at least head-to-head with its competitors in that marketplace and, if possible, well ahead of them.

Training Materials

Training materials are very important, especially at the beginning of a distributor-manufacturer relationship. The manufacturer may supply leaflets, manuals, slide presentations, videotapes, or even on-site trainers. The distributor has every right to assume that the manufacturer will provide instruction in the marketing and sales features of the product. The same applies to customer service and delivery. In addition, the manufacturer may offer full counseling on how to operate key functions in the distribution.

Updates

While updating is often neglected, it is reasonable for a distributor to hope that the manufacturer will provide periodic new information, perhaps in the form of a newsletter about its company, its products, its people, and its industry.

Periodic Visits

Every distributor wants and expects the manufacturer to visit its market. As a general rule, the higher the visitor is on the executive ladder, the better. There is no better way to truly understand a specific market than to visit it, not just overnight, but for several days. Spend time with the distributor, visit the administrators and the sales force, and, most important, visit the end customers. The manufacturer's managerial prowess will be directly related to the time spent with its distributor learning about problems and opportunities in that market. If necessary, the distributor also has the right to expect the manufacturer's technicians—quality control experts, shipping managers, market researchers—to visit its market as well.

Frequent Communication

The distributor expects efficient, clear communications with the manufacturer and its subordinates. This can be in the form of personal visits, phone, fax, or electronic mail. The most important single action is quick follow-up on everything you have discussed and promised. In international distribution management, the worst affronts are inaction and silence.

TRAINING

Once the respective responsibilities are understood, it is incumbent for the manufacturer to embark upon a thorough training of the distributor's staff. One of the better ways of ensuring that distributors perform effectively is to train them. Distributors often lack the skills, knowledge of your product line, and marketing "know-how" to conduct their own training and will feel highly indebted if good programs are made available. It is critical for manufacturers to properly train key employees, not just sales people. In your company, non-sales personnel are constantly being trained to provide necessary support to the various aspects of your organization. The same needs to take place with your distributors.

The training of key employees in your distributor's organization must, however, be tempered with the particular needs of the business. It is important to make people more valuable, but not too valuable. Employees who know more than they need to know can often become ex-employees or even competitors of your distributor's company.

A U.S. manufacturer mistakenly believed it was important to teach all of its Polish distributor's staff English to make the relationship between the two smoother and easier. Unfortunately, after a year, employee turnover was almost 100%, and many of the former workers were now holding jobs in competing companies. After what it had believed was an intelligent dedication of resources, the U.S. firm learned too late it was actually a really bad idea.

Common issues to consider when planning training with your emerging market distributors include:

• Training requirements must be carefully determined prior to reaching an agreement with the distributor.
• The distributor and the manufacturer must budget adequate resources—both time and money—for formal training programs.
• Training must be offered on an ongoing basis.
• Training must be customized to the target country environmental needs.
• Particular attention must be paid to sometimes very basic training, like language and reading skills.

Among the major the benefits of training are:

• Improved distributor relations with the customers.
• Improved manufacturer relations with the distributor.
• Reduced distributor turnover.
• Reduced costs of inefficient territorial coverage, credit, and other losses.
• Reduced need for time invested if distributors are well trained, since they can be left on their own, rather than monitored and supervised.

Effective training programs are oriented to the specific needs of distributors. There is no point in training distributors in fields where their performance is already adequate. Good training starts with concrete objectives developed jointly between manufacturer and distributor. An attempt should be made to determine just what the training needs are and how they can best be met.

Often, distributors must be convinced of the benefits of the program so that they will participate enthusiastically. One of the better ways is for the manufacturer and the distributor to work together in locating weaknesses in distributor personnel and deciding how to develop the personnel (see Table 6.1). Numerous facets of the program must be planned, including:

• Program content.
• Who should be trained?
• The methods to be used.
• Who will do the training?
• The location of the training site.

Table 6.1
Content Areas for Distributor Training Programs

1.   **Manufacturer's Products**

    a.   **Methods of Production & Installation**

    b.   **Product & Service Features**

    c.   **Pricing & Commercial Terms**

2.   **Manufacturer's Marketing Strategy**

    a.   **Targeted Customers for Each Product**

    b.   **How the Marketing Mix is Used to Serve Customers**

3.   **Manufacturer's Resources**

    a.   **Financial**

    b.   **Personnel**

    c.   **Equipment**

4.   **General Business Operations**

    a.   **Computer and Administration Skills**

    b.   **Financial and Cost Accounting Skills**

5.   **Manufacturer's Policies**

    a.   **Pricing**

    b.   **Returns & Service**

    c.   **Delivery**

    e.   **Other Channels of Distribution**

6.   **Major Competitors**

    a.   **Products**

    b.   **Marketing & Promotion Strategy**

    c.   **Distribution Activities**

    d.   **Pricing Policies**

7.   **Self-Improvement**

    a.   **Sales, Service, Installation & Repair Skills**

    b.   **Territory Management**

    c.   **Time Management**

8.   **Other**

Table 6.2
Typical Communication Problems Between Manufacturer and Distributor

- **Physical Separations**

- **Difference in Size and Types of Organisations**

- **Difference in Approaches and Attitudes**

- **Difference in Operating Procedures**

- **Difference in Time Zones**

- **Difference in Native Languages**

- **Basic Human Differences**

- **Inherent Mistrust/Distrust in Business Relationships**

COMMUNICATION BETWEEN MANUFACTURER AND DISTRIBUTOR

The manufacturer needs to develop a communication plan that enhances the quality and quantity of interaction between manufacturer and distributor. Such a plan works to minimize communications problems as well as to avoid future and potentially threatening issues. Some types of communications problems that will inevitably arise without an effective communications plan are shown in Table 6.2.

Two types of communications are needed with distributors. One information flow is required to satisfy operational requirements. This kind of information is called information system data, and it is needed to coordinate internal operations in the channel. Information is required on such matters as buyer needs, product quality, payments, orders (purchases), price levels, delivery, inventory, and credit terms. This kind of input is necessary to keep the channel operating. Day-to-day communication is required to make business operations possible and to ensure that they are carried out as intended.

The second need is for persuasive information, which is used to influence distributor behavior. Advertising, personal selling, and sales promotion are required to persuade, inform, and remind distributors about behaviors that the manufacturer wants to encourage. The manufacturer may also direct persuasive information to distributors in competing channels in an attempt to bring about changes in their purchases.

Nevertheless, for manufacturers to assume that their communication in emerging markets is kept confidential can be a grave mistake. On more than one occasion, Westerners have reported that in Kazakstan, Hungary, and China, their drivers assigned to them were purported to speak little or no English whatsoever. As a result, these unsuspecting businesspeople felt free to talk to their colleagues in the back seat of the car, or, if in the case they were alone, on their mobile phone. The "non-English speaking" driver was in fact listening to every word of every conversation. And, upon his arrival back to the boss's office, the driver gave a detailed analysis of what was said. While this was going on, the unassuming Westerner was waiting outside in the lobby for a meeting with the same boss.

Caslione has on more than occasion been offered the opportunity to purchase faxes from or to his client's competitor from an enterprising hotel clerk.

In the homes of ex-pats in Korea, Brazil, and South Africa, seemingly innocent, hardworking housekeepers have worked as spies, planted there by their own distributors looking to gain valuable information on sensitive business dealings.

In Thailand and India, the homes of many ex-pats as well as their offices, cars, and mobile phones have been consistently bugged by their "business partners."

If there is anything particularly sensitive, it is always better to err on the side of caution and go for a walk. All companies should put forth guidelines for all managers who manage their confidential communications (see Table 6.3).

MONITORING AND CONTROLLING DISTRIBUTOR'S OPERATIONS

Control is monitoring distributors to detect significant differences between actual and desired performance, so as to make appropriate adjustments. Manufacturers begin the control process by converting objectives into performance standards. They are then able to compare actual performance to the standards and note any discrepancies between the two. If the discrepancies are large and further information is not crucial, management initiates action.

Once the standards are formulated, control requires comparing them with actual performance. Take the hypothetical case of a small sporting goods manufacturer using five distributors within one market. The standard for each distributor is a sales forecast, based on past sales in the distributors' territories. The manufacturer needs a feedback mechanism that measures performance. The manufacturer could rely on invoices, shipment records, or order forms to provide sales records by distributor.

The judgment on the significance of discrepancies is largely a policy decision. Sometimes the discrepancies are easily explained and action is unnecessary. It may be that income levels in the territories covered by B, C, and D have recently plunged and sales deterioration is inevitable. Conversely, the sales shortfalls may

Table 6.3
Confidential and Protected Communications

Distributors May Not Always Be Trusted

Protect Your In-Market Communications

- **Offices (Telephones, Faxes, Post/Mail, Etc.)**

- **Hotels (Telephones, Faxes, Post/Mail, Etc.)**

- **Restaurants (Especially In Hotels, Other Popular "Western-Style" Restaurants, Etc.)**

- **Airports, Taxis, Agent/Distributor Vehicles**

Pre-empt Distributor's Activities

- **Secure In-Market Communications**

- **Retain In-Market "Trusted" Sources (Offices, Hotels, Etc.)**

be a result of distributor inadequacies, requiring immediate action. When a manufacturer notes large differences between standards and actual performance, the best response is to seek information that reveals *why* the difference occurred. If the reasons are beyond the control of the manufacturer or distributors and are not expected to recur, action may be unnecessary.

What Should Be Controlled?

Each manufacturer must decide exactly what will be controlled. The five key areas that should be controlled are business operations, prices, promotion, territories, and merchandise handled:

Business Operations. Each manufacturer has particular business operations standards. Some are concerned with the credit policies that distributors offer to customers. Some manufacturers monitor the terms of sale and credit outstanding of each distributor on a monthly basis, which tells manufacturer's executives how well the distributor is serving retailers' credit needs. Other manufacturers concentrate on the adequacies of distributor inventories. Alternatively, the focus may be on the effectiveness of distributor transportation functions.

Prices. The manufacturer may wish to exert control over distributor pricing policies. The manufacturer could be concerned with distributor margins, discounts, allowances, and freight charges. Such control is subject to various laws in each country, however, which may not permit the degree of control desired.

Sales and Product Promotion. One of the more sought-after targets of control is sales and product promotion. Manufacturers expect certain achievements by the distributor's sales force. These include calling on a sufficient number of customers, contacting the right targets, conducting demonstrations, providing customer assistance, and closing sales. Advertising and sales promotion standards are also imposed on wholesalers, who may be expected to spend specified amounts on these functions and to coordinate them with the manufacturer's efforts. Also, control helps ensure that distributors have actually spent the amount of money on cooperative advertising, redeemed coupons, and placed displays that they claim they have.

Territories. Territories may be the object of controls. Some manufacturers restrict the geographical area in which the distributor can sell. In such cases, the distributor is forbidden to sell to any customer who does not have a place of business in the territory. This encourages each distributor to develop its own territory and not to raid those of others. The manufacturer may specify that distributors cannot sell to other intermediaries. This encourages distributors to support the product with ample sales and service effort, rather than pawning off the product to intermediaries in the hope that they will do most of the promotion and merchandising work.

Product Mix. Often manufacturers impose standards on the distributor's product mix. Some want distributors to carry only high-quality products or to offer a full line. Others require distributors to carry products that are complementary to those of the manufacturer. Some manufacturers monitor distributors' product mixes to ensure that these complement but do not overlap its product mix. Some manufacturers have exclusive dealing or tying contracts that block distributors from handling items that compete with those of the manufacturer. Under some conditions, these violate the law in some countries and should be avoided.

Activities to Monitor and Control

There are a number of specific activities that manufacturers can bring into play in controlling distributor performance.

Functional Reports. Manufacturers usually require that distributors periodically summarize their actions and their outcomes in routinely prepared formal reports. This permits comparison of performance levels with standards. Sales reports may be required of distributors, including call reports, which list all prospects contacted during a period of time.

Customer Reports. These detail specific actions by distributors in working with customers. These are common in the soft-drink industry and other fast-moving consumer goods. Other reports may be required for functions such as advertising, inventory management, delivery, processed warranty claims, and price changes. These functional reports point out changes in the achievements of distributors over time.

Financial Ratios. Financial ratios can furnish useful insights into current and emerging problem areas. Innumerable ratios can be calculated, depending on the particular needs of the manufacturer. Inventory turnover can be calculated monthly, quarterly, or annually. Most manufacturers are interested in the turnover of their products rather than the distributor's total product mix. This ratio provides an index of the selling effectiveness and efficient inventory management of the distributor. The ratio of total sales of the manufacturer's products to total expenses incurred in selling the manufacturer's product can be meaningful. If this ratio is too low, the sales force may not be effective in promoting the manufacturer's products or the sales team may be operating inefficiently. On the other hand, if the ratio is too high, the sales force may not be devoting sufficient resources to selling the products.

Sales Analysis. Sales analysis consists of breaking down past distributor sales according to relevant categories. The categories may be geographical areas, product lines, market share, type of customers, or some other dimension. Recent sales can be compared to earlier figures, measuring distributor progress over time. Some firms break down their expenses according to these categories, allowing them to estimate distributor profitability by category from one period to another.

Establishing Standards of Performance for Measuring Distributor Performance

There are a number of criteria or standards of performance that manufacturers can bring into play as a means of assessing distributor performance. The most commonly employed standards of performance are the following.

Distributor Sales Performance. The most widely used standard for assessing distributors is sales performance. This should not be surprising. If distributors are producing adequate levels of sales for the manufacturer, they are likely to be viewed as productive units. For instance, many manufacturers receive reports on each distributor's sales and compare these to past years' data. If possible, the distributor's sale of the manufacturer's products should be studied. This provides a current, up-to-date measure of the movement of product through the channel. Many distributors, particularly larger ones, keep detailed records by each manufacturer they represent and process the sales data in computer systems. Some distributors, however, will not be able or willing to furnish this information. If this is the case, the manufacturer can use measures of its sales to each distributor. Numerous manufacturers keep detailed records of these sales in computerized information systems. It is often meaningful to compare current distributor sales with past distributor sales, to isolate trends and detect shortfalls in distributor effectiveness. Many manufacturers make such analyses for each distributor that stocks the company's products. These comparisons are most meaningful if they are broken down by products or product groups in the manufacturer's product line. Another helpful measure is to establish forecasts for each distributor and compare the distributors' sales to the forecasts. The sales forecasts can be based on the sales potential of each distributor's territory, with adjustments based on the level of competition and difficulty of servicing the territory or on past sales. Rather than imposing forecasts on distributors, the forecasts should be submitted for distributor approval, to promote cooperative efforts. A frequent practice is to have forecasts for individual products or product lines, making detailed comparisons possible. The sales as a percentage of forecast for each distributor can be compared to the same ratio for other distributors, yielding a relative gauge of achievement.

Distributor Inventory Management. A second widely used evaluation standard is inventory management and calculation of distributor's gross margin return on investment (GMROI). Here the manufacturer investigates the extent to which each distributor is carrying an adequate inventory of the manufacturer's products. Pharmaceutical manufacturers, for example, are common users of this criterion, since they are highly concerned with the wholesaler's ability to fill retail customer orders rapidly and completely. It is in the manufacturer's best interest that the distributor adhere to the inventory requirements on which the manufacturer and the distributor originally agreed. Sometimes, inventory levels are not specified in an agreement between the parties. Nevertheless, maintenance of adequate levels is a significant criterion. The manufacturer, however, is less able to require the carrying of specified inventory level than if a contract contains inventory requirements. This means that if the manufacturer believes that inventory maintenance is an important criterion, an agreement on inventory should be made when the parties first decide to do business together.

Distributor Selling Capabilities. Another useful standard is distributor selling capabilities, the ability of the distributor to handle the manufacturer's products effectively. This is a measure of the potential of a distributor to deliver sales. Sales capability depends on the number of salespersons the distributor assigns to the manufacturer's offerings, the competence of individual salespeople, and the enthusiasm of the sales force for the manufacturer's offerings. The number of sales representatives the distributor assigns to the manufacturer's offerings dictates the market exposure that will be achieved. Of equal importance is the amount of time that each sales representative will devote to the line. Large distributors are in a position to furnish superior exposure, provided they are willing to allocate a sufficient number of sales representatives to the manufacturer's offerings. If the distributor's product line is already large, the distributor may not be willing to assist the manufacturer in a satisfactory manner according to this standard. The competence of the distributor's sales force is judged on a scale from very good to very bad. If the sales force has been carefully selected, adequately trained, and highly motivated, good ratings are likely.

Distributor Attitudes. Distributor attitudes toward the manufacturer and its offerings are critical determinants of their ability to represent the manufacturer effectively. Distributors may be selling large volumes of the manufacturer's product but, if their attitudes are negative, a reservoir of resentment is present, which means they may not continue this pattern in the future. It is a mistake to measure attitudes only after sales have plunged. Rather, periodic assessments are needed. Some firms use formal surveys designed to elicit distributors' feelings toward the manufacturer and its offerings and services. These surveys, of course, should not be taken so often as to annoy and alienate distributors.

Competition Facing Distributors. Any comprehensive evaluation of distributors should include an appraisal of the competition they face. This involves examining their performance relative to that of other distributors. The manufacturer's distributors can be compared with other distributors on standards discussed earlier in this section, such as sales performance. If their sales of the manufacturer's lines are substantial relative to sales of competing products by other distributors, good evaluations are likely. Some distributors have developed a reputation of superiority over competitors that is widely known throughout their respective industries. To ensure that their efforts are up to standard, these superior companies ask their customers and suppliers to evaluate them on periodic report cards, rating them from poor to excellent on back orders, invoice errors, and other standards. This provides management with an ongoing assessment of current performance.

Analyses of competition can be utilized in judging particular distributors. One of them may have disappointing sales records, but this may be due to an extraordinary amount of competition in the sales territory. Such an extenuating condition may prompt the manufacturer to assist the distributor, as through increases in margins, training, and missionary sales calls on the distributor's customers.

General Growth Potential of Distributors. The last standard refers to distributor adeptness in accomplishing desired objectives in the future. Some distributors can be expected to contribute multiplying revenues to the manufacturer, whereas others will not. Growth potential is measured by past sales trends, market penetration, performance against competitors, financial health, the capability of management and other personnel, and the speed of reaction changes in the market place. Growth potential is measured subjectively, based on managerial judgment. It is a significant standard if the manufacturer plans future expansion. Manufacturers that have a track record of being strongly motivated to become larger continually are especially interested in distributor growth potential.

Developing Standards of Performance

An important preliminary control step is to establish performance standards. Standards of performance originate in the manufacturer's distribution objectives. If an important objective is to supply fast delivery to retailers, a reasonable standard might be: "Distributors will deliver to customers within three days of the receipt of an order." On the other hand, if the objective is to cover the market extensively, the standard could be: "Distributors will contact at least three-fourths of the customers in their territories once every two weeks." Whatever the objectives, the standards should be measures of progress toward those objectives. It should be recognized that objectives will vary from one company to another.

Standards are determined through answers to the question, "How can we tell if we are making progress toward objectives?" The standards that best provide answers should have priority. Standards should exist for every objective critical to the economic health of the manufacturer.

The Performance Audit

Performance audits consist of comprehensive assessments of distributor performance. Normally, these are conducted from once per quarter to once per year, depending on the stage of the distributor's development. However, they can be undertaken whenever the manufacturer recognizes the need. If there is a reason to believe that a distributor is not pulling its weight in the channel system, for example, a special audit may be conducted.

Manufacturers should take steps to avoid alienating distributors in the auditing process. This is best accomplished by stressing the fact that the audit is conducted to uncover problems and to find solutions to these problems. The manufacturer should avoid the role of a police officer who is attempting to locate transgressions and impose punishment. There are three steps involved in the audit:

1. Developing criteria for measuring performance
2. Evaluating performance against criteria
3. Taking actions to improve performance

Evaluating Performance Against Standards of Performance

In evaluating performance against standards of performance, the manufacturer can follow either of two basic approaches. One is to assess distributor performance on individual standards. If more than one standard is used, however, management does not attempt to combine these assessments. A distributor might be judged as very good on sales performance, fair on inventory maintenance, and poor on selling capabilities, for example. These ratings could be compared with those for other distributors, in an attempt to evaluate the overall worth of each. This method can be carried out rapidly and with minimal effort. It is frequently employed when the number of distributors in considerable, making a more detailed evaluation impractical. Another condition that favors this method is when the number of standards used is small, perhaps consisting of only one or two factors. With many standards, the method becomes unwieldy because it is hard to compare one distributor to another.

A disadvantage of the technique is that it does not supply an index of overall achievement. A distributor may score high on one standard, such as sales performance, and low on another, such as attitude.

An overall method of evaluating distributors considers several standards and provides weights for each, expressing management's opinions about the importance of each standard. This technique necessitates deciding what standards to use and how each standard will be measured. Then weights are assigned to each standard. Every distributor is rated on each standards, and the rating is multiplied by the weight for the appropriate standard. Finally, the resulting figures are added to provide an overall evaluation.

The manufacturer may rate the distributor on each of the three sales performance indexes on a scale from 1 to 10. Gross sales were judged to be high with a score of 7, sales/forecast at an intermediate level with a score of 5, and share of market highest with a score of 8. These ratings are multiplied by the weights to yield an overall weighted rating. The same process is used for distributor inventory maintenance. Finally, all the weighted ratings are added to give a total score, representing management's composite rating of this distributor. The identical process is pursued for other distributors in the channel.

An advantage of this method is that it supplies an overall evaluation of each distributor by combining the standards in a way that recognizes management's judgment of the importance of each. The method is flexible, in that the standards and the weights employed can be changed if management finds, through experience, that alterations are needed.

Taking Actions to Improve Performance

In some cases, the evaluation program will uncover distributor performance that is unsatisfactory. Rather than jumping to conclusions and terminating the low-rated distributors, most manufacturers endeavor to discover why the performance was not better. The reasons can range from poor distributor management to inadequate assistance by the manufacturer. Basically, the manufacturer should take an active role in uncovering distributor problems. Then management can decide what remedial steps, such as providing low-achievement distributors with training, are needed to bring operations up to a satisfactory level. To accomplish this, it may be necessary to exercise some of the sources of power. If the distributor's performance cannot be elevated to an acceptable level through other means, it may be necessary to drop it from the channel.

If the departures between standards and actual performance are large and if distributors appear to be responsible for the inadequate performance, action may be necessary. The manufacturer first decides what changes distributors should make. The manufacturer may determine that distributors should call more often on important customers, add products, do more advertising, or initiate some other action. The best procedure is to make this determination in consultation with the distributors affected, rather than unilaterally. It is one matter to decide what action is needed, but it is another to get it carried out. Sometimes, a simple request that the distributor make a change will suffice. If this does not work, the manufacturer may apply reward, coercive, attraction, legitimate, or expert power to produce the needed results, as by training distributor sales representatives. If all else fails, of course, the manufacturer has the option of dropping the distributor from the channel.

7

Bound Relationships: The Distributor Agreement

Too often, in business like love, you pay as you leave.

Anonymous

Tierra del Fuego is the end of the world. It is where you will find Carmen San Diego and Ushuaia, the world's southernmost city. Looking out over the Beagle Canal toward Antarctica leaves you with an empty feeling. To venture south of here is to leave all of humanity behind. It gives clarity to the common Argentine threat of "kicking you off the end of the world."

The land of Evita and the tango conjures up seductively romantic images. However, ask an Argentine about Evita Peron and more often than not "whore" and/or "thief" will be shouted back at you. Finding a woman who can dance the tango is harder than dining at a vegetarian restaurant in beef-exclusive Buenos Aires.

By the 1930s, Argentina had built the seventh-largest economy in the world. Fifty years later, 5,000% annual inflation, dirty wars, and bad politics had left Argentina in ruins.

The Argentina of today is a great paradox. The superb cuisine and world-famous wine make it a desirable place to visit. However, the social atmosphere can drive the visitor nuts. There are more psychiatrists and plastic surgeons per capita in Argentina than any other country in the world. Everyone has a complex. Even Pope John Paul II has scolded the Argentines for their lack of integrity and self-discipline.

Yet, through it all, Argentina has emerged as one of the fastest-growing economies in the world. Since the early 1990s, foreign investment has been pouring in by the billions of dollars. Ford, IBM, General Motors, Motorola, and Xerox have built factories or established joint ventures in the country. Several other Fortune 500 firms and their European equivalents have headquartered their South American operations there. The self-reliance long preached by Peron and his followers has been forgotten. Argentina is becoming fully integrated into the global economy, seemingly in spite of itself.

Most Western companies will say that although the business climate in Argentina can at best be described as difficult, the opportunities still far outweigh the risks. Nevertheless, a failure to pay attention to the details of the relationship can seriously undermine a company's ability to succeed in "integrity-challenged" Argentina. Nowhere is this attention to detail more important than in the distributor agreement.

The distributor agreement is one of the most misunderstood documents within the world of international business. Time and again, businesspeople fall into the trap of ascribing a higher value to the document than should probably exist. As most agreements are so complex and so detailed, so difficult to follow and understand, and moreover require so much time and energy to construct and execute, it is only natural to justify this effort by placing a strong emphasis upon such documents.

If it is the manufacturer's goal to effectively market and sell its products in a given emerging market, the manufacturer will need to recognize that a document prepared by and agreed to by lawyers will simply not accomplish this formidable task. A distributor will be successful in marketing and selling the manufacturer's products only if it is highly motivated to do so, sales and profits are significant and if an overall constructive business relationship exists between them. In other words, only highly motivated, right-thinking distributors employing solid, cogent business plans will successfully market and sell a manufacturer's product.

Often, distributor agreements seemingly create the impression that the document itself has generated business. Too often, distributor agreements include agreed levels or objectives for opening inventory and ongoing inventory stocking levels and traditional monthly and annual purchase forecasts, giving the document a false illusion of currency and of value to the manufacturer. The enlightened manufacturer understands that although the document appropriately states all of these elements and more, the distributor agreement hardly guarantees any specific inventory stocking levels or any ongoing levels of sales.

Distributors want to perform well for a manufacturer because they can develop profitable businesses selling the manufacturer's products and because they want to retain the franchise—not because there is an agreement. If they honor the territory boundaries, it is because they don't want to jeopardize the relationship with the manufacturer. Further, if distributors adhere to agreed-upon pricing levels, provide certain service facilities, refrain from selling competitive products, and furnish the relevant market and sales information, it is most often because they do not want to lose access to the manufacturer's product line. In the real business world and especially in emerging markets, the moment distributors cease to care, they stop performing.

In emerging markets, however, distributors may only want to enter into an agreement with a manufacturer for the sole purpose of preventing the manufacturer from being successful. A leading manufacturer of farming, construction, and other off-highway equipment unwittingly entered into a distributor agreement in a Middle Eastern market where the selected distributor was the cousin of its biggest competitor's distributor in that same market. Failing to conduct an adequate in-market investigation that would have uncovered such a family relationship and being overly impressed with the elaborate presentations and grand promises made by the prospective distributor, the manufacturer entered into a multiyear agreement with this distributor from which it could not easily extricate itself. Making matters worse, this distributor also filed official documents with its government, effectively registering the brands and trademarks of the manufacturer as the distributor's own.

Not recognizing the need to have local, retained legal counsel in that market, the manufacturer's director of sales for that region signed what appeared to be innocuous, routine forms sent to him by that country's ministry of commerce. The execution of these forms effectively transferred control of his company's rights to its brands and trademarks to the new distributor for an indefinite period of time. In defense of the manufacturer's director of sales, the forms he signed nowhere stated any such assignment of his company's brands or trademarks. Also, his company's attorneys back at corporate headquarters, who write and approve all distributor agreements and who are schooled in foreign law, also believed the forms to be routine and innocuous and gave the director of sales their approval to sign the forms. The apparent effect of signing the form was to name the new "authorized" and "official" distributor in this market, which by definition in this emerging market granted the new distributor certain privileges, including control over the manufacturer's brands and trademarks.

The net effect of this failure to retain local legal counsel, who would be able easily to foresee the consequences of executing what seemingly was a routine forms filing with the local ministry, is that for an indeterminable length of time, if this manufacturer wished to conduct any business in this market it did so only with this distributor and essentially under the terms and conditions laid out by the distributor. Again, this is the same distributor who is very motivated to support a cousin's distribution business and not the business of his newly secured manufacturer. Such a distribution partnership gives new meaning to the phrase, "doing business with a gorilla."

The story clearly illustrates that the normal rules of business law may not apply in all emerging markets and that special diligence is required at all times. In fact, many U.S. and European companies may already have much greater liability or have potentially explosive situations in their businesses as a result of distributor agreements they have entered.

Problems usually do not arise until the manufacturer desires to terminate an underperforming or unwanted distributor. At this moment, the manufacturer will look to the distributor agreement, and the agreement then takes on a new importance. At its most basic level, the distributor agreement between manufacturer and distributor is often little more than a termination document assessing liabilities and costs to the parties upon their separation. On a more constructive level, the distributor agreement is the embodiment of the in-market business operating plan initiated by the manufacturer and then jointly agreed to by both parties.

PROCESS FOR DEVELOPING THE DISTRIBUTOR AGREEMENT

Before we begin this discussion, it must be stated that in no way are the authors dispensing legal advice either directly or by implication. As this discussion seeks to address a most critical aspect of conducting business successfully in emerging markets and in all markets, it is highly recommended that anyone or any company seeking to conduct business with distributors in any market seek out its own legal counsel. As will become apparent from our discussion, the laws governing business dealings in many markets are evolving and need to be addressed by those best qualified to do so, those who are engaged in the practice of law on a full-time basis, both in-market as well as out of market.

First, it should be recognized that the distributor agreement is best approached as having two distinct components. The first is the baseline or underlying agreement, which is generally uniform for all distributors your company may have in a specific market. This baseline agreement recognizes and takes into account all the legal requirements to protect your company in that specific market. It not only embodies the many provisions your company's attorneys routinely require to protect your company's interests in all of your company's distributor agreements, it also conforms to and takes into account the effect of local laws in each individual emerging market where your company intends to conduct business.

The second of these agreement components is the addendum or the appendix. The addendum or the appendix is the part of the distributor agreement that embodies the actual business operating plan of each individual distributor. This component of the agreement is the living and breathing component of the agreement, constantly changing and being modified, usually on a quarterly or semi-annual basis, to reflect the changes and growth in the market and in the distributor's business. Many of the eighteen recommended provisions that follow should be reviewed and considered as addenda to your distributor agreement, if they are not already there.

Second, you should seriously consider engaging in a three-step process in the development of your company's distributor agreement. By adhering to this process you are assured of minimizing any potential problems in dealing with your emerging market distributor. The three-step process is the following:

1. Develop the agreement from an overall business and business plan perspective. In essence, the complete and detailed business plan that you should develop for and with your emerging market distributor can easily be transformed into a series of specific qualifiable and quantifiable objectives and performance standards. For example, specific sales and inventory targets will evolve, and presumably grow, over time; targets need to be set at different levels over different periods of time, that is, monthly, quarterly, and so on. As the business changes, so should your distributor's performance level and its performance targets. This is best accomplished by reviewing the eighteen business provisions presented hereafter and ensuring that all of them have been properly addressed in the objectives and performance standards detailed in your distributor business plan. This portion of the process does not specifically address any of the legal aspects of the manufacturer–distributor agreement, but only the business aspects of the agreement.

2. Once the agreement is prepared, the document should be forwarded to your company's in-house lawyers to be looked at from essentially a legal point of view. It is always advisable to meet with your attorney to explain the business goals and objectives of your plan, as detailed in Step 1, to ensure that the attorney can best support your stated business goals as well as protect your company at times of disagreement and possible distributor termination.

3. Following the internal review of the agreement with your company's in-house attorney, you should then meet with the local, in-market attorney that your company has retained for an opinion, as described in Chapter 4. At this point, any and all provisions and writings in the agreement, from both a business perspective and a corporate legal perspective, should be analyzed by the local in-market attorney to ensure what the local jurisdictional interpretations of the agreement will be, as well as to clarify the enforceability of the agreement and its specific provisions. Often, in a certain market, emerging or otherwise, the wording must change considerably from that utilized to accomplish the same objective elsewhere.

Furthermore, as local in-market attorneys are often "in the know," they can, through their relationships with government and judicial officials, seek changes to or special consideration from potentially unfavorable local laws. This essential next step is overlooked by most companies, and it may very well be the most important.

KEY PROVISIONS IN THE DISTRIBUTOR AGREEMENT

A well-prepared and effective agreement will first embody the business operating plan that will enable both the manufacturer and distributors to be successful in their business together. The agreement will then arm the manufacturer with a multitude of valid opportunities for terminating the relationship and ways to protect the manufacturer during and after termination. It will seek to provide as much protection for the manufacturer as possible, given the individual circumstances of each emerging market.

The best way to approach the agreement is not as a singular document but

Table 7.1
Key Provisions in the Distributor Agreement

1.	Sales Performance	10.	Product
2.	Standards of Performance	11.	Sub-Distributor
3.	Launching	12.	Pricing
4.	Inventories	13.	Payment
5.	Personnel	14.	Returns
6.	Training	15.	Period
7.	Information	16.	Market Development
8.	Exclusivity	17.	Termination
9.	Territory	18.	Right of First Refusal

as a series of business clauses that provide the platform both to execute an effective business plan and to provide the necessary ammunition in the event the manufacturer decides the distributor needs to be terminated. From this, there arise eighteen key provisions in the distributor agreement (Table 7.1). The sample agreement at the end of the chapter contains each of these provisions and illustrates them accordingly.

Provision 1: Sales Performance. This should be defined in volume terms. The contract does not have to be predicated on this figure (although it is preferable to do so), but the manufacturer needs to estimate a number around which performance can be roughly judged. There should be a provision for an agreed annual sales performance figure that would constitute acceptable performance, in other words, sales standards of performance. While this will be a gray area, at least an arbitrator will have a gauge by which to measure performance expectations.

Provision 2: Standards of Performance. The manufacturer should make the effort to specify the kinds of activities or standards of performance it expects in representing the manufacturer's products: ongoing detailing, sales evaluations, advertising, mailings, promotional activities, use of literature, production of local language literature, participation in tenders, and so on. The manufacturer should also take the time to include the types of market areas and customer groups it expects to see covered. Also, there should be a definition of "coverage." If the manufacturer means "actual sales calls," then the agreement should say so. The manufacturer should be as quantitative as possible—listing known customers and defining what is meant by sales calls. The actual media and the type of advertising the manufacturer envisions need to be specified. The manufacturer should also schedule those key customers and decision makers that are important and detail how they should be handled.

Provision 3: Launching. It will take a special effort to get the manufacturer's product off the ground, so the agreement needs to make clear the elements of this effort; such as seminars for key customer groups; evaluations with key decision markets, retailers, and industry leaders; launch advertising; detailing; mailing; and the like.

Provision 4: Inventories. The priority here is to include the agreed-upon formula for maintaining inventory levels. This is usually best phrased by reference to the type of deliveries that end-users should expect. This clause represents an ideal opportunity also to come to grips with the issue of the opening stock order. The manufacturer should try to have the value of the inventory stocking order included in this clause or appended to the contract.

Provision 5: Personnel. The manufacturer should list the teams or staff that are expected to be deployed in the sale of their product and clarify any specialist staff or product managers that have been promised, with the portions of their time that have been pledged. This is an excellent trapping clause. Remember that most distributors will pledge practically anything to get a valued franchise, including full-time product managers, entire sales terms, and so on. The manufacturer should hold distributors to their promises in this clause and hoard this condition for future use.

Provision 6: Training. The agreement should quantify what the manufacturer means by reasonable access to staff for training purposes and establish the right to conduct this training also in the field. If the manufacturer's product proves reasonably active, you won't normally have trouble in participating at sales meetings for training purposes—but field work can become a sticky issue, particularly with distributor managers who fear intrusion and distraction or with resentful salespeople.

Provision 7: Information. The contract needs to clarify what data the manufacturer expects to be made freely available to it and at what intervals. Sales statistics, territory analysis, sales/marketing plans, inventory levels, and competition data are jealously guarded by distributors. Yet, this information will be vital to the manufacturer on a regular basis, for building forecasts, controlling production, and lessening the manufacturer's umbilical relationship with the distributor.

Provision 8: Exclusivity. This section undertakes the questions, Can the distributor handle competitive products? Can the manufacturer supply other distributors in the same territory? Is the exclusive right by region or by product sector or by market sector? The question of exclusivity is one of the thorniest issues in distribution.

Naturally, the distributor wants the maximum amount of exclusivity it can get. If the project proves too much, the distributor can always sub-distribute or relieve the pressure in some other way. Above all, however, the distributor wants to control these issues. The distributor does not want to see the manufacturer engaged in relationships with other companies. Further, its does not want to be subjected to odious performance comparisons or to be pushed into heated competition with competitors.

The manufacturer, on the other hand, will normally be reluctant to part with exclusivity. Even if the mechanism the manufacturer has chosen allows for exclusivity, it will still want the flexibility to expand and change as time goes on. Manufacturers usually want monogamous distributors and will consider swapping exclusivity to get it. In addition, manufacturers are also infinitely better served through well-motivated distributors—not ones who are nervous or uncommitted!

Provision 9: Territory. It is important here to define territory and who is to share it. From this, the relationships with the main importers and other elements in the manufacturer's distribution network can be put forth.

Provision 10: Product. Be certain here to carefully specify the products. Also, who knows how the manufacturer's company may diversify in the future and what different channels might be needed for radically new products? The manufacturer should make sure any new products that would differ significantly from current ones are negotiable.

Provision 11: Sub-Distribution. The manufacturer should reserve the right to veto sub-distributors, some of which may want to buy its products for the wrong reasons, perhaps for resale to a different territory or to get access to pricing information for a competitor.

Provision 12: Pricing. Prices should be appended but with the minimum impact on confidentiality. The manufacturer should keep high-volume discounts off the agenda at contract negotiation time. Discount schedules should be clear and geared to encourage efficient shipments. The manufacturer's FOB factory prices protects from the cost of insurance and bank charges connected with shipments. In addition, the manufacturer should ensure its right to change prices without notice. While the manufacturer will customarily want to give reasonable notice of price changes, it must protect itself against error or traumatic increases in manufacturing costs.

Provision 13: Payment. This clause will be one of the most effective termination clauses, as distributors rarely stick to payment terms. Therefore, it is incumbent upon the manufacturer to be especially clear as to the mode of payment and the precise credit terms.

Provision 14: Returns. Returns is a particularly important clause. Any termination will raise the issue of returns for credit, so it is vital to make returns fully discretionary on the manufacturer's part and to define rules in connection with the costs of transshipment, any necessary refurbishment, obsolescence, methods of shipment, associated declarations, and credit values.

Provision 15: Period. Generally stated, manufacturers want flexibility and therefore look for the shortest possible contract period. Distributors, on the other hand, will want the maximum possible period as a token of security. The trick is to strike a balance where the distributor can be relaxed but not complacent. If an agreement is well peppered with termination clauses and if the term of the agreement is clearly related to fulfillment of obligations, there should be no problem in extrication. Termination notice will need to be specified and, again, negotiated to a minimum.

Provision 16: Market Development. This is a very important clause, particularly in more litigious countries. When a distribution partnership unilaterally ruptures it is not unlike a broken marriage. Bitterness sets in, and pretty soon the wounded party starts thinking in abstracts. It remembers all the time and sweat put into developing the market for the manufacturer's product and establishing the manufacturer's brand with customers. Pretty soon it starts to impute a value to all this effort, this goodwill it helped create. The next step can be a massive claim for reimbursement for so-called market development costs. While a manufacturer may successfully fight off such a claim, the litigation, at the very least, will be used as an excuse for non-payment of invoices due or maybe as a refusal to return samples or exhibiting materials sent on loan.

Provision 17: Termination. By establishing standards of performance for all of the previously mentioned key agreement provisions, the manufacturer has established the basis for fair and just termination. Additional procedural, logistic, and notice provisions will provide the mechanism for effective and efficient distributor termination.

Provision 18: Rights of First Refusal. Agreements should be protected against changes in business ownership. While such changes often make little difference or may even be positive, there is always the hazard of purchase by a competitor or other company with conflicting interests. Should the distributor decide to sell its business, the manufacturer will want to have the first opportunity to purchase the distributor's business.

An agreement must at least appear to be balanced and fair, or targeted distributors are going to have psychological problems. The manufacturer should identify those basic activities it will have to do anyway as a serious manufacturer and position them as concessionary offerings. The manufacturer will be supplying literature, catalogues, mailing pieces, product manuals, posters, and sales demonstration materials. It will be planning special training seminars for distribution staff and inviting certain key personnel to its facilities for more in-depth training. Field work with distributor sales staff will be essential. Contributions are going to be made in time and money terms to promotion and advertising—at the very least by way of artwork, copy, and promotional materials. Usually the manufacturer will also be conceding some sort of exclusivity or voluntary restriction. Many agreements take all such items and, with reasonably skilled use of the pen, turn them into sacrificial clauses in the distributor's favor, dispersed throughout the agreement document.

One way to avoid distributor termination problems is to avoid agency agreements. When entering agreements with foreign agents, here are some ways to mitigate or eliminate risks and penalties.

- "Annulment beats divorce." An agreement of six to nine months is usually a sufficient time to judge a distributor's or agent's performance, motivation, and competency. Generally, as the length of the relationship increases, more liability will flow to the manufacturer under the laws in many countries. Little liability usually attaches to the manufacturer for agreements of under one year.

- Be specific in defining performance. Use phrases like "Agent agrees to sell a minimum of ten thousand units every quarter" to specifically define the distributor's performance.

- Be specific in defining consequences of non-performance. Language similar to "Agent will transfer to principal all legitimate property, including trademarks, patents, company name, and lists of customers and contacts" puts non-performance into a more clearly understood light.

- Be specific as to what laws will govern disputes over agreements. The country and its particular laws governing agreement disputes should be explicitly stated.

- Be specific as to what forum will adjudicate disputes. Almost invariably, from the principal's perspective, arbitration or concillation is preferable to the civil law courts.

- Be specific as to the language in which agreement clauses will be interpreted. Even if the agreement is written in the language of the agent or distributor, consider interpreting the agreement in the language of the manufacturer.

EVALUATION OF THE DOCUMENT BY THE IN-HOUSE LEGAL STAFF

No agreement will be either complete or safe until the manufacturer has consulted with its legal staff, both its company lawyers and its local in-market lawyers. Many will have little grasp of the commercial significance of the clauses the manufacturer's sales executive has drafted, but they can at least check them for any obvious legal heresy. Lawyers start to be useful when it comes to including protective clauses in respect of limitations of warranty, product liability, non-disclosure, consequential damages resulting from breach of contract, product registrations, patents, and so forth.

Finally, of course, a lawyer's most important function is to ensure that the agreement is either enforceable or totally useless in a particular country, depending on the manufacturer's needs.

The necessity for an agreement varies enormously from market to market. In fact, in many cases an actual legal agreement may be a waste of time. They are unenforceable from the distributor's point of view and are of no value in generating sales. Agreements do, however, bring a valuable air of gravity and solemnity into a new commercial relationship, and the sense of occasion generated is another valuable tool in extracting nice opening inventory stock orders. Furthermore, agreements can serve as a useful and permanent statement of policy. They are, in effect, charters of mutual expectation and an excellent reference when chiding, warning, or actually terminating a distributor. An agreement can be a type of permanent rule book, which can prevent useless arguments and bickering—a sort of constitution, to be referred to as final arbitrator when all else fails.

Clearly, nowadays the fail-safe position would be to instigate a distributor agreement in all cases, irrespective of the individual circumstances. This will be mandatory in some cases, particularly in emerging and developing countries and in the Gulf States, where governments are increasingly insisting on distribution agreements, not to protect the national distributor but in fact to protect the final customer or end-user of the product.

Although most of these mandatory agreements are designed to protect the customer from the distributor, they are usually quite severe on the manufacturer and contain clauses in respect of manufacturer liability and exposure that would make any corporate lawyer uneasy. Worse, they are seldom negotiable. Such government involvement takes the simple but effective stance that if a manufacturer wants to do business in, say, India, then he must sign—otherwise, move aside. In these cases there are three choices: The manufacturer could try to negotiate the problematic clauses; to indemnify his company some way, perhaps through self-insurance, against negative consequences; or to conduct his business through a third, but offshore, party, which will buffer or totally absorb the exposure.

At the end of the day, agreements are an inevitable fact of life—at times a mandatory hurdle, more usually a necessary safety measure in a distribution relationship. They are a useful reference for the ground rules during disputes. They are, however, bills of expectations that are rarely commercially significant, in the important sense of generating business.

Table 7.2
Sample Distribution Agreement

SAMPLE DISTRIBUTION AGREEMENT

This agreement hereinafter referred to as the "Agreement", is made between:

MANUFACTURER Marketing & Sales Company
whose registered office is at: address represented by YYY, Managing Director
hereinafter referred to as "Manufacturer"

AND _____

whose registered office is at _____

represented by _____

hereinafter referred to as the "DISTRIBUTOR"

PREAMBLE

Whereas MANUFACTURER is the of MANUFACTURER - a major consumers products manufacturer – involved in the sales and distribution of consumer products in the .

Whereas a distribution system is necessary in order to promote the image of and its brands in .

Whereas the DISTRIBUTOR, represents itself as capable of distributing MANUFACTURER'S products to wholesalers and to retail trade.

Whereas MANUFACTURER wishes the DISTRIBUTOR to distribute the Products, as defined hereinafter, according to the terms of this Agreement, and until 31st December 200X.

THEREFORE, THE PARTIES HAVE AGREED AS FOLLOWS:

Table 7.2 (*continued*)

Article 1:   *Definitions*

In this Agreement the following words and expressions shall have the meaning as set out below:

1.1. The Products
 The Products shall mean the range of products listed in Addendum 1.

 Addendum 1 may, from time to time, be amended by the addition or deletion of products by MANUFACTURER.

1.2.   The Territory
 The Territory shall mean those geographic area, as defined in Addendum 2, which can be amended from time to time by mutual agreement in writing.

1.3.   The Trademark
 The Trademark shall mean those registered trade marks, and brand names belonging world-wide to MANUFACTURER or any of its affiliates.

1.4.   Competing Activity
 Competing activities shall mean any business, trade or occupation which, in MANUFACTURER'S opinion, is the same as, or similar to, or in conflict, or in competition with any business, trade or occupation carried on in respect of the Products.

1.5.   Distribution Network
 Distribution Network shall include MANUFACTURER, the DISTRIBUTOR and all other distributors with which MANUFACTURER has concluded a distribution agreement for another "Emerging Market" Territory.

1.6.   The Information
 The Information shall mean all communications and all information whether written, visual, or verbal, and all other material supplied to or obtained by the DISTRIBUTOR from any company of the Distribution Network during the continuance of this Agreement.

 It includes, but is not limited to, trade secret, confidence, production or marketing or sales data.

 It shall also mean all information, recommendations or advises given to any distributor in the Distribution Network by the DISTRIBUTOR in pursuance of its duties under this Agreement.

1.7.   The Know-How

Table 7.2 (*continued*)

The Know-How shall mean, without limitation, all patentable and non-patentable inventions, discoveries and improvements, processes and copyright works, designs, hardware and software belonging world-wide to MANUFACTURER or any of its affiliates.

1.8.   *Force Majeure*
Force Majeure shall refer to the definition given in Article 27.

1.9.   *Preferred Right*
Preferred Right shall mean access to the full portfolio of The Products, access to the lowest prices, participation in different investment programs which MANUFACTURER may from time to time initiate, a geographic Territory within which MANUFACTURER will not conclude Distribution Agreement with any other company until this Agreement expires/is terminated.

Article 2:   Interpretation

2. 1.   *Headings*
The headings used in this Agreement are included for convenience only and are not to be used in construing or interpreting this Agreement.

2.2.   *Legislation*
Any reference in this Agreement to any statute, decree law, statutory instrument or other regulation having the force of law shall be deemed to include any lawful modifications thereto or re-enactments thereof made after the date of signature of this Agreement.

2.3.   *Proper Law*
The construction, performance and validity of this Agreement shall be governed by the laws of the "Emerging Market".

Article 3:   Right granted

3.1.   *Preferred Right*
MANUFACTURER hereby grants the DISTRIBUTOR, which accepts, a preferred right to distribute and sell the Products in the Territory during the continuance of this Agreement.

Such an appointment is in both parties' interest and not to one or the other party's exclusive interest.

Table 7.2 (*continued*)

3.2.　*Exchange of Information*
MANUFACTURER shall refer to the DISTRIBUTOR any inquiry or order received from a third party located in the Territory, or from a distributor in another territory.

MANUFACTURER agrees to use its best efforts to accept the DISTRIBUTOR'S orders for the Products, and to deliver with priority Products for which orders from the DISTRIBUTOR'S clients were received and were agreed by MANUFACTURER.

The DISTRIBUTOR shall promptly refer to MANUFACTURER any inquiry or orders coming to the DISTRIBUTOR from third parties located outside the Territory.

Article 4:　　*Non-Export*

During the continuance of this Agreement, the DISTRIBUTOR shall not sell outside, export, assist in or be a party to the export of the Products from the Territory unless the prior written consent of MANUFACTURER has been obtained.

Article 5:　　*General Provision*

This Agreement does not constitute the DISTRIBUTOR the agent or legal representative of MANUFACTURER for any purpose whatsoever. The DISTRIBUTOR is not granted any right or authority to assume or to create any obligation or responsibility, express or implied, on behalf of or in the name of MANUFACTURER, or to bind MANUFACTURER in any manner or thing whatsoever without the prior written consent of MANUFACTURER.

For instance, and without limitation, the DISTRIBUTOR cannot:
- enter into or have authority to enter into any engagement
- make any representation or warranty on behalf of
- pledge the credit ot
- bind or oblige the other party hereto

Article 6:　　*No Joint Venture or Partnership*

Nothing in this Agreement shall create a partnership or joint-venture between the parties hereto.

Table 7.2 (*continued*)

Article 7:   *General Undertakings by Distributor*

7. 1.   *Due Diligence*
The DISTRIBUTOR shall, during the continuance of this Agreement:
- diligently and faithfully serve MANUFACTURER as its distributor in the Territory
- use its best efforts to improve the goodwill of MANUFACTURER in the Territory
- use its best efforts in the sale, distribution, merchandising and promotion of the Products so as to increase the retail and wholesale sales coverage in the Territory at à level determined to be satisfactory by MANUFACTURER.

7.2.   *Absence of Interference*
The DISTRIBUTOR shall not do anything that may prevent the sale or interfere with the developments of sales of the Products in the "Emerging Market".

Furthermore, the DISTRIBUTOR refrains from carrying out any actions that could damage the reputation of MANUFACTURER or of the Products.

7.3.   *Sales to Approved Clients*
The DISTRIBUTOR undertakes to sell the Products only to clients agreed upon, in writing, and in advance, by MANUFACTURER, and allows MANUFACTURER'S representatives to maintain contacts with these clients.

7.4   *Facilities*
The DISTRIBUTOR will, on a permanent basis in order to better implement and control the sales and marketing policy of MANUFACTURER do the following free of charge:

- give MANUFACTURER the right to use a room/office of the size agreed in Addendum 4 located within the warehouse of the DISTRIBUTOR, fax, copier, PC and other office appliances as agreed in Addendum 4,
- subsidize phone charges within agreed amount,
- deliver merchandising materials to The Territory as may be requested from time to time by MANUFACTURER,
- provide MANUFACTURER with secure (lockable) warehousing space to store MANUFACTURER merchandising materials.

Table 7.2 (*continued*)

Article 8: *General Undertakings by Manufacturer; Investment Fund*

MANUFACTURER shall make its best efforts to support the DISTRIBUTOR'S business development, under the condition that it has been agreed by both parties, by creating an Investment Fund.

The Investment fund for each quarter will total to X% of quarterly purchases of those Products which are produced in "<u>Emerging Market</u>" from MANUFACTURER in monetary terms.

The Investment fund will be made payable to The DISTRIBUTOR by MANUFACTURER upon meeting specific objectives/investments which should be agreed upon by both parties before beginning of each quarter. Each investment will be assigned a weight.

The Investment fund will NOT be made payable to The DISTRIBUTOR at all or partially (to be decided by MANUFACTURER) if during a quarter:

- The Products with The DISTRIBUTOR'S codes were found on sale out of The Territory,
- The DISTRIBUTOR has sold The Products at a price which is different from the price lists recommended by MANUFACTURER,
- The DISTRIBUTOR has sold The Products without prior approval of DSS,
- The DISTRIBUTOR has not met all targets agreed in Addendum 4 to this Agreement,
- The DISTRIBUTOR has not made all investments agreed in Addendum 4 to this Agreement
- The DISTRIBUTOR has violated any condition of this Agreement.

MANUFACTURER decides which part of Investment Fund will be made payable to The DISTRIBUTOR each time if any condition/objective of this Agreement was not met by The DISTRIBUTOR. This part of The Investment fund will be made payable to The DISTRIBUTOR by MANUFACTURER in the next quarter (no later than 10th day).

Article 9: *Supply of the Product*

9.1. *Exclusive purchase*
The DISTRIBUTOR shall purchase, during the term of this Agreement, the Products which are produced in "<u>Emerging Market</u>" exclusively from MANUFACTURER and the Products which are produced outside of "<u>Emerging Market</u>" as directed by MANUFACTURER.

9.2. *Quantities*

Table 7.2 (*continued*)

The DISTRIBUTOR agrees to forecast, during the continuance of this Agreement, the Products from MANUFACTURER in the manner established in Addendum 3.

MANUFACTURER undertakes to establish with the DISTRIBUTOR monthly volume allocation by brand which may alter from the forecast. While developing monthly allocation MANUFACTURER will do it's best to meet DISTRIBUTOR'S forecast.

9.3.   *Shipment Schedule*
The DISTRIBUTOR agrees to order the Products according to the monthly volume allocation established by MANUFACTURER.

Article 10:   Pricing and Payment

10.1.   *Prices*
The Products (produced in "Emerging Market" are priced by the case in US Dollar amounts and sold by the case in local emerging market currency equivalents at exchange rate of Central Bank of "Emerging Market" effective on date of release of product from MANUFACTURER to DISTRIBUTOR.

Prices are determined by Addendum 5 and are subject for changes by MANUFACTURER. In case of changes MANUFACTURER undertakes to inform the DISTRIBUTOR no later then 3 days in advance of changes validation.

The DISTRIBUTOR agrees to observe the price lists established by MANUFACTURER for all sales of the Products, to the wholesale or retail trade in the Territory, and to use its best efforts to follow the retail selling prices recommended by MANUFACTURER.

Transport charges are attributed to the DISTRIBUTOR and, if MANUFACTURER organizes the delivery of Products are paid to MANUFACTURER in the amount that is stated in the additional contract.

10.2.   *Payments*
The DISTRIBUTOR agrees to make advance payments to MANUFACTURER for all the ordered Products to the bank accounts specified by MANUFACTURER.

10.3.   *Products Produced Outside of "Emerging Market"*
The DISTRIBUTOR agrees to purchase all Products produced out of "Emerging Market" as directed by MANUFACTURER, from a company appointed by MANUFACTURER, on conditions/at prices agreed with a company appointed by MANUFACTURER.

Table 7.2 (*continued*)

Article 11: Sales Volumes

11.1. *Objectives*
The DISTRIBUTOR undertakes to achieve the monthly volume allocations and distribution targets set by MANUFACTURER.

11.2. *Reports*
The DISTRIBUTOR shall send to MANUFACTURER by the Monday following the end of each week, during the continuance of this Agreement, a report of sales made of the Products in the Territory during that week together with such other marketing and other information (distribution) in relation to the operation of the Agreement, as MANUFACTURER may reasonably require.

Forms of these reports will be supplied by MANUFACTURER. For information a model will be joined in Addendum 6.

Article 12: Stocks of the Products

12.1. *Minimum stock*
The DISTRIBUTOR shall at all times during the continuance of this Agreement carry a minimum stock of the Products so that all orders received by its clients can be supplied without undue delay.

Therefore, the DISTRIBUTOR agrees that the minimum stock shall be equal to a one (1) week rolling forecast.

12.2. *Stock reports*
The DISTRIBUTOR shall supply reports as to stock levels and movements to MANUFACTURER on a weekly basis.

Article 13: Storage of the Products

13.1. *Warehouse*
The DISTRIBUTOR undertakes to follow the recommendations issued by MANUFACTURER regarding the warehouse, and especially, their minimum size and their technical requirements.

The DISTRIBUTOR undertakes to store the Product under conditions that will prevent deterioration and also - on the instruction of MANUFACTURER - to store particular Product under such special conditions as may be appropriate to their requirements.

163

Table 7.2 (*continued*)

The DISTRIBUTOR undertakes to follow stock rotation rules issued by MANUFACTURER.

13.2. *Manufacturer's Inspection Right*
The DISTRIBUTOR agrees to allow MANUFACTURER or its authorized representative to have full access for inspection of the Products when in storage under the control of the DISTRIBUTOR, from time to time, without any notice to give.

13.3. *Good Quality Products*
The Products will be kept fresh and sanitary. The DISTRIBUTOR undertakes not to sell damaged, inferior or sub-standard Products.

Article 14:   *Distributor's Records*

14.1.   *Accounts*
The DISTRIBUTOR shall keep accounts together with supporting vouchers, including without limitations: copies of invoices and other relevant documents showing all orders for the supply of the Products by MANUFACTURER to the DISTRIBUTOR, and by the DISTRIBUTOR to its customers.

14.2.   *Manufacturer's Right of Inspection.*
The DISTRIBUTOR shall allow MANUFACTURER or its authorized representative, at all reasonable time whether this Agreement be terminated or not, to inspect, audit and copy invoices and other relevant paper, for the purpose of checking any information given by the DISTRIBUTOR to MANUFACTURER, or of obtaining any information or data relevant to the obligations to be performed by the DISTRIBUTOR under this Agreement.

14.3. *Inventory Report.*
The DISTRIBUTOR shall furnish MANUFACTURER, on a weekly basis, with inventory reports in a format to be agreed with MANUFACTURER that will include among other, stocks by location, by products and by age.

Article 15:   *Sales and Marketing Policies*

15.1.   *Conformity to Manufacturer's Policy*
The DISTRIBUTOR shall conform to the general sales and marketing policies of MANUFACTURER, as communicated from time to time, including but not limited to:

• MANUFACTURER recommendations on wholesale operations (quantity and size of warehouses and their location within The Territory, sub-distributors territories, etc. within wholesale markets, etc.),

• Sales Development plans developed by MANUFACTURER for DISTRIBUTOR.

Table 7.2 (*continued*)

15.2. *Packaging*
The DISTRIBUTOR undertakes not to alter, treat or otherwise deal with any of the Products, or their packaging, or to present any such Products for sale in a group package.

The DISTRIBUTOR undertakes to protect the goodwill and integrity of Manufacturer's products, and not to sell damaged, inferior or sub-standard products.

The proper handling and disposal of damaged, inferior or sub-standard products shall be determined in consultation with MANUFACTURER.

15.3. *Trademarked Items*
The DISTRIBUTOR undertakes:
- not to apply the Trademark to any item not one of the Product
- not to distribute or sell any such items with the Trademark so applied
- not to engage in any other practice or activity likely to mislead potential purchasers into believing that an item is one of the Products when in fact it is not.

Article 16 :   *Advertising and Merchandising*

16.1. *Advertising*
MANUFACTURER shall carry on and be responsible for all advertising for the Products in the Territory.

MANUFACTURER will, from time to time, make contributions as agreed between the parties as incentive programs for retailers and the Distributor's sales staff to promote sales of the Products.

16.2. *Prior Approval of Manufacturer*
All advertisements, point of sale, promotion merchandising and publicity material for the Products issued by the DISTRIBUTOR shall be subject before issue to the prior approval of MANUFACTURER.

16.3. *Sales Promotion Activities*
All sales promotion activities carried on by the DISTRIBUTOR for the Products of whatever nature must receive the prior written approval of MANUFACTURER which reserves the right to veto the same entirely at its discretion.

Table 7.2 (*continued*)

Article 17:   *Distributor's Staff*

17.1.   *Sufficient Staff, Distributor Sales Supervisor*
The DISTRIBUTOR shall maintain, during the continuance of this Agreement, sufficient staff to sell, distribute and promote the sale of the Products throughout the Territory as specified in Addendum 4.

The DISTRIBUTOR undertakes to follow the indications of Addendum 4, in order to have a staff proportionate to its activity, which will enable him to fulfill its obligations, especially, but not limited to, regarding to sales, in a efficient manner.

Distributor's staff involved in selling, merchandising and/or marketing The Products should report to DISTRIBUTOR Sales Supervisor who will be a MANUFACTURER employee permanently located with the DISTRIBUTOR. Any personal action (hiring, firing, salary change, promotion, etc.) can happen only with a prior written approval of DSS.

Distributor's staff involved in selling, merchandising and/or marketing The Products should be dedicated to The Products exclusively and should not be involved in any selling activity for any competitor's products.

17.2.   *Minimum Salary*
The DISTRIBUTOR undertakes to remunerate its employees with a minimum salary following the program set out in Addendum 4.

17.3.   *Training Program*
MANUFACTURER agrees to establish specific training programs for the Distributor's employees covering sales techniques, presentation of the Products and merchandising skills.

17.4.   *"Manufacturer's Brands Uniform"*
MANUFACTURER will provide the Distributor's employees with Manufacturer's brand promotional clothing, in order for them to promote the reputation and the quality of the brands belonging to MANUFACTURER.

The employees have the obligation to take care of these clothing, to wash them, and to always keep them fit.

Table 7.2 (*continued*)

Article 18: Industrial Property Rights

18.1. *Trade Mark and Copyright*
The DISTRIBUTOR undertakes not to sell, produce, make, modify or manufacture, or assist any other party to sell, produce, make, modify or manufacture the Products or any part thereof for use sale or any other purpose.

18.2. *Brand Notices*
The DISTRIBUTOR shall leave in position and not cover or erase any notices or other marks - including, without limitation, details or notices that a Trade Mark design or Copyright relating to the Product is owned by MANUFACTURER or any of its affiliates or a third party - which MANUFACTURER may place on or affix to the Products.

18.3. *Exclusive Property of Manufacturer*
It is agreed that all rights to the Trade Mark are and shall remain the exclusive property of MANUFACTURER or any of its affiliates.

18.4. *Additional Use of the Trademark*
The Trademark shall not be used in any manner liable to invalidate the registration thereof.

The right to use the Trademark in connection with the appropriate Product is only granted to the extent that MANUFACTURER is able to do so without endangering the validity of the registration.

18.5. *Information Obligation*
The DISTRIBUTOR shall - insofar as it becomes aware thereof - notify MANUFACTURER of any unauthorized use in the Territory of the Trade Mark or of any other intellectual or industrial property rights in the control or ownership of MANUFACTURER or any of its affiliates.

At the request and cost of MANUFACTURER, the DISTRIBUTOR shall:
- take part in or give assistance in respect of any legal proceedings
- execute any documents
- do any things reasonably necessary to protect Manufacturer's intellectual and industrial property rights in the Territory

Article 19: Commencement of Agreement

This Agreement shall, subject to earlier termination as herein provided, commence upon the date of signature hereof, and continue in force until 31st December 200X.

Table 7.2 (*continued*)

Article 20   *Termination*

In addition to any other remedies the parties may have, upon the occurrence of any of the following events or conditions, this Agreement may be terminated at any time, with a ten (10) days written notice:

20.1. By MANUFACTURER, upon non-payment of any amounts due by the DISTRIBUTOR to MANUFACTURER in a timely manner.

20.2. By MANUFACTURER, if the Distributor's legal organization has been altered by merger, consolidation or sale of all or à substantial part of its shares or assets; or if the control of the DISTRIBUTOR shall pass from the present shareholders, or owners, or controllers, to other persons whom MANUFACTURER shall, in its absolute discretion, regard as unsuitable.

20.3. By MANUFACTURER, upon the failure by the DISTRIBUTOR to maintain adequate inventories of the Products which are necessary to avoid non-delivery to, or out-of-stock situations at the trade level.

20.4. By MANUFACTURER, if Manufacturer's share in Distributor's business is less than specified in this Agreement.

20.5. By MANUFACTURER if the DISTRIBUTOR sells the Products outside the Territory.

20.6. By MANUFACTURER if the DISTRIBUTOR discloses any confidential or secret information (as defined in Sect 1.6) of MANUFACTURER.

20.7. By MANUFACTURER if the DISTRIBUTOR alters the image of MANUFACTURER and/or of its Products.

20.8. By MANUFACTURER if the DISTRIBUTOR makes any representation or conducts any advertising which has not been previously authorized by MANUFACTURER.

20.9. By MANUFACTURER if the DISTRIBUTOR breaks down the packaging of the Products.

20.10. By MANUFACTURER if the DISTRIBUTOR fails to achieve three (3) sales targets in a period of six (6) months, unless such failure was caused by a default of MANUFACTURER to fulfill its obligations under the present Agreement, or if it is the result of a cause of "force major".

Table 7.2 (*continued*)

> 20.11. By either party upon the insolvency, bankruptcy, dissolution or liquidation of either party, or upon the filing of a legal proceeding, or the entry of a legal order or restraint, limiting the rights of creditors of a party.
>
> 20.12. By either party, in the event of a breach by the other party of any material provision, representation or obligation of this Agreement.
>
> 20.13. By the DISTRIBUTOR if MANUFACTURER fails to ship the Products ordered by the DISTRIBUTOR in reasonable amounts within a reasonable time, in accordance with the parties' course of dealings.

Both parties recognize and expressly agree that the causes and notice for termination as stipulated above, are adequate and sufficient under all circumstances; and therefore, neither party shall be entitled to and hereby waive any compensation, damages, indemnity or claim solely by reason of such termination.

Article 21: *Proceedings Costs*

The DISTRIBUTOR undertakes that it will indemnify MANUFACTURER against all damages, costs liabilities, injury, loss or damage arising out of the breach or negligent performance or failure in performance by the DISTRIBUTOR of the terms of this Agreement.

Article 22: *Effect of Termination*

22.1. *Documentation*
Upon termination of this Agreement – from any cause whatsoever - the DISTRIBUTOR shall, at the request of MANUFACTURER, promptly return to MANUFACTURER all the documentation of any nature whatsoever in his possession or control, relating to the Products or to MANUFACTURER and to the activities of the DISTRIBUTOR in relation to the Products or MANUFACTURER.

22.2. *Products*
Upon such termination, the DISTRIBUTOR, if so required by MANUFACTURER, shall send back to MANUFACTURER, at the acquisition price in local emerging market currency, the products purchased by the DISTRIBUTOR from MANUFACTURER and remaining unsold.

Table 7.2 (*continued*)

22.3. *Intellectual Property Rights*
Upon such termination, the DISTRIBUTOR shall have the further rights to use the Trade Mark or know-how, in any way whatsoever, and in particular, but without any limitation, shall cease to use the Trade Mark on its letterheads, vehicles or elsewhere.

22.4. *Customers*
Upon such termination, the DISTRIBUTOR shall, if so requested, supply MANUFACTURER with a list of the Distributor's customers for the Product.

22.5. *No Right to Indemnification*
The termination of this Agreement, for any reason whatsoever, shall not give the DISTRIBUTOR any right whatsoever to any indemnification for any reason whatsoever. In particular, upon termination of this Agreement, for whatever reason, the DISTRIBUTOR is not entitled to severance payment. The DISTRIBUTOR acknowledges that there will be no compensation for clientele and agrees moreover that he has no claim of any nature with respect to goodwill in the Territory concerning the Product and the business attached thereto, such goodwill being the exclusive property of MANUFACTURER.

Article 23: Competing Activity

The DISTRIBUTOR and its shareholders undertake that within X months after this Agreement has been signed Manufacturer's share in total (insert manufacturer's product category) sales turnover of The DISTRIBUTOR measured by volume will reach X%, and will be no lower than X+% after that results.

Article 24: Confidentiality

The DISTRIBUTOR agrees, except with the prior written consent of MANUFACTURER, never to divulge, disclose or otherwise furnish to a person not a party hereto any trade secret, confidential or other sensitive information (including, but not limited to, Manufacturer's production, sales and marketing data) with which it becomes familiar in connection with the relationships established by this Agreement.

The provisions of this section shall survive the expiration or termination of this Agreement.

Table 7.2 (*continued*)

Article 25:   *Transmission of Rights*

This Agreement and the benefit of the rights granted to the DISTRIBUTOR by this Agreement shall be personal to the DISTRIBUTOR who shall not, without the prior consent of MANUFACTURER:
- mortgage or charge the same to any third party
- sub-contract or assign the same or part with any of its rights or obligations thereunder

The foregoing shall not prevent the DISTRIBUTOR from factoring or mortgaging, or in any way creating a charge or security, over Products the title in which shall have passed to it or over-book debts created by the sale of such Products.

Article 26:   *Disputes*

26.1. *Amicable Resolution*
The parties agree to use their best endeavors to resolve amicably all and any dispute arising in connection with this Agreement.

26.2. *Arbitration*
In the event that the parties fail to solve such disputes they shall be finally settled by arbitration.

The rules applying to the Arbitration proceedings shall be the one of the "Emerging Market" arbitration association.

Arbitration will be held in , and the proceedings shall be held in the local "Emerging Market" language.

26.3. *Severability*
In the event that any or more of the provisions contained in this Agreement shall, for any reason, be held unenforceable, illegal, or otherwise invalid in any respect, under the law governing this Agreement or its performance, such illegality or invalidity shall not affect any other provisions of this Agreement, and this Agreement shall then be construed as if such unenforceable illegal or invalid provisions had never been contained herein.

26.4. *Compliance With Laws*
In the performance of this Agreement, both parties shall comply with all laws, rules, regulations, decrees and other ordinances issued by any governmental or other state authority relating to the subject matter of this Agreement and the performance by the parties hereto of their obligations thereunder.

Table 7.2 (*continued*)

Article 27: Force Majeure

27.1. *Situations*

Neither party shall be liable to the other for any failure to perform or delay in performance of its obligations thereunder - other than an obligation to pay moneys - caused by, but not limited to:

- act of God
- outbreak of hostilities, civil disturbance, act of terrorism
- the act of any government or authority
- fire, explosion, flood
- default of suppliers or sub-contractors
- theft, malicious damage, strike, lock-out, industrial action of any kind
- any cause or circumstance whatsoever beyond its reasonable control

27.2. *Notification*

Upon the occurrence of any such event, the party suffering therefrom shall immediately give the other notice of the cause of the delay by telephone and confirm it by telefax and by a registered mail letter.

27.3. *Proof*

This notification has to be followed by all useful information. The proofs shall be notified with a twenty-one (21) days delay upon notification.

27.4. *Sanction*

Any unjustified delay in respect of the above mentioned formalities shall lead to the loss of the exoneration right provided by Force Majeure.

Article 28: Manufacturer's Right of First Refusal

Distributor grants Manufacturer the right of first refusal to purchase Distributor's business if Distributor elects to sell or otherwise terminate its interest in its distribution business during the term of this agreement.

Distributor is in no way obligated to sell its business at any time nor is Manufacturer obligated purchase Distributor's business if neither chooses to do so.

Distributor must make Manufacturer aware of any and all credible offers to purchase Distributor's business. If Manufacturer elected to meet the highest credible purchase offer, Distributor must sell its business to Manufacturer

Table 7.2 (*continued*)

Article 29: *Whole Agreement*

29.1. *Previous Agreements*
This Agreement shall constitute the entire Agreement between both the parties with respect to the subject matter hereof and shall supersede any prior agreement and any and all promises, representations, warranties or other statements whether written or oral made by or on behalf of one party to the other of any nature whatsoever or contained in any document given by one party to the other concerning such subject matter.

29.2. *Amendment*
This Agreement may not be released, discharged, supplemented, interpreted, amended, varied or modified in any manner except by an instrument in writing signed by a duly authorized officer or representative of each of the parties.

Article 30: *Notice and communication*

30.1. *Support of Communication*
Any notice and any permission, consent, license, approval or other authorization to be served upon, or given, or communicated to one party hereto by the other, shall be in the form of a document in writing including without limitation a registered letter, a telex or a facsimile.

30.2. *Address*
All the communications shall be made to MANUFACTURER at the following address or to the following fax number:

Address:
Tel Number:
Fax Number:
E-Mail Address:
To the attention of:

And to the DISTRIBUTOR at the following address or to the following fax number:

Address: _____

Tel Number: _____

Fax Number: _____

To the attention of: _____

173

Table 7.2 (*continued*)

30.3. *Hand Delivery*
All communications by hand delivery shall be done during normal business hours.

30.4. *Effect of the Communication*
À communication shall have effect for the purpose of this Agreement and shall be deemed to have been received by the party to whom it was made:

- if delivered by hand, upon written receipt by the relevant person

- if sent by telex or facsimile, upon the transmission of the communication to the relevant number and the receipt by the machine that the message has been received properly.

- if sent by registered post, upon the registration receipt provided by the relevant postal authority.

30.5. *Change of Address*
Each party shall be obliged to send a notice to the other of any change in the details mentioned in Article 29.2., which details shall then be deemed to have been amended accordingly.

Article 31:   *Authority to Execute*

Each individual executing this Agreement on behalf of a party hereto, represents and warrants that he has been fully powered to execute this Agreement and that all necessary action to authorize the execution of this Agreement has been taken.

Done in four (4) originals, two (2) in local "Emerging Market" language and two (2) in English, one (1) in each language were retained by each party.

Made this _____ day of _____ 19__ in _____

MANUFACTURER Marketing & Sales Company   For the DISTRIBUTOR

_____   _____

YYY   ZZZ
Managing Director   Managing Director

ADDENDUM 1

THE PRODUCTS

List Products

ADDENDUM 2

THE TERRITORY

Exclusive territory for the Distributor should be specified here. If necessary a map may be attached.

ADDENDUM 3

THE FORECAST: MONTHLY OBJECTIVES

Distributor _____	Qty		Cases
Month _____			
To be submitted 7 days before beginning of each month.			
	Signature		_____ __
	Name		_____ __
	Position		_____ __

ADDENDUM 4

QUARTERLY BUSINESS DEVELOPMENT PLAN

For "_____" Quarter of 200__

The DISTRIBUTOR during the continuance of this Agreement will employ sales force of ___ sales agents equipped with ____ delivery vans (type, cargo carrying capacity). Minimal net salary for a sales agent will be $____ net base and $____ net in commissions paid against achieving _____.

The DISTRIBUTOR will, on a permanent basis in order to better implement and control the sales and marketing policy of MANUFACTURER do the following free of charge:

- give MANUFACTURER the right to use a room/office of _____ sq.m. in size located within the warehouse of the DISTRIBUTOR,
- provide MANUFACTURER with the following office furniture _____,
- give MANUFACTURER access to fax, copier, PC and other office appliances as needed,
- subsidize phone charges within $X per month,
- deliver merchandising materials to The Territory as may be requested from time to time by MANUFACTURER,
- provide MANUFACTURER with secure (lockable) warehousing space of _____ sq.m. in size to store MANUFACTURER merchandising materials.

INVESTMENT PLAN

Nature of Investment	Qty	Weight	Amount	Specification
Recruitment of sales agents	?	?%	$____	Sourced by the local recruitment agency, interviewed by DSS and a Distributor's representative
Purchase vans	?	?%	$____	Carrying capacity of at least X number of Product each able to maneuver within the city center
Purchase computer	?	?%	$____	IBM compatible, processor - Pentium XXX or higher, etc.
TOTAL:		?%		

ADDENDUM 5

THE PRICES

Prepayment	Quantity Per Unit		Price Per Unit
Selling prices for Products			
Effective from 31st December 200X			
Received from the Warehouse X			

ADDENDUM 6

THE WEEKLY DISTRIBUTOR REPORT

Distributor: _____	Stock Beginning of Week (Units)	Incoming Shipments (Units)	Sold (Units)	Stock End of Week (Units)
Week of: _____				
To be submitted each Monday.				
	Signature			_____
	Name			_____
	Position **DSS**			

8

The Final Imperative: Forging Global Manifest Destiny

> We are like a big fish that has been pulled from the water and is flopping wildly to find its way back in. In such a condition the fish never asks where the next flip or flop will bring it. It senses only that its present position is intolerable and that something else must be tried.
>
> Anonymous Chinese saying

Arriving at the old Shanghai airport in the early 1990s, one could expect to spend at least two hours clearing immigration. By that time, your baggage might have arrived on conveyor belts that worked only when the temperature was above 20° C. In the middle of the conveyor belts was a Chinese-built moped on display, advertised for about US$800. Today, at the brand new US$8 billion airport in the Pudong section of town, it takes only ten minutes to clear immigration and customs. In between the conveyor belts sits a German-built Mercedes that sells for around US$125,000.

The economic integration of humankind has been a march throughout recorded history. Punctuated by periods of equilibrium, Global Manifest Destiny, the inevitability of all of the world's citizens being brought together by economic means, at times has expanded rapidly across the planet and at other moments has retrenched itself, seemingly waiting for another day. The breakneck pace of recent events has caused a complete reevaluation of all of our old beliefs and explanations. Asia's meteoric rise and apparently overnight collapse seems at times inexplicable, more for our failure to anticipate it rather than its actual occurrence. America's unimpeded economic expansion for more than a decade seems to defy the conventional models. China's rise as a global super-power appears on the horizon like a hazy sunrise, easy to see but difficult to define.

"Experts" try to rationalize and explain such occurrences using popular but failed paradigms like "globalization" and "global economy." Such terms are more often merely used to explain, justify, permit, and endorse the actions of one particular group against another. The financial markets tell us that because of "globalization," seemingly stable economies and companies can be brought to their knees almost overnight—workers are bankrupted, national banks looted, currencies devalued, and companies degraded. The absurd preoccupation with instant gratification has become a "day-trading mentality," terribly shortsighted and inherently dangerous for government and business leaders alike. Yet, no models currently exist that truly explain how this happens. We are seemingly left flipping and flopping like the big fish, not sure where we are headed, only certain that the current situation is just not right.

However, there is hope, and Global Manifest Destiny holds the promise. By recognizing, embracing, and assimilating Global Manifest Destiny as part of the very fabric of their organizations, forward-thinking leaders will undoubtedly be the ones who benefit from the inevitable economic integration of humankind. Those who fail to do so will eventually be disregarded and easily forgotten.

Global Manifest Destiny is not merely the "Americanization" of the world's economy. Just as the Europeans, Chinese, Africans, Romans, Greeks, Egyptians, and Phoenicians before them, the Americans of today are simply the most visible, yet unknowing, flag bearers of Global Manifest Destiny.

In fact, the best place to view the march of Global Manifest Destiny is not in the nations traditionally defined as the "industrialized world," but in what are called the emerging markets. The magnitude and ferocity of the economic integration of humankind is most evident in places like Ciudad del Este, Mumbai, Almaty, Guangzhou, and even Timbuktu.

Within these emerging markets, the two distinct phases of Global Manifest Destiny are easily discerned. In the first phase—Accelerated Re-Activity—the pace of commercial interchange is faster and more subject to wild fluctuations in the marketplace. Additionally, there is clear evidence of heightened competition for limited resources as well as arrogance on the part of suppliers, customers, and governments. During the Accelerated Re-Activity phase, a special infrastructure and unique behavioral mode of collective thinking and actions prevail. It is here where astute companies are most likely to build their best and sometimes easiest profits. The scarcity and higher costs associated with the Accelerated Re-Activity phase place an increasingly heavier burden on the existing infrastructure to create more and more of what is needed to sustain the phase. Moreover, since the focus is almost exclusively on profits, little if any attention is paid to maintaining and preparing the infrastructure against the unstoppable forces working to bring this phase to an end. When the infrastructure fails, it is no longer possible to simply "re-act."

Once the high profits and relatively "easy money" begin to ramp down and eventually evaporate, priority is placed upon shoring up or even completely rebuilding the current overburdened infrastructure in an attempt to "kick start" the economy and resume the Accelerated Re-Activity phase. At this point, we enter the other, distinct phase of Global Manifest Destiny—Decelerated Pro-Activity—which is characterized by comparatively lower sales and profits as well as reduced competition for limited resources. Here, enlightened, forward-thinking companies embrace initiatives to repair and minimize the shortcomings of the current system and build new infrastructures in a "pro-active" manner during these times of economic deceleration. For these firms, the Decelerated Pro-Activity phase is the time to keep and build market share, with an eye to building even greater profits once the Accelerated Re-Activity phase begins again.

Beyond how successful companies respond to the phases of Global Manifest Destiny, savvy investors all over the world are also paying close attention to how a company's strategic planning manages each phase of Global Manifest Destiny. To focus only on the short term in the face of Global Manifest Destiny is utter folly for both the investor and the business leader.

The spectacular economic growth in emerging markets is the beginning of the biggest "consumer boom" in history. More consumers with more income than ever before will provide companies with the greatest money-making opportunity in the Industrial Age. The place to "strike it rich" is in the emerging markets of the world, and the time is now. Conversely, that may also be the place to "lose it big" if one is not careful.

In comparison to the industrialized nations, emerging markets over the past two decades have been growing at an increasingly faster rate. The factors leading to the high rate of growth of emerging markets within the pillars of Global Manifest Destiny include demographics, communication, positive governmental action, and urbanization. The products of these factors are the creation of a new consumer class and a need for substantial infrastructure development. Within the next twenty-five years, more than 900 million new consumers with the buying power of an average American household will be created. Well over 90 percent will come from high-growth, emerging markets in Latin America, Southeast Asia, India, Central and Eastern Europe, Russia, Africa, and China. India, for example, currently has a middle-class market segment of approximately 180 million people. In the next twenty-five years, the nation will add between 75 million and 150 million new middle-class consumers, bringing the total middle class in India to between 240 and 320 million—a number greater than the entire population of the United States! China has an estimated 70 million consumers with the same buying power as the average American household. This number is expected to quadruple in the next twenty-five years.

In addition, the World Bank estimates more than US$2 trillion will continue to be spent on infrastructure over the next ten years. Energy exploration and generation, airports and air traffic control systems, telecommunications and satellite-ready technology, hospitals and health care services, automotive and spare parts production, banking and insurance, and environmental cleanup will absorb tens of billions of dollars as emerging markets seek to move into the first world.

The commercial environment in North America and Europe allows for a substantial amount of flexibility. However, the atmosphere in emerging markets is not nearly as accommodating and can be downright hostile. In order to take advantage of the phenomenal opportunities that exist in high-growth emerging markets, it is critical to identify the inherent realities of those nations. All that glitters isn't gold. A failure to realize this can result in terribly expensive and even dangerous consequences. Emerging market realities, however, are not merely value judgments about what is wrong in those places. They are customs, traditions, and ways of doing things that work for the people who live there. They are not right or wrong. Not good or bad. They just are.

Currency issues like hyperinflation and devaluation, the failings of infrastructure, the lack of adequate staffing, antiquated governmental policies, the proliferation of tax-free markets, and the chronic shortage of market information contribute to the extreme difficulties Western companies face in successfully doing business in emerging markets. Beyond recognizing the realities inherent in emerging markets, companies need to constantly examine what their expectations and tolerance levels should be. Each company must address three fundamental questions before making determinations about their business involvement in emerging markets:

• What is the level of risk the company is willing to accept in light of the inherent volatility emerging markets present?

• What is the level of investment the firm is willing to make to succeed in high-growth, emerging markets?

• What is the level of control the company is seeking for its emerging market operations?

Of course, every company will respond to each question differently, depending on its corporate culture and the market in question. However, before embarking on any venture into emerging markets, these answers need to be analyzed carefully and quantified wherever possible; commitments must be made upon on a market-by-market basis. Enlightened and more serious companies address these critical issues while being completely aware of the inherent realities and "minefields" characteristic of doing business in emerging markets. Further, leading firms design and implement a primary strategy that guides them in their emerging markets activities. Once the primary strategy is in place, the issues of risk tolerance, the amount of investment to be made, and the level of control desired can be placed into proper perspective for each market considered.

Simply stated, ascertained risk is manageable risk. Without question, certain undeniable risks come with pursuing any commercial activities in emerging markets. Notwithstanding this truth, there are proven ways in which to minimize the level of risk and make it palatable with your firm's emerging-market appetites. To best evaluate risk, the expectations of your company in an emerging market, and the realistic objectives for that market, it is crucial to analyze both the external and internal factors. Setting your company's realistic objectives is the net result of several varying and conflicting forces. The scope of these forces, the determination of their importance, and the need to anticipate their direction combine to give your company a greater sense of the amount of risk involved and serve to guide the establishment of your genuine expectations.

The recognition of a primary strategy compatible with the corporate culture and the combination of these factors—external and internal—provide a blueprint from which a company can realistically determine its emerging market objectives. Once in place, this framework can be built around the company's desire for profits, revenues/sales, and market share in the chosen market—factors otherwise known as outputs.

The vast majority of the time, it is in a manufacturer's interest to better monitor and control the sales and distribution of its products. For most companies, properly monitoring and controlling critical aspects of a distributor's business rather than "owing" the local business may be a much better approach to developing one's business in emerging markets. This is the basis of the Distributor Monitoring and Control Strategy (DMC). The DMC approach provides greater leverage and better leads to the appropriate allocation of resources to maximize the effectiveness of the relationship. Solid distribution also encourages the development of a more constructive and balanced relationship built upon "mutual self-interest." By better monitoring and controlling those activities within the distributor's business that are essential to successful sales and distribution, the distributor is more effectively managing its resources—its own money, staff, and other resources—for the manufacturer's direct benefit as well as its own. This frees up scarce resources that might be better spent elsewhere.

The same resources and people that would be employed by the manufacturer cost much less if employed by the local emerging market distributor. For example, whereas the foreign manufacturer must pay all social costs and taxes for its employees, the local emerging market distributor is oftentimes able to creatively avoid payment of such costs. Moreover, the wage and salary levels for comparable jobs are much lower in the local distributor's business than in the foreign manufacturer's business.

The underlying presumption here is that the manufacturer recognizes its role in dealing fairly and reasonably with its selected distributors. As often as distributors operate in a purely "self-interested" mode, so do most manufacturers. The collective goal of both manufacturer and distributor should be the development of constructive, mutually beneficial, long-term relationships.

Unfortunately, in the industrialized world, many manufacturers have historically failed to recognize the critical importance of monitoring and controlling their key business activities within their distributors' businesses. Some have even proactively abdicated what little monitoring and control ability they have had through the years in an effort not to antagonize a key distributor.

Fortunately, emerging markets are more malleable, only because they are new. Distributors in emerging markets may be more receptive to the guidance of foreign companies in implementing a mutually beneficial relationship between manufacturer and distributor. The current phase of Decelerated Pro-Activity in emerging markets allows manufacturers not to repeat the mistakes of the past; they can still proactively affect the evolution of distribution networks and distribution structures within selected distributors in a given emerging market. In determining a company's distribution strategy, an eleven-step process, as described in Chapter 4, is undertaken by which an enlightened manufacturer can begin to formulate its entry sales and distribution strategies for emerging markets.

It is estimated that more than US$7 trillion of world trade is annually conducted through traditional distribution channels. Unfortunately, many Western firms fail in emerging markets because they do not have sufficient firsthand knowledge about and experience in their targeted emerging markets. Additionally, most firms fail to properly select and recruit appropriate emerging market distributors or fail to develop strategies that best enable their companies to sufficiently monitor and control their emerging markets distributors in a particular market. Neglecting to implement the proper strategies and select the appropriate emerging markets distributors will almost certainly guarantee failure in the sales and distribution of their products.

The best way for many companies to prosper in emerging markets is through the proper application of new and different distribution strategies quite different from the ones used in mature, industrialized markets. Outdated strategies include passing or affixing Western value judgments upon the businesses and business people in emerging markets.

Many of America's and Europe's most successful companies have initially sold their products into new markets with great expectations, only to realize later that they were blocked either entirely or effectively from doing the business they intended because of unknown local factors. Undisclosed family relationships, unknown representation of competitive products in other companies set up by the same distributor for the sole purpose of deceiving the foreign manufacturer, and unstated real intentions are all the ways in which unsuspecting companies have been blindsided in emerging markets. While such lessons may be considered invaluable, they usually come at exceptionally high prices.

The "Black Hole Syndrome" of distribution is an all too common occurrence for those aspiring to succeed in emerging markets. Orders are filled and shipped to foreign customers only to have the product disappear into a "black hole" of distribution analogous to the distant vacuums that astronomers have recently discovered in outer space. After a few months, manufacturers sometimes cannot even locate their products, or their products are sold differently and at prices never intended by the manufacturer. Stories abound of companies selling their products with all the right intentions to a customer only to discover later that their units were being used for completely different purposes.

Fortunately, help may be available that allows us to avoid such hazards. Setting up the right distribution channels with the right distributor is one of the biggest challenges facing foreign companies entering an emerging market. New entrants often find themselves competing against multinational and local companies with well-established distribution networks. Moreover, companies are increasingly spending more on improving distribution, inventory management, and merchandising as they strive to maintain or gain a marketing advantage.

Although its critical importance cannot be overstated, distribution is generally the most globally differentiated and least understood of all marketing mix components. It is also the component most likely to hinder success in foreign markets for small and mid-size companies. These companies simply do not have access to the sizable resources of much larger companies. Proper distribution planning aims to ensure that the best available channels and physical distribution methods are in place to efficiently and economically get the right products and services to the right customers at the right time and right place and in the right form. In the global marketplace, where channels lengthen and materials handling problems multiply, sometimes exponentially, effective sales and distribution strategies coupled with efficient channel and physical distribution systems can help offset high costs and help level the competitive playing field.

Once a foreign company acquires a reasonably good understanding of the situation in the marketplace, it is necessary to embark upon the eleven critical steps leading firms use to recruit and select an emerging market distributor. The goal in this process is to establish a relationship which is forthright, mutually beneficial, and built upon a strong foundation. Moreover, the key theme that permeates the eleven-step process is to quickly and solidly establish the manufacturer on an "equal footing" with the emerging market distributor so to preempt any deception or "gamesmanship" being applied by the distributor to establish control of the relationship with the manufacturer. Although some of the steps may appear less relevant than others in light of a given situation, the proper application of these comprehensive steps will minimize the likelihood of choosing the wrong distributor.

Before considering how to integrate your company into your distributor's business, it is important to consider what you expect from your relationship with your distributor and the distributor with you. The relationship between a company and its distributors can be highly complex. On the side of the distributor, several responsibilities must dominate its thinking. These responsibilities need to be communicated by the manufacturer to the distributor in order to assist in the process of training and communicating with the distributor. Further, the responsibilities of the manufacturer are equally important to the development of the relationship.

Once the respective responsibilities are understood, it is incumbent for the manufacturer to embark upon as thorough a training of the distributor's staff as your company's resources can permit. The overriding benefit of training is the exertion of control and the ability of the manufacturer to influence the distributor's business and its people. Moreover, distributors often lack the skills, knowledge of your product line, and marketing know-how to conduct their own training and feel highly indebted if good programs are made available. It is critical for manufacturers to properly train key employees, not just sales people. Like in your company, non-sales personnel are constantly being trained to provide the necessary support to the various aspects of your organization. The same needs to take place with your distributors.

The training of key employees in your distributor's organization needs, however, to be tempered with the particular needs of the business. It is important to make people more valuable, but not too valuable. Employees who know more than they need to know can often become ex-employees or even competitors of your distributor's company.

The manufacturer also needs to develop a communications plan that enhances the quality and quantity of interaction between manufacturer and distributor. Such a plan works to minimize communication problems as well as avoid future and potentially threatening issues.

At the core of distributor control is the continuous monitoring of distributor's key operations that are integral in the successful marketing, sales, distribution, and servicing of your products. Control is monitoring these key operations to detect differences between actual and desired performance standards, so as to make appropriate adjustments.

Most Western companies will say that, although the business climate in emerging markets can at best be described as difficult, the opportunities still far outweigh the risks. Nevertheless, a failure to pay attention to the details of the relationship can seriously undermine a company's ability to succeed in high-growth emerging markets. Nowhere is this attention to detail more important than in the distributor agreement. Still, the distributor agreement is one of the most misunderstood documents within the realm of international business. Time and again, businesspeople fall into the trap of ascribing a higher value to the document than should probably exist. As most agreements are so complex and so detailed, so difficult to follow and understand, and moreover, require so much time and energy to construct and execute, it is only natural to justify all of this by placing a strong emphasis upon them.

If it is the manufacturer's goal to effectively market and sell its products in a given emerging market, the manufacturer will need to recognize that a document prepared by and agreed to by lawyers will simply not accomplish this formidable task. A distributor will be successful in marketing and selling the manufacturer's products only if it is highly motivated to do so, if there is significant sales and profit, and if there exists an overall constructive business relationship between them. In other words, only highly motivated, right-thinking distributors employing solid, cogent business plans will successfully market and sell a manufacturer's product.

Often, distributor agreements seemingly create the impression that the document itself has generated business. Too often, distributor agreements include agreed levels or objectives for opening inventory and ongoing inventory stocking levels and traditional monthly and annual purchase forecasts that may give the document a false illusion of currency and of value to the manufacturer. The enlightened manufacturer understands that although the document appropriately states all of these elements and more, the distributor agreement hardly guarantees any specific inventory stocking levels or any ongoing levels of sales performance.

The process for establishing successful sales and distribution strategies in high-growth emerging markets is undoubtedly formidable. However, nothing that is worth having comes easy. Through the application of this process, companies in the United States, Western Europe, and Japan will be able to better understand what is needed in order to maximize the opportunities found in emerging markets.

Global Manifest Destiny is producing a new economic game, with new rules requiring new strategies to win. Moreover, these new influences are compelling corporations, investors, governments, non-profits, and, most important, individuals to look at the world in a completely different way. Some of today's players in this new game will adapt and learn how to win. They will be those who understand the march of Global Manifest Destiny. They will become the top of the food chain, the "fittest of the fit" individuals, organizations, firms, or nations. Those who fail to understand will be relegated to irrelevance and obscurity, rolled over by the unstoppable advance of Global Manifest Destiny.

Appendix: Emerging Market Local Information Sources

In the following pages, we have put together a set of basic contact information for several economies. While we have done our best to include the very latest and most complete information, we cannot guarantee that some details will not have changed by or after publication.

Listings of foreign, private, or non-governmental organizations in this directory do not suggest their endorsement.

ARGENTINA

Country Government Agencies

Adminstracion Nacional de Aduanas (Customs Administration)
Contact: Lic. Gustavo A. Parino, National Administration
Azopardo 350
Buenos Aires
Tel: 54–1-331–7606/35
Fax: 54-1-331–9881; 345–1778

Ministerio De Economia (Ministry of Economy)
Contact: Dr. Domingo F. Cavallo (Minister)
Hipolito Yrigoyen 250
Buenos Aires
Tel: 54–1-342–6411; 342–6421/29
Fax: 54–1-331–0292

Secretaria De Comercio E Inversiones (Secretariat of Trade and Investment)
Contact: Dr. Carlos Sanchez
Hipolito Yrigoyen 250
Buenos Aires
Tel: 54–1-331–2208
Fax: 54–1-349–5422

Secretaria De Hacienda (Secretariat of Finance)
Contact: Mr. Ricardo Angel Guiterrez
Hipolito Yrigoyen 250
Buenos Aires
Tel: 54–1-331–0731; 342–2937
Fax: 54–1-349–6116

Secretaria De Industria (Secretariat of Industry)
Contact: Lic. Carlos A. Magarinso
Av. J.A. Roca 651
1322 Buenos Aires
Tel: 54–1-349–3406/07/08
Fax: 54–1-331–3218

Ministerio De Relaciones Exteriores (Ministry of Foreign Affairs)
Contact: Ing. Guido Mario Di Tella (Minister)
Reconquista 1088
1003 Buenos Aires
Tel: 54–1-331–0071/9
Fax: 54–1-312–3593/3423

Secretaria de Relaciones Economicas Internacionales (Secretariat of International Economic Relations)
Contact: Ing. Jorge Campbell
Reconquista 1088
1003 Buenos Aires
Tel: 54–1-331–7281/4073
Fax: 54–1-312–0965

Law Firms in Argentina

Brons and Salas
Contact: Dr. Thomas Boywitt, Partner
Marcelo T. de Alvear 624, Piso 1
1058 Buenos Aires, Argentina
Tel: 54–1-331–9271/79
Fax: 54–1-331–7025

Camara Argentina de Supermaercados (Association of Supermarkets)
Dr. Ovidio Vicente Bolo, President
Paraguay 577, Piso 3
1057 Buenos Aires

Tel: 54–1-312–3790/5419
Fax: 54–1-312–5846

Associacion de Importadores Y Exportadores De La Rep. Argentina (Association of Argentine Importers and Exporters)
Lic. Fernando A. Raimondo, President
Belgrano 124, Piso 1
1092 Buenos Aires
Tel: 54–1-342–0010/0018/0019
Fax: 54–1-342–1312

Camara de Importadores de La Republica Argentina (Chamber of Importers)
Mr. Diego Perez Santisteban, President
Av. Belgrano 427, Piso 7
1092 Buenos Aires
Tel: 54–1-342–1101/0523
Fax: 54–1-331–9342

Camara de Comercio Exteriordel Centro de La Republica
(Chamber of Foreign Trade of Central Argentina)
Eng. Victor Muscaria, President
Av. Callao 332, P.B.
1022 Buenos Aires
Tel: 54–1-46–6912

Camara de Comercio, Industria y Produccion de La Rep. Argentina
(Chamber of Commerce, Industry and Production of the Argentine Republic)
Dra. Maria Arsenia Tula, President
Florida 1, Piso 4
1005 Buenos Aires
Tel: 54–1-342–8252; 343–5638; 331–0813
Fax: 54–1-331–9116

Bolsa de Comercio Buenos Aires (Buenos Aires Stock Exchange)
Dr. Jullio A. Maccki, President
Sarmiento 299, Piso 1
1353 Buenos Aires
Tel: 54–1-331–5231/33/1174; 313–4812/4544
Fax: 54–1-312–9332

Country Market Research Firms

R.G. Asociados
Defensa 649, P.5 "A"
1265 Buenos Aires
Tel: 54–1-342–9355

A&C
Salta 1007

1074 Buenos Aires
Contact: Dr. Carlos Kaplan
Tel: 54–1-27–9007; 304–6309/8213
Fax: 54–1-27–8800

Guillermo Bravo y Associado
Av. De Mayo 1480 E.P.
Buenos Aires
Contact: Dr. Guillermo Bravo
Tel/Fax: 54–1-381–7892/2540/5625

Mercados Direcxtos
Lavalle 1515, Piso 1
1048 Buenos Aires
Tel: 54–1-375–0772/73
Fax: 54–1-375–2012

Country Commercial Banks

Banco de la Nacion Argentina
Bartolome Mitre 326
Contact: Dr. Aldo Antonio Dadone, President
1036 Buenos Aires
Tel: 54–1-343–1011/21
Fax: 54–1-331–8745

Banco de la Provincia De Buenos Aires
San Martin 137
1004 Buenos Aires
Contact: Lic. Rodolfo Figeri, President
Tel: 54–1-331–2561/9/4011/3584

Citibank N.A.
Bme. Mitre 530
1036 Buenos Aires
Contact: St. Jorge Bermudez, President
Tel: 54–1-329–1000; 331–8281/4031
Fax: 54–1-331–8180

Banco Rio de La Plata S.A.
Bme. Mitre 480
1036 Buenos Aires
Contact: Sr. J. Gregorio Perez Companc, President
Tel: 54–1-331–0555/7551/8361

BRAZIL

Country Government Agencies

Banco Central do Brasil
Brazilian Central Bank
SBS—Edificio Sede do Banco Central do Brasil
70074–900 Brasília, DF
Tel: 55–61–214–1020–214–1000
Fax: 55–61–224–4119

Banco do Brasil S-A-BB
Bank of Brazil
SBS, Qd.4, Lote 32, Bloco C,
Ed, Sede III, 20 andar
70073–900 Brasília, DF
Tel: 55–61–212–2211
Fax: 55–61–2230156

Empresa Brasileira de Telecomunicacoqes—Embratel
Brazilian Long Distance Telephone Company
Av. Presidente Vargas 1013
Edificio Sede, 15 andar
20179–900 Rio de Janeiro, RJ
Tel: 55–21–216–8182
Fax: 55–21–224–1175

Instituto Nacional da Propriedade Industrial (INPI)
Brazilian Industrial Property Institute
Praca Maua 7, 18 andar-Centro
20081–240 Rio de Janeiro, RJ
Tel: 55–21–291–1224
Fax: 55–21–263–2539

Ministerio da Industria e Comercio-MIC
Ministry of Industry and Commerce
Esplanada dos Ministerios, Bloco J, 6 andar
70056–900 Brasília, DF
Tel: 55–61–225–8105

Secretaria de Comercio Exterior
Secretariat of Foreign Trade
Esplanada Dos Ministrios
Bloco J, 8 andar
70056–900 Brasília, DF
Tel: 55–61–224–0639
Fax: 55–61–225–7230

Ministerio da Fazenda—MF
Ministry of Finance

Esplanada dos Ministrios—Bloco P
70048–900 Brasília, DF
Tel: 55–61–314–2000
Fax: 55–61–223–5239

Country Trade Associations

Automotive Components Manufacturers—Sindpecas
Rua Abilio Soares 1487
04005–005 Sao Paulo, SP
Tel: 55–11–884–4599
Fax: 55–11–884–0584

Dental, Medical, and Hospital Equipment
Sindicato Da Industria De Artigos E Equipamentos Odontologicos Medicos E
Hospitalares E De Laboratorios
Av. Paulista 1313, 8 andar, CJ 806
01311–923 Sao Paulo, SP
Tel: 55–11–285–0155
Fax: 55–11–285–0018

Electric and Electronics Industry
Associacao Brasileira Da Industria Eletrica E Eletronica—Abinee
Av. Paulista 1313, 7 andar
01311–923 Sao Paulo, SP
Tel: 55–11–241–1577
Fax: 55–11–285–0607

Electrical Energy
Sindicato Da Industria De Energia Eletrica
Almeda Campinas 433, 10 andar
01404–901 Sao Paulo, SP
Tel: 55–11–288–1166
Fax: 55–11–288–8524

Food Processing—Dairy Products
Sindicato Da Industria De Latcinios E Produtos Derivados
Praca Dom Jose Gaspar, 30, 10 andar
01047–901 Sao Paulo, SP
Tel: 55–11–259–3251
Fax: 55–11–259–8482

Franchising
Associacao Brasileira De Franchising—ABF
Travessa Meruipe 18
04012–000 Sao Paulo, SP
Tel: 55–11–571–1393
Fax: 55–11–575–5590

Food
Associacao Brasileira Das Industrias Da Alimentaco—Abia
Av. Brig Faria Lima 2003
11 andar cjs. 1104–1116
01451–001 Sao Paulo, SP
Tel: 55–11–816–5733
Fax: 55–11–814–6688

Machine Manufacturers
Associaca Brasileira De Maquinas—Abimaq
Av. Jabaquara 2925, 3 andar
04045–902 Sao Paulo, SP
Tel: 55–11–579–5044
Fax: 55–11–579–3498

Material Handling and Storage
Instituto de Movimentacao E Armazenagem de Materiais—Imam
Rua Topazio 243
04105–904 Sao Paulo, SP
Tel: 55–11–277–9188
Fax: 55–11–277–9144

Motor Vehicles: Importers
Associacao Brasileira Dos Importadores De Veiculos Automotores—Abeiva
Rua Bento da Andrade 103
04503–010 Sao Paulo, SP
TeleFax: 55–11–884–1622

Motor Vehicles: Independent Importers
Associacao Brasileira Dos Importadores Independents de Veiculos Automotores
Av. Brigaderio Faria Lima 1885, 4 andar cj 420
01451–001 Sao Paulo, SP
TeleFax: 55–11–211–9447

Pharmaceuticals
Associacao Brasileira De Industria Farmaceutica—Abifarma
Rua Beira Rio 57, 7 andar
04548–050 Sao Paulo, SP
Tel: 55–11–820–3775
Fax: 55–11–822–6628

Plastics
Sindicato Da Industria De Material Plastico
Av. Paulista 24.39, 8 andar, cjs, 81–82
01311–936 Sao Paulo, SP
Tel: 55–11–282–8288
Fax: 55–11–282–8042

Printing
Associacao Brasileira Da Industria Grafica
Rua Marques de Itu 70, 12 andar

01270–900 Sao Paulo, SP
Tel: 55–11–231–4733

Railway and Highway Equipment
Sindicato Interestadual Da Industria De Materiais E Equipamentos Ferroviarios E
Rodoviarios-Simefre
Av. Paulista 1313, 8 andar cj. 811
01311–923 Sao Paulo, SP
Tel: 55–11–289–9166
Fax: 55–11–289–5823

Road Transportation
Associacao Nacional Das Empresas De Trasportes Rodoviarios De Carga—NTC
Rua da Gavea 1390
02121–020 Sao Paulo, SP
Tel: 55–11–954–1400
Fax: 55–11–954–1127

Software
Associacao Brasileira Das Empresas De Software
Av. Brig Faria Lima 1857, 3 andar, cj 307
01451–001 Sao Paulo, SP
Tel: 55–11–813–2057–9511–0704
Fax: 55–11–815–0359

(State of Sao Paulo Federation of Industries)
Federacao Das Industrias Do Estado De Sao Paulo—Fiesp
Av. Paulista 1313
01311–923 Sao Paulo, SP
Tel: 55–11–251–3522
Fax: 55–11–284–3971

(State of Rio de Janeiro Federation of Industries)
Federacao Das Industrias Do Estado Do Rio de Janeiro
Av. Calgeras 25, 9 andar
20030–070 Rio de Janeiro, RJ
Tel: 55–21–292–3939
Fax: 55–21–262–6705

Country Market Research Firms

A.C. Nielsen S-C Ltda
Av. Bernardino de Campus, 98, 9° andar
04004–040 Sao Paulo, SP
Tel: 55–11–889–7077
Fax: 55–11–889–8220

Booz, Allen & Hamilton Do Brasil Consultors Ltda
Rua Gomes De Carvalho, 1765, 5 andar

04547–901 Sao Paulo, SP
Tel: 55–11–820–1900
Fax: 55–11–820–6750

Bichuetti Consultoria Empresarial S-C Ltda
Av. Brig. Faria Lima 1541–6B
01451–000 Sao Paulo, SP
Tel: 55–11–813–9744
Fax: 55–11–816–0908

Barros Riebeiro Planejamento, Consultoria E Representacoes Ltda
Rua Dr. Joao Climaco Pereira 46
04532–070 Sao Paulo, SP
Tel: 55–11–820–7422
Fax: 55–11–820–0720

Adela Empreendimentos E Consultoria Ltda
Av. Brig. Faria Lima 1541, 7 andar, cj 7D
01451–000 Sao Paulo, SP
Tel: 55–11–813–711
Fax: 55–11–212–7675

Lindsey Consultores S-C Ltda
Rua Bela Cintra 1932
01415–002 Sao Paulo, SP
Tel: 55–11–280–8122
Fax: 55–11–853–7787

Country Commercial Banks

Most Banks in Brazil operate as multiple banks, accumulating the functions of commercial and investment banks, and are also active in the capital market.

Banco Brasilerio de Descontos—BRADESCO—Sao Paulo

Banco itau—Sao Paulo

Banco Nacional—Minas Gerais

Banco Bamerindus—Parana

Uniao de Bancos Brasileiros—UNIBANCO

Banco Safra—Sao Paulo

Banco Econmico—Bahia

Banco de Credito Nacional—BCN—Sao Paulo

Banco Bozano Simonsen—Rio de Janeiro

Banco Mercantil de Sao Paulo—Sao Paulo

CHINA

Country Government Agencies

Minstry of Foreign Trade and Economic Cooperation
2 Dongehangan Avenue
Dongeheng District
Beijing 100731
Tel: 8610–519–8804
Fax: 8610–519–8904

Ministry of Communications
10 Fuxing Road, Haidian District
Beijing 100845
Tel: 8610–326–5544

Ministry of Power Industry
137 Fuyoujie, Xicheng District
Beijing 100031
Tel: 8610–602–3816
Fax: 8610–601–6077

Ministry of Agriculture
11 Nongzhanguan Nanli
Beijing 100026
Tel: 8610–500–4363
Fax: 8610–500–2448

Environmental Protection Agency
15 Xizhimennei Nanziaojie, Xicheng District
Beijing 100035
Tel: 8610–601–5642
Fax: 8610–601–5641

Country Trade Associations

China Council for the Promotion of International Trade
1 Fuzingmenwai Street
Beijing 100860
Tel: 8610–851–3344
Fax: 8610–851–1370

China Chamber of International Commerce
1 Fuxingmenwai Street
Beijing 100860
Tel: 8610–851–3344
Fax: 8610–851–1370

All-China Federation of Industry and Commerce
93 Beiheyan Dajie, Dongcheng
Beijing 100006
Tel: 8610–512–7232/513–6677
Fax: 8610–513–1769

Country Market Research Firms

Beijing Explorer Design and Communications Corporation
44 A Baishiiao Road
Beijing 100081
Tel: 8610–831–4488
Fax: 8610–823–3164

China International Economic Consultants, Inc.
13/F Capital Mansion
6 Xin Yuan Nan Road
P.O. Box 9412
Beijing 100004
Tel: 8610–455–0088; 466–3012
Fax: 8610–466–2468

All China Marketing Research Company
No. 3 Yuetan Beijie
Beijing 100037
Tel: 8610–835–4703
Fax: 8610–835–4718

The Gallup Organization
G-202 Huiyuan Gongyu International
Asian Games Village, Beijing 100101
Tel: 8610–499–1749
Fax: 8610–499–1749

Pinnacle Management
Room 359 Shangrila Hotel
Beijing 100081
Tel: 8610–841–2211 or 842–5669
Fax: 8610–842–8271

Country Commercial Banks

People's Bank of China
32 Chengfang Street
Beijing, China 100800
Tel: 86–1-601–6705/601–6707
Fax: 86–1-601–6704

Bank of China
410 Fuchengmennei Daije
Beijing, China 100034
Tel: 86–1–601–1829

Industrial and Commercial Bank of China
26 Xichangan Street
Beijing, China 100031
Tel: 86–1–603–1062
Fax: 86–1–603–1056

Investment Bank of China
B11 Azuo Fuxing Road, Meidya Hotel Office
Bldg. #4455
Beijing, China 100038
Tel: 86–1–851–5900
Fax: 86–1–851–6088

State Development Bank
Yulong Hotel, 40 Fucheng Road, Haidian District
Beijing, China 100046
Tel: 86–1–843–7253
Fax: 86–1–843–7254

INDIA

Country Government Agencies

Central Board of Excise and Customs
Tel: 91–11–301–2849

Department of Revenue
Ministry of Finance
Government of India
156 E, North Block
New Delhi, 100 001 India
Fax: 91–11–301–6475

Bureau of Indian Standards (BIS)
Manah Bhavan
9 Bahadur Shah Zafar Marg
New Delhi 110 002 India
Tel: 91–11–331–0131
Fax: 91–11–331–4062

Drugs Controller
Director General of Health Services
Nirman Bhavan
New Delhi 110 011 India

Tel: 91–11–30–8438
Fax: 91–11–30–4252

Reserve Bank of India (RBI)
Shaheed Bagat Singh Road
P.O. Box 1055
Bombay 400 023 India
Tel: 91–22–286–1602
Fax: 91–22–286–5330

Department of Industrial Development
Secretariat for Industrial Approvals (SIA)
Udyog Bhavan
New Delhi 110 011 India
Tel: 91–11–301–1983
Fax: 91–11–301–1770

Country Trade Associations/Chambers of Commerce

Federation of Indian Chambers of Commerce & Industry
Foreign Investment & Trade Promotion Office (FITPO)
Federation House, Tansen Marg.
New Delhi 110 001 India
Tel: 91–11–331–9251
Fax: 91–11–332–0714

Confederation of Indian Industry
23.26 Institutional Area
Lodi Road
New Delhi 110 003 India
Tel: 91–11–462–9994
Fax: 91–11–463–3168

The Associated Chambers of Commerce and Industry of India (ASSOCHAM)
Allahabd Bank Building (2nd Floor)
17 Parliament Street
New Delhi 110 001 India
Tel: 91–11–310704
Fax: 91–11–312193

Indian Merchants Chamber
Secretary General Churchgate
Bombay 400 020 India
Tel: 91–22–204–6633
Fax: 91–22–204–8505

The Chairman
Indian Investment Centre
Jeevan Vihar Blg.

Sansad Marg
New Delhi 110 001 India
Tel: 91–11–373–3673
Fax: 91–11–373–2245

INDONESIA

Country Government Agencies

Minister, Department of Agriculture
JL Harsono R.M. 3
Ragunan, Bldg. A
Pasar Minggu, Jakarta 12550
Indonesia

Minister, Department of Foreign Affairs
Ali Atlatas, SH
I. Taman Pejambon 6
Jakarta, Indonesia
Tel: 62–21–345–6014
Fax: 62–21–384–9412

Minister, Department of Industry
Kav 52–53
Jakarta, Indonesia
Tel: 62–21–520–0700
Fax: 62–21–520–1606

Minister, State Ministry for Investment
Capital Investment Coordinating Board
JI. Jend Gatot Subroto 44.
2nd Floor
Tel: 62–21–525–0023
Fax: 32–21–525–4945

Minister, Department of Trade
JI. M. I. Ridwwan Rais 5
3rd Floor
Jakarta, Indonesia
Tel: 62–21–384–8667
Fax: 62–21–374–361

Minister, Department of Communications
JI. Merdeka Barat 8
9th Floor
Jakarta, Indonesia

Tel: 62–21–345–6332
Fax: 62–21–345–1657

Country Trade Associations/Chambers of Commerce

Kadin (Indonesian Chamber of Commerce)
Jalan M.H. Thamrin 20
Jakarta 10350
Tel: 62–21–315–0242
Fax: 62–21–525–1589

Importers Association of Indonesia (GINSI)
CTC Building, 4th Floor
Jl. Kramat Raya 94–96
PO Box 2744, Jakarta 10027
Tel: 62–21–390–1559, 390–8480
Fax: 62–21–390–479

Indonesian Exporters Association (GPEI)
Jalan Kramat Raya 4–6,
Jakarta Pusat
Tel: 62–21–356–099

HPMI (Himpunan Pengusaha Muda Indonesia)
(Young Businessmen Association of Indonesia)
Jl. Raya Pasar Minggu 1-A
Jakarta 12780
Tel: 62–21–797–2233/2299
Fax: 62–21–797–2233

Country Market Research Firms

Inkindo, The Association of Indonesian Consultants
Jalan Bendungan Hilir Raya
No. 29. Jakarta Pusat
Indonesia
Tel: 62–21–573–8577/78
Fax: 62–21–573–3474

Importers Association of Indonesia (GPEI)
Jalan Kramat Raya 4–6
Jakarta Pusat
Tel: 62–21–356–099

National Agency for Export Development
Jl. Gajah Madfa No. 8
Jakarta 10130

Tel: 62–21–362–666, 384–5096, 385–7184
Fax: 62–21–384–4588, 384–8380, 385–3135

P.T. SRI International
Wisma Bank Dharmala, 15th Floor
JI. Jend Sudirman Kav 28
Jakarta 12920, Indonesia
Tel: 62–21–521–2200
Fax: 62–21–521–2203

Business Advisory Indonesia
Kuningan Plaza, Suite 304 North
JI. H.R. Rasuna Said CII-14
Jakarta 12941, Indonesia
Tel: 62–21–520–7696, 520–7689
Fax: 62–21–525–0604

Harvest International
Wisma Metropolitan I, 10th Floor
Jalan Jendral Sudriman, KAV 29
Jakarta Pusat, 12920 Indonesia
Tel: 62–21–525–1641
Fax: 62–21–520–7789

Country Commercial Banks

Indonesia has one of the most deregulated, market-based banking systems in the developing world. Since the 1988 banking deregulation package, the Indonesian banking sector has expanded rapidly, presenting numerous financing options to exporters.

Bank Umum Nasional
JI. Prapatan 50
Jakarta
Tel: 62–21–365563

Bank Niaga
JI. M.H. Thamrin 55
Jakarta Pusat
Tel: 62–21–333936

Bank Bali
Bank Bali Building, 7th Floor
JI. Hayam Wuruk No. 84.85
Jakarta
Tel: 62–21–649–8006

MALAYSIA

Country Government Agencies

Ministry of International Trade and Industry (MITI)
Blk. 10, Government Offices Complex
Jalan Duta
5–622 Kuala Lumpur
Tel: 60–3-254–0033
Fax: 60–3-255–0827

Ministry of Energy, Telecommunications and Posts
1st Floor, Wisma Damansara
Japan Semantan
59668 Kuala Lumpur
Tel: 60–3-256–2222
Fax: 60–3-255–7901

Malaysian Industrial Development Agency (MIDA)
Wisma Damasara, Jalan Semantan
P.O. Box 10618
50720 Kuala Lumpur
Tel: 60–3-255–3633
Fax: 60–3-255–7970

Country Trade Associations/Chambers of Commerce

Federation of Malaysian Manufacturers (FMM)
17th Floor, Wisma Sime Darby
Jalan Raja Laut, 50359 Kuala Lumpur
Tel: 60–3-293–1244
Fax: 60–3-293–5105

Malaysian International Chamber of Commerce and Industry
Wisma Damansara
P.O. Box 10192
50706 Kuala Lumpur
Tel: 60–3-254–2205
Fax: 60–3-255–4946

PITO Malaysia
(Private Investment and Trade Opportunities)
Yee Seng Building, 7th Floor
15 Jalan Raja Chulan
50200 Kuala Lumpur

Tel: 60–3-238–9491
Fax: 60–3-238–9493

Country Market Research Firms

J. Walter Thompson SDN, BHD
21st Floor, Wisma Sime Darby
Jalan Raja Laut
50350 Kuala Lumpur
Tel: 60–3-291–7788
Fax: 60–3-293–9363

Burson-Marsteller (M) SDN, BHD
11th Floor, Bangunan Getah Asli
148 Jalan Ampang
50450 Kuala Lumpur
Tel: 60–3-261–7900
Fax: 60–3-261–3828

Leo Burnett Advertising SDN, BHD
10th Floor, MCB Plaza
6 Changkat Raja Chulan
50200 Kuala Lumpur
Tel: 60–3-201–0998
Fax: 60–3-201–0972S

Lintas Worldwide SDN, BHD
Wisma Perdana, Jalan Dungun
Damansara Heights
50490 Kuala Lumpur
Tel: 60–3-254–5122
Fax: 60–3-255–9985

McCann Erikson SDN, BHD
18th Floor, Menara Aik Hua
Changkat Raja Chulun
50200 Kuala Lumpur
Tel: 60–3-230–5677
Fax: 60–3-230–5598

Country Commercial Banks

European exporters should encourage their Malaysian clients to seek financing assistance from banks and financial institutions in the country. The banking sector is now generally very liquid and flush with cash. The banking system comprises Bank Negara (the Central Bank), commercial banks, merchant banks, finance companies, the National Savings Bank, the Islamic Bank, and development and finance intermediaries such as unit trusts and the provident fund.

Bank Bumiputra Malaysia Berhad
Menara Bumiputra, Jalan Melaka
50100 Kuala Lumpur
P.O. Box 10407
50913 Kuala Lumpur
Tel: 60–3-298–8011

Malaysian Banking BHD
Menara Maybank, Bukit Mahkamah
100 Jalan Tun Perak
50050 Kuala Lumpur
Tel: 60–3-230–8833

Security Pacific Asian Bank
Plaza See Hoy Chan
Jalan Raja Chulan
50200 Kuala Lumpur
Tel: 60–3-238–7922

United Malayan Banking Corporation
Banguan UMBC
Jalan Sultan Sulaiman
50935 Kuala Lumpur
Tel: 60–3-230–5833

Standard Chartered Bank
2, Jalan Ampang
50450 Kuala Lumpur
Tel: 60–3-232–6555

Bank of Commerce
6 Jalan Tun Perak
50050 Kuala Lumpur
Tel: 60–3-292–1722
Fax: 60–3-298–6628

MBF Finance Berhad
Plaza MBF
P.O. Box 10027
50901 Kuala Lumpur
Tel: 60–3-261–1177
Fax: 60–3-261–8124

MEXICO

Country Government Agencies

Secretaria de Comercio y Fomento Industrial (SECOFI)
(Secretariat of Commerce and Industrial Development)

Alfonso Reyes 30, Piso 9
Colonia Hipodromo-Condesa
06140 Mexico, D.F.
Tel: 52–5-729–9100
Fax: 52–5-729–9343

Instituto Mexicano de la Propiedad Industrial y Desarrollo Tecnologico
(Mexican Insitute of Industrial Property and Technological Development)
Azafran 18, Piso 3
Colonia Granjas Mexico
08400 Mexico, D.F.
Tel: 52–5-650–4928
Fax: 52–5-654–0771

Secretaria de Medio Ambiente Recursos Naturales y Eso (SEMARNAP)
(Secretariat for the Environment, Natural Resources, and Fisheries)
Rio Elba 20, Piso 16
Colonia Cuauhtemoc
06500 Mexico, D.F.
Tel: 52–5-553–9538
Fax: 52–5-286–6625

Secretaria de Comunicaciones y Transporte (SCT)
(Sectretariat of Communications and Transport)
Centro Nacional SCT
Edificio "C", 1er Piso
Xola y Avenida Universidad
Colonia Narvarte
03028 Mexico, D.F.
Tel: 52–5-530–3060/538–0945/519–5201/0680
Fax: 52–5-559–8708

Country Trade Associations/Chambers of Commerce

Camara Nacional de Comercio de la Ciudad de Mexico (CANACO)
(National Chamber of Commerce of Mexico City)
Paseo de la Reforma 42
Colonia Centro
06048 Mexico, D.F.
Tel: 52–5-705–0424
Fax: 52–5-705–5310

Confederacion de Camaras
Nacionales de Comercio (CONCANACO)
(Confederation of National Chambers of Commerce)
Balderas 144, Piso 3
Colonia Centro
06079 Mexico, D.F.

Tel: 52–5-709–1559
Fax: 52–5-709–1152

Camara Nacional de la Industria de la Transformacion
(National Manufacturing Industry Chamber)
Avenida San Antonio 256
Colonia Ampliacion Napoles
03849 Mexico, D.F.
Tel: 52–5-563–3400
Fax: 52–5-598–9467

Confederacion de Camaras Industriales de los Estados Unidos Mexicanos
(CONCAMIN)
(Confederation of Industrial Chambers of Mexico)
Colonia San Rafael
06570 Mexico, D.F.
Tel: 52–5-566–7822
Fax: 52–5-535–6871

Associacion Nacional de Importadores y Exportadores de la Republica Mexicana
(ANIERM)
(Association of Importers and Exporters of Mexico)
Monterrey 130
Colonia Roma
Tel: 52–5-584–9522
Fax: 52–5-584–5317

Country Market Research Firms

Arthur D. Little de Mexico, S.A.
Sinaloa 149, Piso 10
Colonia Roma Norte
06700 Mexico, D.F.
Tel: 52–5-208–7564
Fax: 52–5-207–7592

Bisma S.A. De C.V.
Ingenieros Militares No. 91
Colonia Lomas de Sotelo
11200 Mexico, D.F.
Tel: 52–5-395–2181
Fax: 52–5-395–8648

Buro de Investigatcion de Mercado S.A.
Avenida Irrigacion No. 108
Colonia Irrigacion
11500 Mexico, D.F.
Tel: 52–5-557–2643
Fax: 52–5-557–1440

Marketing Services Mexicana, S.A.
Blvd. Adolfo Lopez Mateos 138, 1er Piso
Colonia Merced Gomez
03930 Mexico, D.F.
Tel: 52–5-651–3864
Fax: 52–5-660–4936

Norris & Elliott, S.A. De C.V.
Leibnitz 11, 4o Piso
Colonia Veronica Anzures
11590 Mexico, D.F.
Tel: 52–5-254–6402
Fax: 52–5-254–6434

Wilsa S.A.
Cozumel 60
Colonia Condesa
05140 Mexico, D.F.
Tel: 52–5-286–1531
Fax: 52–5-286–9457

Country Commercial Banks

Banco Nacional de Mexico S.A. (Banamex)
Palma 43, 3er Piso
Colonia Centro
06089 Mexico, D.F.
Tel: 52–5-225–6508
Fax: 52–5-225–5389

Bancomer
Eximbank Financing
Avenida Universidad 1200
Colonia Xoco
03339 Mexico, D.F.
Tel: 52–5-621–3434
Fax: 52–5-621–7635

Banco Internacional
Paseo de la Reforma 156, Piso 16
Colonia Juarez
06600 Mexico, D.F.
Tel: 52–5-721–2733
Fax: 52–5-721–2393

Multibanco Comermex
Lorenzo Boturini 206, 1er Piso
Colonia Transito
06920 Mexico, D.F.

Tel: 52–5-229–1678
Fax: 52–5-728–1795

PHILIPPINES

Country Government Agencies

Bangko Sentral NG Pilipinas
(Central Bank of the Philippines)
Malate
Manila
Tel: 632–507–051; 593–380
Fax: 632–522–3987

Board of Investments
(Investment and Marketing Department)
385 Sen. Gil J. Puyat Avenue
Makati City
Tel: 632–897–6682
Fax: 632–895–3521

Bureau of Customs
Port Area
Manila
Tel: 632–471–329; 474–421
Fax: 632–530–0966

Bureau of Export Trade Promotion
Department of Trade and Industry
357 Sen. Gil J. Puyat Avenue
Makati
Metro Manila
Tel: 632–817–5298; 817–5203
Fax: 632–817–4923; 819–1816

Bureau of International Trade Relations
Department of Trade and Industry
361 Sen. Gil J. Puyat Avenue
Makati
Metro Manila
Tel: 632–817–9695
Fax: 632–818–7846

Bureau of Trade Regulation and Consumer Protection
Department of Trade and Industry
2nd Floor, Trade and Industry Bldg.
361 Sen. Gil J. Puyat Avenue
Makati
Metro Manila
Tel: 632–817–5280; 817–5340
Fax: 632–810–9363

Department of Labour and Employment
DOLE Executive Bldg.
San Jose Street
Intramuros
Manila
Tel: 632–527–3466
Fax: 632–527–3568

Department of Trade and Industry
4th Floor, BOI Bldg.
385 Sen. Gil J. Puyat Avenue
Makati City
Tel: 632–816–0121; 818–456
Fax: 632–851–166

Export Processing Zone Authority
4th Floor, Legaspi Towers 300
Roxas Blvd.
Metro Manila
Tel: 632–521–9725
Fax: 632–521–8659

National Development Authority
Amber Avenue
Ortigas Complex
Pasig City
Tel: 632–631–3716; 631–0945
Fax: 632–631–3747

Securities and Exchange Commission
Corporate and Legal Department
7th Floor, SEC Bldg.
EDSA Greenhills
Mandaluyong City
Tel: 632–780–931
Fax: 632–722–0990

Country Trade Associations/Chambers of Commerce

Bankers Association of the Philippines
11th Floor, Sagitarius Bldg.
Dela Costa Street
Salcedo Village
Makati
Metro Manila
Tel: 632–851–711; 810–3858
Fax: 632–812–2870

Chamber of Real Estate & Builders Associations, Inc. (CREBA)
3rd Floor, CREBA Center
Don Alejandro Roces Avenue
cor South 'A' Street
Quezon City
Tel: 632–983–511
Fax: 632–998–401

Chemical Industries Association of the Philippines
c/o Rohm & Haas Phils., Inc.
12th Floor, PCI Tower II Bldg
Makati Avenue
cor. H.V. dela Costa Street
Makati City
Tel: 632–891–2140; 815–2088
Fax: 632–891–2140

Computers and Distributors and Dealers Association of the Philippines
7th Floor, SEDCCO 1 Bldg.
Legaspi cor Rada Streets
Legaspi Village
Makati City
Tel: 632–810–3814
Fax: 632–815–6531

Council of Engineering Consultants of the Philippines
2283 Manila Memorial Park Bldg.
Pasong Tamo Extension
Makati City
Tel: 632–815–2409
Fax: 632–818–0921

European Chamber of Commerce of the Philippines
5th Floor, Kings Court II Bldg.
Pasong Tamo
Makati
Metro Manila
Tel: 632–854–747; 866–9966
Fax: 632–815–2688

Garment Industry Association of the Philippines
Room 608, Dona Narcisa Bldg.
8751 Paseo de Roxas
Makati
Metro Manila
Tel: 632–813–7418; 883–943

Hospital, Medical, Laboratory Equipment & Supply Importers Association of the Philippines, Inc.
c/o 3–1 Philippines

704 Aurora Blvd.
Quezon City
Tel: 632–721–5211
Fax: 632–721–7012

Hotel and Restaurant Association of the Philippines
Room 205, Regina Bldg.
Aguirre Street
Legaspi Village
Makati
Metro Manila
Tel: 632–815–4659
Fax: 632–815–4663

Market Opinion and Research Society of the Philippines
3rd Floor, #60 Libertad Street
Mandaluyong City
Tel/Fax: 632–635–0130

Philippine Chamber of Commerce and Industry (PCCI)
Ground Floor, East Wing
Secretariat Bldg.
Philippine International Convention Center
CCP Complex
Roxas Boulevard
Pasay City
Tel: 632–833–8591; 833–8592
Fax: 632–833–8895

Philippine Chamber of Food Manufacturers, Inc.
8th Floor Liberty Bldg.
Pasay Road
Makati
Metro Manila
Tel: 632–865–011
Fax: 632–865–011

Philippine Constructors Association (PCA)
3rd Floor, Padilla Bldg.
Emerald Avenue
Ortigas Complex
Pasig City
Tel: 632–631–3135
Fax: 632–631–2788

Philippine Electronics and Telecommunications Federation
6th Floor, Telecoms Plaza

316 Sen. Gil J. Puyat Avenue
Makati City
Tel: 632–815–8921
Fax: 632–818–6967

Philippine Software Association, Inc. (PSA)
Mezzanine, Republic Glass Building
196 Salcedo Street
Legaspi Village
Makati City
Tel/Fax: 632–810–7391

Pollution Control Association of the Philippines (PCAPI)
Rms. 2114–2115, V.V. Soliven Bldg.
EDSA
Greenhills
San Juan
Metro Manila
Tel: 632–701–487
Fax: 632–701–487

Market Research Firms

Anderson Consulting
SGV Development Center
105 de la Rosa Street
Legaspi Village
Makati
Metro Manila
Tel: 632–817–0301
Fax: 632–817–2397

Applied Market Research, Inc.
No. 11 2nd Street Barrio Kapitolyo, Pasig City
Tel/Fax: 632–635–2419

Asia Pacific Center for Research
Rm. 411, Marbella I Condominium
2223 Roxas Boulevard
Pasay City
Tel: 632–831–5390
Fax: 632–833–3831

Philippine Survey and Research Center, Inc.
PSRC Bldg.
Calbayog cor. Kanlaon Streets
Mandaluyong City
Tel: 632–774–802
Fax: 632–774–805

Pulse Research Group
Pulse Research Bldg.
San Miguel Avenue
Ortigas Center
Pasig City
Tel: 632–631–1810
Fax: 632–631–6148

Total Research Needs-MBL, Inc.
149 Panay Avenue
Quezon City
Tel: 632–961–102
Fax: 632–922–2860

Country Commercial Banks

Allied Banking Corp.
6754 Ayala Avenue
Makati City
Tel: 632–810–2448
Fax: 632–810–2362

Bank of the Philippine Islands
BPJ Bldg. Ayala Avenue
Makati City
Tel: 632–816–9600
Fax: 632–818–8092

Development Bank of the Philippines
Makati and Sen. Gil J. Puyat Avenues
Makati
Metro Manila
Tel: 632–892–1866; 818–9511
Fax: 632–892–1866

Far East Bank & Trust Company
Muralla Street
Intramuros
Metro Manila
Tel: 632–530–0071
Fax: 632–49–2770

Philippine Banking Corporation
Ayala Avenue
Makati City
Tel: 632–812–9201; 817–0901
Fax: 632–817–0892

Philippine Commercial International Bank
PCI Bank Tower

Makati Avenue
Makati City
Tel: 632–817–2424
Fax: 632–818–3946

Philippine National Bank
PNB Financial Center
Roxas Blvd.
Manila
Tel: 632–891–6258
Fax: 632–891–626

Standard Chartered Bank
7901 Makati Avenue
Makati City
Tel: 632–817–2680
Fax: 632–815–5895

POLAND

Country Government Agencies

Ministry of Finance
ul. Swietokrzyska 12
00–490 Warsaw
Tel: 48–2–694–5555
Fax: 48–22–266–3552

Ministry of Foreign Economic Relations
Pl. Trzech Krzyzy 5
00–507 Warsaw
Tel: 48–2–693–5000 or 628–6125
Fax: 48–2–628–6808 or 625–4944

Ministry of Industry
ul. Wspolna 2/4
00–926 Warsaw
Tel: 48–2–628–0694 or 661–8111
Fax: 48–2–628–1758

Ministry of Privatization
ul. Krucza 36
00–049 Warsaw
Tel: 48–2–628–9531
Fax: 48–2–625–1114

The State Foreign Investment Agency
Aleja Roz 2
05–559 Warszawa

Tel: 48–22–295–717
Fax: 48–2–621–8427

Country Trade Associations/Chambers of Commerce

National Chamber of Commerce of Poland
ul. Trebacka 4
00–950 Warsaw
Tel: 48–22–260–0275
Fax: 48–22–274–6733

Business Foundation
ul. Krucza 38/42, Room 117
00–512 Warsaw
Tel: 48–2–628–2148
Fax: 48–2–621–9761

Polish Distributors Federation
ul. Okrezna 2
00–916 Warszawa
Tel: 48–22–409–154
Fax: 48–22–427–986

Company Assistance Ltd.
ul. Podwale 13
00–950 Warsaw
Tel: 48–2–635–8650
Fax: 48–22–317–920

Coopers & Lybrand
ul. Mokotowska 49
02–950 Warsaw
Tel: 48–2–660–0666
Fax: 48–2–660–0572

Deloitte & Touche
Small Business Chamber
ul. Smocza 27
01–048 Warszawa
Tel: 48–22–380–172
Fax: 48–22–383–553

Country Market Research Firms

Alcat Communications
ul. Karlowicza 9a
02–501 Warsaw

Tel: 48–22–484–640
Fax: 48–22–486–782

Ernst & Young
ul. Wspolna 62
00–844 Warsaw
Tel: 48–22–295–241
Fax: 48–22–294–263

Price Waterhouse
ul. Emilii Plater 28
00–688 Warsaw
Tel: 48–2-630–3030
Fax: 48–2-630–3040

Country Commercial Banks

Bank Handlowy W Warzawie SA (Commercial Bank SA)
ul. Chalubinskiego 8
00–950 Warszawa
Tel: 48–22–303–000
Fax: 48–22–300–113

Bank Depozytowo Kredyt Owy SA
ul. Chopina 6
20–928 Lublin
Tel: 48–81–217–12
Fax: 48–81–713–153

Bank Polska Kasa Opieki SA
ul. Traugutta 7/9
00–950 Warszawa
Tel: 48–2-269–211
Fax: 48–2-275–807

Bank Rozwoju Eksportu, SA
(Export Development Bank)
Plac Bankowy 2
00–950 Warszawa
Tel: 48–2-635–5926
Fax: 48–2-635–2713

Pomorski Bank Kredytowy SA
Pl. Zolnierza Polskiego 16
70–952 Szczecin
Tel: 48–91–334–769
Fax: 48–91–533–114

Bank Slaski SA
ul. Warzawska 14

40–950 Katowice
Tel: 48–3-1537–281
Fax: 48–3-1537–734

SINGAPORE

Country Government Agencies

Ministry of Trade and Industry
8 Shenton Way #48–01
Treasury Building 0106
Tel: 65–225–9911
Fax: 65–320–9260

Singapore Trade Development Board
1 Maritime Square, #10–40 (Lobby D)
World Trade Center
Telok Blangah Road (0409)
Tel: 65–271–9388
Fax: 65–274–0770, 278–2518, 271–0985

Registry of Companies and Business
18 Anson Road 05–01/15
International Plaza (0207)
Tel: 65–227–8551
Fax: 65–225–1676

Registry of Trademarks and Patents
51 Bras Basah Road #04–01
Plaza by the Park (0718)
Tel: 65–330–2700
Fax: 65–339–0252

Customs and Excise Department
1 Maritime Square #03–01/#10–01
World Trade Center (0409)
Tel: 65–272–8222
Fax: 65–277–9090

Economic Development Board
250 North Bridge Road
#24–00 Raffles City Tower (0617)
Tel: 65–336–2288
Fax: 65–339–6077

Ministry of Law
250 North Bridge Road #21–00
Raffles City Tower (0617)

Tel: 65–2336–1177
Fax: 65–330–5887

Ministry of Communications
460 Alexandra Road
#39–00 PSA Bldg. (0511)
Tel: 65–270–7988; 279–9734

Ministry of National Development
5 Maxwell Road #21–00 & 22–00
Tower Block MND Complex (0160)
Tel: 65–222–1211
Fax: 65–322–6254

Ministry of Labour
18 Havelock Road #07–01 (0105)
Tel: 65–534–1511
Fax: 65–5334–4840

Country Trade Associations/Chambers of Commerce

Singapore International Chamber of Commerce
6 Raffles Quay #10–01
Johan Hancock Tower (0104)
Tel: 65–224–1255
Fax: 65–224–2785

Singapore Federation of Chambers of Commerce and Industry
47 Hill Street #03–01 Chinese Chamber of Commerce Bldg. (0617)
Tel: 65–338–9761/2
Fax: 65–339–5630

Singapore Manufacturers Association
(The Singapore Export Centre)
20 Orchard Road SMA House (0923)
Tel: 65–338–8787
Fax: 65–336–5385

Association of Small and Medium Enterprises
Blk. 139 Kim Tian Road #02–00 (0316)
Tel: 65–271–2566
Fax: 65–271–1257

Singapore Retailers Association
2 Bukit Merah Central
#15–03 NPB Bldg. (0315)
Tel: 65–272–3106
Fax: 65–271–3091

Information Technology Institute
NCB Building 71 Sciences Park Drive (0511)
Tel: 65–772–0967
Fax: 65–779–5996

Singapore Federation of Computer Industry
NCB Building, 71 Science Park Drive (0511)
Tel: 65–775–1927
Fax: 65–778–4968

Institute of Microelectronics
Block 750E Chai Chee Road
#07–03/04 Chai Chee Industrial Park (1646)
Tel: 65–442–0881
Fax: 65–449–6158

Singapore Economic Development Board
#24–00 Raffles City Tower
North Bridge Road (0617)
Tel: 65–336–2288
Fax: 65–339–6077

Singapore Trade Development Board
10–40 World Trade Centre (0409)
Tel: 65–271–9388
Fax: 65–274–0770

Singapore Association of Food Equipment Manufacturers and Suppliers
c/o Focus Management Pte. Ltd.
#06–03 Maxwell House
20 Maxwell Road
Singapore 0106
Tel: 65–222–8291
Fax: 65–222–3703

Pharmaceutical Industry Association of Singapore
151 Chin Swee Road #02–13A
14 Manhattan House (0316)
Tel: 65–738–0966
Fax: 65–738–0977

Telecommunication Authority of Singapore
31 Exter Road Comcenter #05–00 (0923)
Tel: 65–738–7788
Fax: 65–733–0073

Country Market Research Firms

D. Richmond Associates Pte. Ltd.
150 Orchard Road #08–12

Orchard Plaza
Singapore 0923
Tel: 65–738–7550
Fax: 65–732–9727

Applied Research Corporation
Engineering Block E4–04–11
National University of Singapore
Singapore 0511
Tel: 65–775–5822
Fax: 65–773–0924

Market Behaviour (Singapore) Pte. Ltd.
1 Sophia Road #04–01 Peace Center
Singapore 0922
Tel: 65–337–6117
Fax: 65–337–6127

Country Commercial Banks

Several large commercial banks offer a variety of banking services to manufacturing firms and other clients. Most banks extend credit for five to ten years at competitive interest rates covering up to 50% of plant and machinery costs and up to 65% of the value of factory buildings. Higher percentages are available for particularly desirable projects and for expansion loans.

In addition to providing loans, many larger Singapore banks also have subsidiaries that carry out merchant banking, insurance, property development, securities trading as members of the stock exchange, and underwriting issues of government bonds. Seventy-seven merchant banks also provide a wide range of services not covered by some commercial banks, including investment portfolio management, investment advisory services, advice on corporate restructuring, takeovers and mergers, arranging finance, lending or participating in syndicated loans, capital equipment leasing and underwriting, and floating bond and stock issues.

The Association of Banks in Singapore
10 Shenton Way #12–08 MAS Bldg. (0207)
Tel: 65–224–4300
Fax: 65–224–1785

General Insurance Association of Singapore
1 Shenton Way #14–01 Robina House (0106)
Tel: 65–221–8788
Fax: 65–227–2051

Monetary Authority of Singapore
10 Shenton Way, MAS Bldg. (0207)
Tel: 65–225–5577
Fax: 65–229–9491

Stock Exchange of Singapore Ltd.
1 Raffles Place #25–00 OUB Centre (0104)
Tel: 65–535–3788
Fax: 65–535–0769

SOUTH AFRICA

Country Government Agencies

Ministry of Trade and Industry
Mr. Trevor A. Manuel
Private Bag ×274
Pretoria 0001
Tel: (27 12) 322–07677
Fax: (27 12) 322–7851

Director-General Department of Trade and Industry
Dr. Zav Rustomjee
Private Bag ×84
Pretoria 0001
Tel: (27 12) 310–9791
Fax: (27 12) 322–0298

Minister of Finance
Mr. Chris Liebenberg
Private Bag ×115
Pretoria 001
Tel: (27 12) 323–8911
Fax: (27 12) 323–3262

National Economic Forum
PO Box 2352
Johannesburg 2000
Tel: (27 11) 614–2251
Fax: (27 11) 618–2078

South African Chamber of Business (SACOB)
P.O. Box 91267
Auckland Park 2006
Tel: (27 11) 482–2524
Fax: (27 11) 726–1344

South African Foreign Trade Organization (SAFTO)
P.O. Box 782706
Sandton 2146
Tel: (27 11) 883–3737
Fax: (27 11) 883–6569

Johannesburg Chamber of Commerce and Industry (JCCI)
Private Bag X34
Auckland Park 2006
Tel: (27 11) 726–5300
Fax: (27 11) 726–8421

Durban Regional Chamber of Business
P.O. Box 1506
Durban 4000
Tel: (27 31) 301–3699
Fax: (27 31) 301–3699

Cape Town Chamber of Commerce
P.O. Box 204
Cape Town 8000
Tel: (27 21) 23–2323
Fax: (27 21) 24–1878

Association for the Promotion of the Western Cape (Wesgro)
P.O. Box 1678
Cape Town, 8000
Tel: (27 21) 45–3201
Fax: (27 21) 45–3751

Computer Users Industry Council of South Africa
3 Alexandra Avenue
Halfway House Box
1688 Halfway House
Tel: (27 11) 805–3151

Electronics and Telecommunications Industry Association
P.O. Box 1338
Johannesburg 2000
Tel: (27 11) 833–6033
Fax: (27 11) 838–1522

Motor Industries Federation
P.O. Box 2940
Randburg 2125
Tel: (27 11) 789–2542

S.A. Direct Marketing Association
P.O. Box 85370
Emmarentia 2029
Tel: (27 11) 482–1419
Fax: (27 11) 726–3807

Computing Services Association
Private Bag X34
Aukland Park 2006

Tel: (27 11) 726–5300
Fax: (27 11) 726–8421

Business Equipment Association
P.O. Box 3277
Randburg 2125
Tel: (27 11) 789–3805
Fax: (27 11) 789–3327

National Clothing Federation of South Africa
P.O. Box 75755
Gardenview 2047
Tel: (27 11) 622–8125
Fax: (27 11) 622–8316

The Grocery Manufacturer's Association of South Africa
P.O. Box 34
Randburg 2125
Tel: (27 11) 886–3008
Fax: (27 11) 886–5375

Black Management Forum
P.O. Box 197
Booysens 2061
Tel: (27 11) 337–7661
Fax: (27 11) 337–8744

Foundation for African Business and Consumer Organisations
PO Box 8785
Johannesburg 2000
Tel: (27 11) 832–1911
Fax: (27 11) 836–5920

South African Franchisor's Association
PO Box 80
Meadowlands 1851
Tel: (27 11) 939–2121
Fax: (27 11) 939–2013

South African Import and Export Association
PO Box 9736
Johannesburg 2000
Tel: (27 11) 839–1385/6
Fax: (27 11) 839–1386

South African Marketing Research Association
PO Box 91879
Auckland Park 2006
Tel: (27 11) 482–1419
Fax: (27 11) 726–3639

Country Commercial Banks

Commercial Banks operating in South Africa can be located through:

Registrar of Financial Institutions
Private Bag ×238
Pretoria 0001
Tel: (27 12) 325–2550

SOUTH KOREA

Country Government Agencies

Board of Finance and Economy
1 Chungang dong, Kwacheon shi
Kyunggi do, 427 760
Securities Policy Division
Securities Bureau
Tel: 82–2-503–9252

Ministry of Trade, Industry and Energy
Trade Cooperation Bureau
1 Chungang dong, Kwacheon shi
Kyunggi do, 427 760
Tel: 82–2-503–9443

Ministry of Information and Communications
100 Sejong to, Chongro ku Seoul
Tel: 82–2-750–2001

Chambers of Commerce

Korean Foreign Trade Association
Rm. 4720
KOEX Bldg
1591 Samsung dong
Kangnam ku Seoul
Tel: 82–2-552–5301
Fax: 82–2-551–5100

Korean Trading International, Inc.
11th Flr, KWTC
159 1 Samsung dong
Kanguam ku Seoul
Tel: 82–2-551–3012
Fax: 82–2-551–3100

Federation of Korean Industries
281 Yoido dong, Yongdongpo ku

Seoul 150 756
Tel: 82–2-780–0821
Fax: 82–2-782–6425

Korean Chamber of Commerce and Industry
45 Namdaemuntro 4 ka
Chung ku
Seoul 100 743
Tel: 82–2-316–3523
Fax: 82–2-757–9475

Korean Federation of Small Businesses
16 2 Yoido dong, Youngdeungpo ku
Seoul 150 010
Tel: 82–2-785–0892
Fax: 82–2-782–0247

Association of Foreign Trading Agents of Korea
AFTAK Bldg. 218 Hangang to 2ka
Yongsan ky Seoul
Tel: 82–2-780–3377
Fax: 82–2-785–4373

Korea Construction Equipment Association
Daeyoung Bldg. 44 1, Yoido, Yungdeungpo ku
Seoul 150 010
Tel: 82–2-783–4001/3
Fax: 82–2-780–4001

Korea Machine Tool Manufacturer's Association
4th Floor Tower Crystal Building
1008 1 Daechi Dong
Kangnam Ku, Seoul 135–280
Tel: 82–2-565–2721
Fax: 82–2-564–5639

Korea Automobile Manufacturer's Association
8th Floor, Daesang 63 Bldg.
60 Yoido dong
Youngdongpo ku Seoul
Tel: 82–2-782–0534
Fax: 82–2-782–0464

Electronic Industries Association of Korea
648 Yeoksam dong, Kangnam ku Seoul
Tel: 82–2-922–6612
Fax: 82–2-927–6615

Korea Software Industry Association
Room No. 905
Local Administration Bldg.

234 2 Mapo ku, Kongduk dong, Seoul
Tel: 82–2-713–4185
Fax: 82–2-704–3415

The Federation of Korean Information Industry
13th Floor 28 1 Yoido dong
Youngdongpo ku, Seoul
Tel: 82–2-780–0206
Fax: 82–2-780–1266

The Korean Pharmaceutical Manufacturers' Association
990 2 Bangbae dong, Seocho ku, Seoul
Tel: 82–2-581–2101
Fax: 82–2-581–2106

Korea Customs' Association
16 1 Hangangro 3 ga, Yongan gu. Seoul
Tel: 82–2-701–1456/9
Fax: 82–2-701–1459

Country Market Research Firms

Alliance Research Consultants
5th Floor, Geona Bldg.,
839 13 Yoksam dong, Kangnam Ku, Seoul
Tel: 82–2-558–1240
Fax: 82–2-558–5888

Pacific Consultants
Room No. 5, 33rd Floor
Korea World Trade Center Bldg.
Tel: 82–2-551–3352
Fax: 82–2-551–3360

S.H. Jang Associates, Inc.
Room No. 1409, the Korea Herald Bldg.
112 Hoehyun Dong 3 Ka, Chung Ku Seoul
Tel: 82–2-753–4531
Fax: 82–2-756–3635

Korea Research Centre, Ltd.
6th Floor, Seo Hyuan Bldg.
Seocho Dong, Seocho Ku, Seoul
Tel: 82–2-535–3130
Fax: 82–2-535–3488

Asia Market Intelligence Korea
Room No. 1001, Poong Lim Bldg.
823 Yoksam dong, Kangnam Ku, Seoul

Tel: 82–2-566–3979
Fax: 82–2-566–4684

Country Commercial Banks

Cho Hung Bank
CPO Box 2997
Seoul 100 629
Tel: 82–2-733–2000
Fax: 82–2-732–0835

The Citizens National Bank
CPO Box 815
Seoul 100 608
Tel: 82–2-754–1211
Fax: 82–2-757–3679

The Commercial Bank of Korea
CPO Box 126
Seoul 100 601
Tel: 82–2-775–0050
Fax: 82–2-754–7773

Hanil Bank
CPO Box 1033
Seoul 100 610
Tel: 82–2-771–2000
Fax: 82–2-775–5628

Korea First Bank
CPO Box 2242
Seoul 100 622
Tel: 82–2-733–0070
Fax: 82–2-720–1301

TAIWAN

Country Government Agencies

Taiwan Authority Agencies
Ministry of Foreign Affairs
2 Chiehshou Road, Taipei
Tel: 886–2-311–9292

Ministry of Finance
2 Aiko W. Road, Taipei
Tel: 886–2-322–8000

Ministry of Economic Affairs
15 Foochow Street, Taipei
Tel: 886–2–321–2200

Ministry of Transportation and Communication
Changsha Street Section 1
Taipei
Tel: 886–2–349–29002

THAILAND

Country Government Agencies

Office of the National Economic and Social Development Board
962 Knung Kasem Road
Bangkok 10100
Tel: 662–281–0947
Fax: 662–282–4192

Office of the Board of Investment
555 Vipavadee Rangsit
Bangkhen, Bangkok 10900
Tel: 662–537–8555
Fax: 662–537–8130

Trade Associations/Chambers of Commerce

Board of Trade of Thailand
150 Rajopit Road
Bangkok 10200
Tel: 662–221–0555
Fax: 662–225–3995

Thai Chamber of Commerce
150 Rajbopist Road
Bangkok 10200
Tel: 662–221–0555
Fax: 662–225–3995

Federation of Thai Industries
394/14 Samsen Road
Dusit Bangkok 10200
Tel: 662–225–0086
Fax: 662–225–3372

Board of Trade of Thailand
150 Rajbopist Road

Bangkok 10200 Thailand
Tel: 662–221–0555/221–1827

Office of the Board of Investment
555 Vi pavadee Rungsit Road
Bangkok 10300, Thailand
Tel: 662–537–811, 537–8155
Fax: 662–537–8177

Country Market Research Firms

The Brooker Group Ltd.
2nd Floor, Zone D. Room 201/2
Queen Strikit National Convention Centre
60 New Rachadapisek Road
Klongtoey, Bangkok 10110, Thailand
Tel: 662–229–3111
Fax: 662–229–3127

Business Advisory Thailand
2nd Floor, SMC Building
285 Sukhumvit Road
Bangkok 10110, Thailand
Tel: 662–253–6291–2-6295
Fax: 662–254–4576

Business International Dataconsult
Orient Research Ltd.
54 Soj Santipharp Nares Road
Bangkok 10500
Tel: 662–236–2780, 233–5606
Fax: 662–236–8143

Development Services Ltd.
130/13 Soi Orapin (Soi 12)
Rama VI Road
Bangkok 10400, Thailand
Tel: 662–279–9500, 279–2913
Fax: 662–278–3722

Tara Siam
21st Floor, CP Tower, 313 Silom Road
Bangkok 10500
Tel: 662–231–0463/4
Fax: 662–213–0465

Country Commercial Banks

Bank of Asia Public Company, Ltd.
191 South Sathorn Road
Khet Sathorn, Bangkok 10120
Tel: 662–287–2211/3
Fax: 662–213–2652

Krung Thai Bank, Ltd.
35 Sukhumbit Road
Bangkok 10110
Tel: 662–255–2222
Fax: 662–255–9391

Siam City Bank, Ltd.
1101 New Petchburi Road
GPO Box 488, Bangkok 10400
Tel: 662–253–0200/9
Fax: 662–253–7061

Siam Commercial Bank, Ltd.
1060 New Petchburi Road
GPO Box 1644, Bangkok 10400
Tel: 662–256–1234
Fax: 662–253–6697
For more information about the recently established Ex-Im Bank bundling facility, the contact point is as follows:

Bank of Asia Public Company, Ltd.
Tel: 662–287–2956
Fax: 662–213–2624

TURKEY

Country Government Agencies

Devlet Planlama Teskilati
(State Planning Organisation)
Iktisadi Planlama Genel Mudurlugu
Necatibey Caddesi No. 108
06100 Bakaniklar, Ankara, Turkey
Tel: 90–312–230–8720
Fax: 90–312–231–3498

Dis Ticaret Mustesarligi
(Undersecretariat of Foreign Trade)
Eskisehir Karayolu, Inonu Bulvari
06510 Emek, Ankara, Turkey

Tel: 90–312–212–8724
Fax: 90–312–212–8765

Basbakanlik Ozellestirme
Idaresi Baskanligi
(Prime Minister's Office, Privatization Administration)
Huseyin Rahmi Gurpinar Cad, No. 2
06680 Cankaya, Ankara, Turkey
Tel: 90–312–439–9916
Fax: 90–312–439–8477

Devlet Istatistik Enstitusu
(State Institute of Statistics)
Necatibey Caddesi No. 114
06100 Ankara, Turkey
Tel: 90–312–417–6440
Fax: 90–312–418–5027

Turk Standartlari Enstitusu
(Turkish Institute of Standards)
Necatibey Caddesi No. 112
06100 Bakaniliklar, Ankara, Turkey
Tel: 90–312–417–0020
Fax: 90–312–425–4399

Ulastirma Bakanligi
(Ministry of Communications and Transportation)
Babcelievler Son Durak
Emek, Ankara, Turkey
Tel: 90–312–212–4632
Fax: 90–312–212–4187

Country Trade Associations/Chambers of Commerce

Deik Dis Ekonomik Iliskiler Kurulu
(Foreign Economic Relations Board)
Odakule Beyoglu, Istanbul, Turkey
Tel: 90–212–243–4180
Fax: 90–212–243–4184

Tusiad Turk Sanayicileri Ve Isadamlari Dernegi
(Turkish Indstrialists and Businessmen's Association)
Mestrutiyet Caddesi No. 74
80050 Tepebasi, Istanbul, Turkey
Tel: 90–212–249–1929
Fax: 90–212–249–1350

Yem Sanayichileri Dernegi
(Food Industries Association)

Tuna Caddesi, Halk Sokak 207
Lenisehir, Ankara, Turkey
Tel: 90–312–431–1685
Fax: 90–312–431–2704

Otomotiv Sanayii Dernegi
(Automotive Manufacturers' Association)
Atilla Sokak No. 6
81190 Altunizade, Istanbul, Turkey
Tel: 90–216–318–2994
Fax: 90–216–321–9497

Kimya Sanayichileri Dernegi
(Chemical Manufacturers' Association)
Yildiz Posta Caddesi
Ayyidiz Sitesi No. 28/5, 55 Blok
Esentepe, Istanbul, Turkey
Tel: 90–212–266–0830
Fax: 90–212–273–0898

Turkiye Bilisim Dernegi
(Information Association of Turkey)
Selanik Caddesi No. 17/4
06650 Kistlay, Ankara, Turkey
Tel: 90–312–418–4755
Fax: 90–312–425–4817

Turkiye Giyim Sanayicileri Dernegi
(Turkish Clothing Manufactures' Association)
Yildiz Posta Caddesi
Dedeman Is. Hani 48/8
80700 Gaytrettepe, Istanbul, Turkey
Tel: 90–212–274–2525
Fax: 90–212–272–4060

Chambers of Commerce

Ankara Chamber of Commerce
Anaturk Bulvari 193/4
Kavaklidere, Ankara, Turkey
Tel: 90–312–417–1200
Fax: 90–312–417–2060

Istanbul Chamber of Commerce
Ragip Gumuspala Caddesi No. 84
34378 Eminonu, Istanbul, Turkey
Tel: 90–212–511–4150
Fax: 90–212–526–2197

Ismir Chamber of Commerce
Araturk Caddesi No. 126
35210 Pasaport, Ismir, Turkey
Tel: 90–232–441–7777
Fax: 90–232–483–7853

Aegean Chamber of Industry
Cumhuriyet Bulvari No. 63
Ismir, Turkey
Tel: 90–232–484–4330
Fax: 90–312–483–9937

Country Market Research Firms

Turkiye Is Bankasi A.S.
Ataturk Bulvari, No. 191
06680 Kavakalidere, Ankara, Turkey
Tel: 90–312–428–1140
Fax: 90–312–425–0750

Yapi Ve Kredi Bankasi A.S.
Yapi Kredi Plata A. Blok
Buyukdere Caddesi
80–620 Levent, Istanbul, Turkey
Tel: 90–212–280–111
Fax: 90–212–280–1670

Akbank T.A.S.
Sabanci Cnetere, 4 Levent
80745 Istanbul, Turkey
Tel: 90–212–270–3355
Fax: 90–21–269–7383

Turkiye Imar Bankasi T.A.S.
Buyukdere Caddesi, Dogus Han No. 42 46
80290 Mecidiyekoy, Istanbul, Turkey
Tel: 90–212–275–1190
Fax: 90–212–272–4720

VIETNAM

Country Government Agencies

Ministry of Finance
8 Phan Huy Chu Street
Hanoi
Tel: 844–262789
Telex: 805–412232 MOFI VT

Ministry of Trade
Head Office
31 Trang Tien Street
Hanoi
Tel: 844–262521, 262522
Telex: 805–411251, 411528 BNT VT

Ministry of Foreign Affairs
1 Ton That Dam Street
Hanoi
Tel: 844–258201

State Committee for Cooperation and Investment
56 Quoc Tu Giam Street
Hanoi
Tel: 844–253666, 232494
Fax: 844–259271

Vietnam Trade Information Centre/Research Institute for Foreign Economic Relations
46 Ngo Quyen Street
Hanoi
Tel: 844–263198
Fax: 844–263177

Ho Chi Minh City External Office of Economic Relations
145–47 Ben Chuong Duong
District 1 Ho Chi Minh City
Tel: 848–298116

Country Trade Associations/Chambers of Commerce

Investment and Foreign Trade Association
92–96 Nguyen Hue Blvd.
District 1 Ho Chi Minh City
Tel: 848–22912
Fax: 848–255682

Vietnam Chamber of Commerce and Industry
33 Ba Trieu St. Hanoi
Tel: 844–252962
Fax: 844–256446

Ho Chi Minh City
171 Vo Thi Sau St.
District 1 Ho Chi Minh City
Tel: 848–230301
Fax: 848–294472

Country Market Research Firms

Foreign Trade and Investment Development Centre
92–96 Nguyen Hue Blvd.
District 1 Ho Chi Minh City
Tel: 848–230072
Fax: 848–222983

Investment and Management Consulting Corporation
District 1 Ho Chi Minh City
PO Box 572
Tel: 848–299062
Fax: 848–296125

Country Commercial Banks

The central bank, the State Bank of Vietnam, is an organization of the Council of Ministers and has a monopoly on the issuance of money and management of monetary, credit, and payment operations to stabilize the value of the currency. All commercial banks must be licensed by the State Bank, which enforces minimum reserve requirements. As of September 1998, there were approximately 1,000 commercial banks operating in Vietnam.

Bank for Foreign Trade of Vietnam
47–49 Ly Thai To
Hanoi
Tel: 844–269951
Fax: 844–269951

Industrial and Commercial Bank of Vietnam
79A Ham Night
Q.I. Ho Chi Minh City
Tel: 848–297266

Vietnam Export-Import Bank
7 Le Thi Hong Gam
Q.I. Ho Chi Minh City
Tel: 848–293938
Fax: 848–296063

Indovia Bank
36 Ton That Dsam
Q.I. Ho Chi Minh City
Tel: 848–298450
Fax: 848–231141

Banque Francaise Du Commerce Exterieure
11 Me Linh Square
Q.I. Ho Chi Minh City

Tel: 848–222830
Fax: 848–299126

MULTILATERAL AND REGIONAL DEVELOPMENT BANKS AND ORGANIZATIONS

Loosely associated with the UN are the World Bank and the International Monetary Fund, two large, powerful organizations whose purpose is to assist in development in the less modern areas of the world. In addition, there are four regional development organizations with similar objectives.

In addition to being possible financing sources, directly or indirectly, the international development banks through their many projects also offer numerous supply opportunities for equipment manufacturers, engineers, consultants, construction firms, and similar businesses. The banks produce publications indicating their procurement needs.

The World Bank
1818 H Street, NW
Washington, DC 20433
USA
Telephone: (202) 477–1234
Fax: (202) 477–6391
The primary goal of the World Bank and its affiliates is to raise the standard of living in developing countries. The bank finances a broad range of capital infrastructure projects, but particularly focuses on investments that improve the quality of life of the masses. It also promotes economic development and structural reform in the countries in which it is involved. There are two parts of the bank, the International Bank for Reconstruction and Development (IBRD) and the International Development Association (IDA), which lend funds, give advice and try to get investments moving, with IDA specifically concentrating on the poorer countries and providing easier financial terms. An affiliate, the International Finance Corporation, relates directly to the private sector. It invests its own funds as well as seeking out other monies for commercial enterprises. Another affiliate is the Multilateral Investment Guarantee Agency, which seeks to protect the investor from political risks.

The World Bank will speak with you and may produce or lead you to your needed financing. The bank has offices throughout the world, but Washington, DC, is the location of its world headquarters. The bank also publishes an International Business Opportunities Service, to which you can subscribe by contacting World Bank Publications at Room T8094 at the above address, or calling in the USA (202) 473–1964 or fax (202) 676–0635.

International Finance Corporation (IFC)
1818 H Street, NW
Room I 9163
Washington, DC 20433
USA
Telephone: (202) 477–1234 (general)
(202) 473–9119 (corporate relations)
Fax: (202) 676–0365

The IFC is an institution within the World Bank group that provides support to the private sector in its effort to promote growth in developing countries. It actually invests in commercial enterprises. If interested, companies should contact the corporate relations unit to make proposals or obtain information.

Multilateral Investment Guarantee Agency (MIGA)
1818 H Street, NW
Washington, DC 20433 USA
Telephone: (202) 473–6168
Fax: (202) 477–9886

The MIGA provides guarantees against loss from non-commercial risks in foreign investment.

International Monetary Fund (IMF)
700 Nineteenth Street, NW
Washington, DC 20431
USA
Telephone: (202) 623–7000

Depending upon how much you want to know about the financial stability and performance of countries and their economies, you may want to explore the many publications of the International Monetary Fund. In particular, the monthly magazine accompanied by an annual yearbook, entitled *Information Financial Statistics*, contains a wealth of economic data difficult to come by elsewhere.

Inter-American Development Bank
1300 New York Avenue, NW
Washington, DC 20577
USA
Telephone: (202) 623–1000 (general), 623–6278 (external relations)

The Inter-American Development Bank (IDB) was established in 1959 and focuses on economic and social development in Latin America and the Caribbean. The IDB supplements private funds as needed to support development in the borrowing member countries. As with the World Bank and IMF, it may provide technical advice to the government of the countries in which it is working. Projects are all over the lot and include sewage treatment, road construction, support for entrepreneurs, education and training, farming and fishing, and so on.

African Development Bank Headquarters
01 BP 1387
Abidjan 01
Cote d'Ivoire
Telephone: 225–20–4444
Fax: 225–21–7753

The African Development Bank seeks to aid the development of African member nations by financing projects and promoting private investment in Africa. Related to the bank is the African Development Fund, which provides financing to the poorer countries of Africa at especially low rates.

Asian Development Bank
P.O. Box 780
1099 Manila, Philippines

Street Address:
6 ADB Avenue, Mandaluyong
Metro Manila, Philippines
Telephone: 63–2-711
Fax: 63–2-741–7961

With the past progress in several Asian countries, the Asian Development Bank is planning to focus its resources on specific needy nations in the area. The bank mostly finances and supports infrastructure projects.

European Bank for Reconstruction and Development
One Exchanges Square
London EC2A 2EH
England
Telephone: 44–71–338–6000
Fax: 44–71–338–6100

The European Bank for Reconstruction and Development was established in 1991 to aid in the development and transition of the countries of Central and Eastern Europe and the former Soviet Union. The bank seeks to promote private initiative. It can make loans to private enterprise, invest in equity capital, and confirm guarantees.

European Investment Bank
100 Bd Konrad Adenauer
L-2950 Luxembourg
Tel. 4379–1
Fax: 43 77 04

The mission of the European Investment Bank is to further the objectives of the European Union by making long-term finance available for sound investments. Financing is often provided in the form of individual loans and global loans to assist with development in Africa, Latin America and the Caribbean, Eastern and Central Europe, Asia, and the Mediterranean.

The European Development Fund
European Commission
Directorate General for Development
"General Financial Affairs; Relations with European Investment Bank"
Rue de la Loi, 200
B-1040 Brussels
Tel: 32–2-295–1908
Fax: 32–2-296–9842

The European Development Fund is the main financing instrument of the Lome Convention and provides grants for aid programs for the seventy African, Caribbean, and Pacific countries that are signatories to this agreement with the European Union.

PHARE
European Commission, Information Unit
Directorate General External Relations
Europe and the New Independent States MO 34 3/80
Westraat 200 Rue de la Loi
B-1049 Brussels

Tel: (32–2) 299–1600/299–1444
Fax: (32–2) 299–1777
E-mail: phare.info@dgla.cec.be
World-Wide-Web Address: http://www.cec.lu/en/comm/dgla/phare.html

The Phare Programme is a European Union initiative that supports the development of a larger democratic family of nations within a prosperous and stable Europe. Phare provides know-how from a wide range of non-commercial public and private organizations to its partner countries. It acts as a multiplier by stimulating investment and responding to needs that cannot be met by others. Phare can unlock funds for important projects from other donors through studies, capital grants, guarantee schemes, and credit lines.

TACIS
European Commission
Tacis Information Office
Directorate General for External Political Relations
AN 88 1/06
Westraat 200 Rue de la Loi
B-1049 Brussels
Belgium
Tel: (32–2) 295–2585/296–6065
Fax: (32–2) 231–0441

The Tacis Programme is a European Union initiative to help the Newly Independent States move away from centrally planned to market economies. It provides support in the form of grant finance to foster exchange and knowledge and expertise through partnerships, links, and networks.

EUROPEAN OFFICES OF TRADE AND INDUSTRY

European Government Websites

This list of web addresses provides a starting point for those wishing to locate and explore citizen-oriented information disseminated by the European governments.

Austria
http://gov.austria.info.at/ForeignAffairs

Belgium
http://www.online.be/belgium

Denmark
http://www.SDN.DK/

Finland
http://www.vn.fi/

France
http://www.france.diplomatie.fr/

Germany
http://www.auswaertiges-amt.government.de/

Germany (Bavaria)
http://www.bayern.de/

Greece
http://web.ariadne-t.gr/

Ireland
http://www.ir/gov.ie

Italy
http://www.aipa.it/

Luxembourg
http://www.restena.lv/gover/

Netherlands
http://145.10.251.249/

Portugal
http://infocid.sma.pt/

Spain
http://www.la-moncloa.es/

Sweden
http://www.sb.gov.se/

United Kingdom
http://www.open.gov.UK/

Austria

Ministry of Economics
Stubenrint 1
1010 Vienna

Belgium

Belgium Foreign Trade Office
Emile Jacqmainlaan 162-box 36
B-1210 Brussels
Tel: 32–2–219–44–50
Fax: 32–2–217–61–23

Flemish Foreign Trade Board
Koningsstraat 80
B-1000 Brussels

Tel: 32–2-504–87–11
Fax: 32–2-504–88–99

Belgium Nationale Delcrederedienst (Export Insurance)
Square de Meeus 40
1040 Brussels
Belgium
Tel: 01132–2-509–42–11
Fax: 01132–2-513–50–59

France

Department of Trade and Commerce
Yves Galland
139 Rue de Bercy
75572 Paris, Cdex 12
France
Telephone: 140–04–04–04

Germany

Ministry of Economic Affairs
Villemombler Stra 76
53123 Bonn
Germany
Telephone: 49–228–6150

Greece

Ministry of Trade
Kanigos Square
Athens, Greece
Telephone: 301–361–6241
Fax: 301–384–2642

Iceland

Ministry of Trade
Arnarhavali
150 Reykjavik
Iceland
Telephone: 354–560–9070

Ireland

Department of Tourism and Trade
Kildare Street
Dublin 2
Telephone: 353–1–662–1444
Fax: 353–1–676–6154
Web Site: http://www.irlgov.ie/dtt

Italy

Ministero Del Commercio
Viale America 341
001 44 Rome, Italy
Telephone: 39–6–599–31
Fax: 39-6-59-647-494

Luxembourg

Minister of the Economy
19 Boulevard Royale
2914 Luxembourg
Grand Duchy of Luxembourg
Telephone: 352–4781

Norway

Ministry of Trade and Commerce
P.O. Box 8148 DEP
0033 Oslo, Norway
Telephone: 47–22–24–9090

Sweden

Ministry of Trade and Commerce
1033 Stockholm
Sweden
Telephone: 84052131

United Kingdom

Department of Trade and Industry
Ashdown House

123 Victoria Street
London SW1E 6RB
Telephone 441–215–5000

Welsh Office of Overseas Trade Services
The Welsh Office
Cathays Park
Cardiff CF1 3NQ
Tel: 01222 823547
Fax: 01222 823964
Email: exports@welsh-ofce.gov.uk

OTHER HELPFUL INTERNET SITES

Export and International Trade

http://lib.lsu.edu/bus/marketin.html
http://ciber.bus.msu.edu/busres.htm
http://www.dis.strath.ac.uk/business/index.html
http://www.isomeric.com/islink.html

Country Information

http://www.tradeport.org/ts/countries
http://www.odci.gov/cia
http://strategis.ic.gc.ca
http://www.embassy.org
http://lcweb.loc.gov

Addresses of Foreign Companies

http://www.globalyp.com
http://s17.bigyellow.com
http://www.europages.com
http://www.i-trade.com/exhibit/search

Selected Bibliography

Banjerjee, Neela. "Hoping Bear Will Awaken." *The New York Times*, May 1, 1999.

Dunning, John. *The New Globalism and Developing Countries*. New York: United Nations University Press, 1997.

Eichengreen, Barry. "Trade Blocs, Currency Blocs, and the Disintegration of World Trade in the 1930's." *National Bureau of Economic Research Working Paper Series*, No. 4445. 1993.

Kristoff, Nicholas. "At This Rate We'll Be Global in Another Hundred Years." *The New York Times*, May 23, 1999.

Kurylko, Diana. "Makers Develop Hybrids for Emerging Markets." *Automotive News Europe* 3, June 22, 1998.

World Almanac Book of Facts 1999. New York: World Almanac Corporation.

Index

ABB (Asea-Brown-Boveri Ltd.), 32
Accelerated Re-Activity Phase, 9–13, 29
Age of populations, emerging markets, 20–22
Amway Corp., 66
Argentina, 55, 65, 145–149
Asian economic crisis, origins, 10–12
AT & T Corp., 68, 75

Black hole syndrome. *See* Distribution, black hole syndrome
Blockbuster Video, 31
Bolivia, 67
Bombardier Corp., 108
Brazil: 108; imports, 23, 50; relationship with Portugal, 68

Caslione, John A., 59–60
Channel analysis, 86–90
China: communications, 22–25, 29; foreign direct investment to, 27, 31; infrastructure improvements, 34; Shanghai, 181; tax-free markets, 54; transport, 68
Ciudad del Este, 53–54, 83
Coca-Cola Corp.: in Africa, 32; global strategy, 61

Colombia, 39–40
Communications: emerging markets 22–25; with distributors, 134–135
Congo, 25, 91–94
Control: of distributors, 126–130; level desired, 60–62
Corporate DNA, 46–47, 76, 80
Currencies, emerging markets, 40–44

Danzas Corp., 33
Decelerated Pro-Activity Phase, 9–13, 34, 57, 81
Democratic Republic of the Congo, 91–94
Developing world, cities, 65
DIC Inland Chemical Corp., 30
Distribution: black hole syndrome, 63, 95, 186–187; channel analysis, 86–90; emerging markets, 77–80; exclusive, 85; industrialized world, 75–76; intensive, 84; selective, 84–85; typologies, 96
Distributor agreements: key provisions, 149–155; process of development, 148–149
Distributor Monitor and Control Strategy (DMC), 77–80

Distributor Profile Evaluation Worksheet, 101

Distributors: agreements, 148–155; communicating with, 134–135; control and monitor of, 126–138; ideal, 100–102; identification program, 119; initial inventory, 110–113; initial product training, 115; joint sales and service plan, 114; key contract provisions, 149–154; minimal, 101–102; performance evaluations, 138–144; personal interview, 103–104; profiles, 100–109; responsibilities, 118–127; sales forecast, 109–110; standards of performance, 138–143; survey of potential, 102–103; training of, 131–133

Dresdner Bank Ltd., 10

Eastman Kodak Corp., 30
Egypt, 93–99
Emerging markets: age of populations, 20–22; communications, 22–25; currencies, 40–44; distribution, 76–77; GDP growth, 16–18; governmental action, 25–27, 50–53; infrastructure, 44–48; market information, 55–57; population growth, 18–19; population movements, 19–20; realities, 40–57; tax-free markets, 53–55; urbanization, 27–28
End-User Survey, 99–100
Europe, colonialism, 6–7
Exclusive distribution, 85, 86; typologies, 96–98, 128

Federal Express Corp., 33
Ford Corp., 146
Foreign direct investment: Africa, 32; Central and Eastern Europe, 32; China, 31; India, 30; Latin America, 31–32

GDP growth, emerging markets, 16–18
General Motors Corp., 32, 146
Global Manifest Destiny, 2–7; phases, 8–13, 57, 181–184, 189
Globalization, 3, 5–6
Governmental action, emerging markets, 25–27, 50–53

Home Depot Corp., 75
Honda Motor Corp., 55
Hughes Communications Corp., 33

IBM Corp., 146
Ideal distributors, 100–102
Identification, potential distributors, 119
India: Bangalore, 31; foreign direct investment, 30; imports, 50; infrastructure development, 33–34; middle class, 30; transport, 68
Industrialized world, distribution, 75–76
Infrastructure development: China, 34; emerging markets, 44–48; India, 33–34; Latin America, 33
Initial inventory, 110–113; product training, 115
Intensive distribution, 84
Investments, assessments of, 60–62
Ivestor, Donald, 32

Japan, 69
J. C. Penney Corp., 31
Joint sales and service plan, 114
Joint ventures, 62

Kazakhstan, 39
Kenya, 93

Letters of credit, 22–23
Long Airdox Corp., 29

Madagascar, 37–38, 68
Manufacturers: communicating with distributors; 134–35; controlling distributors, 136–143; developing distributor agreements, 148–149; provisions, 149–155; responsibilities, 127–133; training distributors, 131–133
Manufacturer's agents, 73–74
Market information, emerging markets, 55–57
Maucher, Helmut, 4
Minimal distributors, 100–102
Mohamad, Mahatthir, 4
Motorola Corp., 146

NAFTA, 27, 68
Nestle S. A., 4
Nigeria, 38

Objectives, setting realistic, 62–73

Performance: evaluation of distributor performance, 141–142; improvements, 142–143; performance audit, 141; standards, 138–142
Population: growth in emerging markets, 18–19; movements, 19–20

Renaissance, 6
Ringer, Nick, 3
Risk assessment, 60–64
R. J. Reynolds International Corp., 3, 39
Russia: alcohol consumption, 59–60; decelerated re-activity phase, 12–13; direct foreign investment, 12–13; education, 64; imports, 51; Moscow, 32, 38; staffing, 48–49

Sales and distribution flowchart, 82–84
Sales forecasts, 109–110
Selective distribution, 84–85
Sese Seko, Mobutu, 93
Setting objectives, 62–77
South Africa, 68–69

Southeast Asia, economic crisis, 10–13
Standards of performance, 138–143
Suzuki, S. A., 32

Tax-free markets: China, 45; Ciudad del Este, 53–54, 83; emerging markets, 53–55
Tenneco Ltd., 33
Thailand, 10–11
Thomas, Andrew R., 37, 91–95
3–Com Corp., 33
Timbuktu, 4–5
Trading companies, 74
Training, distributor, 131–134

Ukraine, 39
United Colors of Benneton, Ltd., 31–32
Urbanization, emerging markets, 27–28
Uzbekistan, 39

Venezuela, 51, 117–118
Vietnam, 48

Wal-Mart Corp., 31, 75

Xerox Corp., 31, 143, 146

Zaire, 91–94

About the Authors

JOHN A. CASLIONE is the President and CEO of Andrew-Ward International, Inc. and Global Distribution Services, Inc., both global marketing, sales and distribution firms. He also serves on the faculty of Southern Methodist University's Executive Education Department of the Edwin L. Cox School of Business.

ANDREW R. THOMAS is the Managing Director of Erhart Enterprises, S.A., a worldwide distributor of consumer and industrial products. He has served on the faculties of the University of Toledo, La Universidad de Guayaquil in Ecuador and the University of Akron.